Liberating Christianity

Liberating Christianity

*Overcoming Obstacles to Faith
in the New Millennium*

THOMAS C. SORENSON

WIPF & STOCK · Eugene, Oregon

LIBERATING CHRISTIANITY
Overcoming Obstacles to Faith in the New Millennium

Copyright © 2008 Thomas C. Sorenson. All rights reserved. Except for brief quotations in critical publications or reviews, no part of this book may be reproduced in any manner without prior written permission from the publisher. Write: Permissions, Wipf and Stock Publishers, 199 W. 8th Ave., Eugene, OR 97401.

Wipf & Stock
A Division of Wipf and Stock Publishers
199 W. 8th Ave., Suite 3
Eugene, OR 97401
www.wipfandstock.com

ISBN 13: 978-1-60608-072-6

www.wipfandstock.com

Manufactured in the U.S.A.

Except as otherwise noted, the Scripture quotations contained herein are from the New Revised Standard Version Bible, © 1989 by the Division of Christian Education of the National Council of Churches of Christ in the U.S.A., and are used by permission. All rights reserved.

Contents

Acknowledgments vii
Introduction ix
Questions for Reflection and Discussion xxviii

PART ONE: OVERCOMING THE OBSTACLE OF PHILOSOPHICAL MATERIALISM

1 The Rise of the Materialist Worldview and Its Effect on Christianity 3

2 The Reality and Nature of the Spiritual 9

PART TWO: OVERCOMING THE OBSTACLE OF BIBLICISM

3 The Language of Faith: Symbol and Myth 23

4 The Nature of Religious Truth 31

5 The Limits of Literalism 45

6 Relationship and Decision: The Nature of Spirituality and Faith 56

7 The Bible: Myth and Spiritual Experience 67

PART THREE: OVERCOMING THE OBSTACLE OF THE DENIAL OF GRACE

8 Beyond the Classical Theory of Atonement 91

9 The Meaning of the Cross: The Demonstration of God's Solidarity 110

10 The Dynamics of Salvation 126

11 Christian Social Ethics: The Teachings of Jesus for Our Time 153

Epilogue 195
A Philosophical Appendix 199
Glossary 209

Acknowledgments

To my father, Lloyd R. Sorenson, Ph.D., Professor Emeritus of History, University of Oregon, Eugene, Oregon. He taught me the joy and the value of the life of the mind and never to be satisfied with superficial answers. His reading of various drafts of this book helped me avoid some significant errors.

And to the members of the adult education forum of Monroe Congregational United Church of Christ, who taught me that the people of the church are open to new ideas and willing to be challenged to stretch their Christian faith in new directions.

I also wish to thank my daughter Mary Yuhas for her encouragement and help in proofreading and editing the text. Her insightful questions helped clarify several points that were unclear or on which I had contradicted myself.

I wish most of all to thank my wife the Rev. Jane Sorenson for her help with the text and most of all for her patience with my preoccupation during my months of work on this book.

Introduction

"For I am convinced that neither death, nor life, nor angels, nor rulers, nor things present, nor things to come, nor powers, nor height, nor depth, nor anything else in all creation, will be able to separate us from the love of God in Christ Jesus our Lord."

—St. Paul[1]

CHRISTIANITY IS THE MOST successful faith tradition in history. Today Christians number two billion people.[2] Christianity is the largest of the world's faith traditions, far exceeding the numbers of Islam, the second largest faith in the world.[3] Christianity has adherents in every corner of the earth, in every nation, in every culture. The beliefs and stories of Christianity have shaped the culture of Europe; and that culture has spread, for better or for worse, around the globe. Even those cultures that have not embraced the Christian faith have not escaped its influence, for they are conditioned today (to a greater or lesser extent) by their reaction to and interactions with Christianity and the dominant world culture that it produced. Certain types of Christianity are on the march in South America and Africa, where Evangelical and Pentecostal Christianity are increasing their numbers at the expense of the Roman Catholic Church and indigenous spiritual traditions. Neither world history nor today's cultural and geopolitical dynamics are comprehensible without an understanding of the role Christianity, in its own right and as the dominant faith of the world's dominant culture, has played in shaping them.

Yet the greatness of Christianity is not merely a matter of numbers and geopolitical influence. The legitimate function of any religion is to connect people to God, and Christianity has connected more people to

1. Rom 8:38–39.
2. http://www.religioustolerance.org/worldrel.htm.
3. Ibid.

Introduction

God than any other religion. We do not have to diminish the spiritual truth and power of other faiths (something I have no intention of doing in this study) to say that our Christian faith is unsurpassed in its power to save, that is, in its power to connect us to God and to bring us the gifts of the spiritual life. Countless people all over the world have found and continue to find hope, strength, courage, peace, consolation, joy, inspiration, and meaning in and through the great stories and beliefs of the Christian faith. Just why this is so we hope to discover in the course of this study. Suffice it to say here that if Christianity were wanting in spiritual power it would not have survived and become the significant force in world history and in the lives of real people that it has been and continues to be.

Yet in our context, the English-speaking dominant culture of North America at the beginning of the twenty-first century, Christianity is in crisis.[4] It is of course true that Evangelical and Fundamentalist types of Christianity are riding a wave of popularity and political influence today, especially in the United States. Yet this reality only masks the underlying loss of influence that the faith has experienced over the past several decades. The truth is that Christianity has become simply unbelievable to a majority of Americans. The faith's loss of credibility is most pronounced among the cultural elite, those writers, artists, and educators who in the long run shape the culture of any nation. In particular, educated, articulate, socially and politically aware and involved men and women of progressive views—people we used to call liberals before liberal became a dirty word among us—find Christianity not only unattractive and unpersuasive but downright distasteful or even abhorrent. The great challenge facing progressive, or what I will here call liberated and liberating Christianity, is to demonstrate to the people of our context that Christianity can be a nurturing spiritual home for them and their social and political beliefs.

The reasons why Christianity has become unacceptable to many modern people are both generally applicable to all religions and specific to Christianity. The general reason many people today reject Christianity is that they reject the spiritual view of reality, adhering instead to a materialist ontology (the understanding of the nature of being, of what is real) that denies the spiritual dimension of reality and holds that only the material is real. A dominant version of this ontological materialism is scientism,

---

4. On the nature and importance of contextual theology see Douglas John Hall, *Thinking the Faith: Christian Theology in a North American Context* (Minneapolis: Fortress Press, 1991), Chapter One and pp. 69ff.

Introduction

the belief that only that is real which can be demonstrated by the methods of science. I will examine the validity of this materialist worldview in Part One of this study. Suffice it to say for now that philosophical materialism denies the universal experience of humanity that there is more to reality than the physical, that there is a spiritual dimension to reality that is as real as the physical. Indeed, most human cultures have held the spiritual to be *more* real than the physical, to be in fact ultimate reality. One aim of this study is to open up the reality of the spiritual dimension and to show that acknowledgement of its reality is both reasonable and consistent with human experience, to show that spiritual experience is every bit as valid as sensory experience and indeed not fundamentally different from it.

Which brings us to the things about Christianity itself that make our faith unacceptable to so many people today. The first of them is the history of the faith. Seen from the outside, or for that matter to a considerable extent from the inside, the history of Christianity appears to be a parade of horrors. Its prominent features include Crusades against Muslim believers in the name of Christ that were in reality motivated as much by economic considerations as by misguided religious ones; the slaughter of Christians the official church deemed to be heretics and the burning of women accused of being witches; religious wars, especially those that ravaged Europe in the sixteenth and seventeenth centuries; the forced conversion and virtual annihilation of indigenous peoples around the world but especially in the Americas; the oppression of women in the name of a male deity whose male servants created and perpetuated a culture of patriarchy, androcentrism, and misogyny; the creation of authoritative institutional structures that dictate what the people are to believe; anti-Judaism so endemic and virulent that the entire history of the faith up to the 1930s can legitimately be seen as preparation for the Holocaust; the denial of the full and equal God-given humanity of gay and lesbian people; and, at least since the time of Galileo, an anti-intellectualism that has resisted (and in some forms of Christianity, including the most vocal and visible ones among us, continues to resist) the discoveries of modern science and the insights of the higher Biblical criticisms. The list could go on and on. The point here is not to bash the faith but to acknowledge the sinful side of our history as the first step in overcoming it. Given that sordid and brutal history, it is no wonder that sensitive, well-intentioned, even spiritual people find Christianity not merely unattractive but downright repugnant.

Introduction

We can't change Christianity's history. All we can do is repent of the sinful parts of it, strive to do better, and spread the word that, while the faith has a dark side to its history, it has also been from the very beginning an immense blessing, a life-giving, life-enhancing, life-transforming spiritual path for countless generations of Christians. We can, however, do something about the other major reasons specific to Christianity that so many people reject the faith, and doing something about them is the major intent of this study. A second cause of the disrepute of Christianity among sensitive, educated Americans today, and the one that is a major focus of this study, is what I will here call Biblicism. It is the focus of Part Two of this study. As I understand the concept, Biblicism is the belief that to be Christian one must believe the Bible to be the literal, inerrant Word of God. It consists of two parts. One is the belief, in effect, that God is the author of the Bible. It is the belief that even if it does have various human authors the Bible originated with God and that it accurately reflects the word and will of God throughout all of its books. The other part of Biblicism is literalism. Literalism is, among other things, the belief that all of God's words in the Bible are to be understood literally. Christian Biblicists, whether Fundamentalist, Evangelical, or Pentecostal, have so dominated the public awareness of Christianity in recent times that most people both inside the churches and outside them equate Biblicism with Christianity and are completely unaware of any other way of understanding the faith.

Literalism today undeniably causes many decent, caring, loving people to reject Christianity; but, perhaps ironically, they reject it because they share at least the literalist if not the divine origin assumptions about the Bible with the very Biblicist Christians whose faith they are rejecting. Today people both inside the churches and outside the churches know of no way of understanding Christianity other than the literal way. Yet there is another way. This matter is so central to this study that I need to say a bit more about it here.

Christian theology has known of another way of understanding the stories of the faith almost from the very beginning. In the third century, the Church Father Origen wrote of the second creation story in Genesis, the story of Adam and Eve in the Garden of Eden:

> Who is so silly as to imagine that God, like a husbandman, planted a garden in Eden eastward, and put in it a tree of life, which could be seen and felt.... And if God is also said to walk in the garden in the evening, and Adam to hide himself under a tree, I do not

Introduction

suppose that anyone will doubt that these passages, by means of seeming history, though the incidents never occurred, figuratively reveal certain mysteries.[5]

Eighteen hundred years ago Origen, and the rest of the church fathers, knew how to read Scripture nonliterally.

More recently, for at least the last century, mainline seminary students (and since Vatican II Catholic seminary students as well) have been taught that the stories of the Bible are not necessarily literally true. They have been taught to see the Bible as a collection of stories. They have been taught that religion consists not of objective factual truths but of myths[6] and symbols, the power of which far surpasses that of any mere fact. They have been taught the so-called higher Biblical criticisms, which demonstrate the very human nature of the books of the Bible, their historical settings, their cultural assumptions, their editorial development, and their linguistic ambiguities. Yet for the most part when the graduates of those seminaries have gone into the churches as pastors and teachers they have not taught the lay people of the church what they themselves were taught.[7] A major focus of this study is helping lay people to learn what seminary students have known for decades, to help them understand the Bible as story, myth, and symbol and to help them discover the power and truth of the faith understood in this way.

Those same seminary students have long been taught that the Bible is a very human creation. That statement is not necessarily inconsistent with a belief in at least some divine inspiration behind the writing of the Bible, although asserting the divine inspiration of the Bible creates its own problems that I will address in the course of this study. Whether one believes in some degree of divine inspiration or not, the undeniable fact is that a belief in the divine origin of scripture has, in many Christian circles, made critical analysis of the Bible impossible. Another major theme of this study is to focus our attention on the human origins of the Bible. I

---

5. Quoted in Richard Smoley, *Inner Christianity: A Guide to the Esoteric Tradition* (Boston: Shambhala, 2002), 4.

6. I use the term myth here not in its popular sense of something believed to be true that is not true but in its technical sense as a story about the divine and our relationship to the divine. Chapter Three deals with this understanding of myth in more detail.

7. See Oliver Thomas, *10 Things Your Minister Wants to Tell you (But Can't Because He Needs the Job)* (New York: St. Martin's, 2007).

Introduction

will examine what that very human origin means for our understanding of the nature of the Bible and of Biblical authority.

There are other important reasons why Christianity as it is popularly understood is so unattractive to many people in our context as well. These reasons are the subject of Part Three of this study, "Overcoming the Obstacle of the Denial of Grace." This part deals with several different subjects. While they may at first glance appear unrelated, they all have in common that they amount in one way or another to a denial of grace. They include the classical theory of atonement, the idea that Jesus Christ, the Son of God Incarnate, became human for the purpose of dying as an atonement for human sin that was a necessary precondition of God's forgiving that sin. I will offer a critique of that theory and present an alternative understanding of the meaning of Christ's death called theology of the cross. I will consider this theology's implication that God's grace is truly free and truly universal. I will consider what liberated and liberating Christianity means for Christian teaching on some of the major social issues of our day, namely, violence, economic justice, and inclusivity versus exclusivity. Finally, I will take a close look at the issue of homosexuality as the defining issue in American Christianity today.

Challenging people's comfortable, unexamined assumptions about the faith can be difficult and frightening. People resist the new (for them) truths of a liberated Christianity. The things that are here interpreted as barriers to the faith are, for some people, the sure and reassuring truths they have known for a lifetime. The pastor fears that introducing a new way of thinking about the faith may cause some of the flock to lose their faith altogether. Worse, at least in the minds of many pastors, it may cause some to leave the church and take their pledge dollars with them. These concerns are real, and I hope that this study will be a tool to help pastors guide their parishioners beyond traditional conceptions of the faith in a way that actually strengthens people's faith and their commitment to the church.

Yet whether this study succeeds in that goal or not, the underlying fact remains. Biblicism and the denial of God's grace are killing Christianity in our context today. They have Christianity imprisoned; they have the faith in a straightjacket. They are burying Christianity alive, and if we cannot liberate Christianity from that tomb it will surely die. Not today, not tomorrow, perhaps not for a long time, but die it surely will. For this reason those of us who love the Christian faith, who have committed our lives to it, and who find our connection to God in its life-giving, life-transforming

Introduction

stories and in its magnificent myths and symbols, have no choice but to seek to liberate our great faith from the prison it finds itself in today. We can give Christianity a future if we can free the Bible to be the profoundly human document that it is and free the faith to be myth, to be symbol. As myth and symbol it can save us. As mere fact it can't even save itself. We can give Christianity a future if we can free it to be truly a religion of grace. As a religion of universal, unconditional grace it can free the world to live in love. As a system of ancient and outmoded moral laws and of conditions for obtaining God's grace it is unconvincing and untrue to the God it claims to follow.

The title of this study suggests more than that, however. God calls us to liberate Christianity; but the great good news is that if we can do that, Christianity will liberate us. Popular Christianity today imprisons not only Christianity but Christians as well. It imprisons Christians in a denial of their God-given intellectual capacities. It imprisons Christians in a judgmental, legalistic moral system that reduces the life of faith to a set of rules, of dos and don'ts that must be obeyed. With its pervasive focus on sin and redemption, it imprisons Christians in fear for their immortal souls. With its insistence that it, and it alone, possesses absolute truth, it imprisons people in a we/they mentality that makes outsiders the enemy and directs our attention and energies only inward, toward our own group. It cuts us off from other people and other cultures. Christianity liberated from Biblicism frees us to become the whole, complete people God intends us to be. It frees us to be open to the wonders and the goodness of all of God's people, to celebrate and learn from them ways they are different from us. Christianity liberated from Biblicism frees us to find goodness in all people and in all life-affirming and life-enhancing relationships. Liberated Christianity liberates our spirits to respond to God not in fear but in love and joy. In liberating Christianity, we liberate ourselves too.

It is not uncommon for authors of works in the realm of theology and spirituality to begin their work with an account of their own spiritual history, an account of how they have come to hold the beliefs they advance in their book. Theology is an academic discipline, but it is inextricably linked with spirituality, which is a much more personal matter. That is perhaps why an account of the author's personal spiritual journey is not inappropriate in a work such as this. Perhaps a brief telling of my personal spiritual story will aid the reader in understanding what follows

Introduction

or at least will lead the reader to a more charitable attitude toward me when the views I express here seem difficult or misguided.

I was raised in an academic family. My father, to whom this work is dedicated despite the fact that he does not share all of the views I express in it, was a history professor his entire professional career and is, to this day, the most intelligent person I have ever met.[8] My mother was a feminist pioneer of sorts, although she always denied that honorable title. She received a law degree in the early 1940s in, of all places, North Dakota. So I was raised by highly educated parents, and education was always highly valued in our home either for its own sake (my father's position) or for the potential it can create for worldly success (my mother's position). That my twin brother and I would receive at least an undergraduate university education was an unspoken assumption that I imbibed with my infant formula and that I never doubted.

I was raised in the Congregational Church, specifically First Congregational Church of Eugene, Oregon. My father was raised in the Roman Catholic Church, but in college he had a crisis of faith and left the Church. He never went back. My mother was raised a Congregationalist by her mother, although her father, after whom I am named, was Catholic. Through my mother, Congregationalism became the family faith. For the first half of my life, faith wasn't very important to me. I left the church when I was in high school. I thought it was because I had concluded in my youthful arrogance that the people of Eugene First Congregational were all hypocrites. In reality, it was probably more because I didn't understand the faith or feel much need for it. I felt that I didn't fit in at church. I felt I didn't fit in anywhere, but I couldn't just walk out of school. I could just walk out of church, so I did.

My journey back to faith and the church began in the 1970s when I was in graduate school at the University of Washington studying for a Ph.D. in Imperial Russian history with Professor Donald W. Treadgold,

---

8. My father's path into academia began with an act of pure serendipity, or divine Providence depending on how you look at it. He was the son of a blacksmith in the tiny town of Sheldon, North Dakota. The Great Depression wiped out his father's business, and my dad faced what must have seemed a bleak and even hopeless future. Then the director of the University of North Dakota band came through town and heard my father play the clarinet in the high school band. Dad was quite a good clarinet player. The director said he couldn't offer any money, but if dad would come to Grand Forks and play in the band he would help him find a job. That was the best offer dad had had to that point, so off to Grand Forks he went. The rest, no pun intended, is history.

Introduction

one of the premier Russian historians of his generation.[9] Don Treadgold was one of those rarest of creatures in academia in the early 1970s—a believing, practicing Christian. At the time I had little interest in and less knowledge of Christianity, but I respected Dr. Treadgold's combination of an active faith and world-class scholarship.[10] Under his influence I chose as my dissertation topic a study of Konstantin P. Pobedonostsev, the Over Procurator of the Holy Synod of the Russian Orthodox Church from 1880 to 1905 and the tutor of the last two Russian Tsars, Alexander III and Nicholas II.[11] My dissertation then is on a topic from the history of the Russian Orthodox Church, although honesty compels me to state that my interest in Pobedonostsev was more as a figure in the intellectual history of Russia than in that country's religious history.

My journey back to the church gained speed in 1975, when my wife Francie, our infant son, and I went to Moscow for a year so I could do dissertation research. For reasons I can't truly recall, we began attending the Anglo-American Church at the American Embassy. The dreary reality of Soviet life contrasted sharply with the warmth of that American church. I began for the first time to feel the attraction of life in the Spirit. That the Spirit was so sorely lacking from everyday life in the Soviet capital made that attraction all the stronger. Upon our return to Seattle, we joined Pilgrim Congregational UCC in Seattle. I was a church member again for the first time since my youth.

Two years later I entered the University of Oregon School of Law because there were no jobs to be had in my chosen academic field of Imperial Russian history. During those years I attended a Presbyterian church in Eugene with my father (who had temporarily left First Congregational because of an intense dislike of the pastor at the time), but my understand-

---

9. Coincidentally, Professor Treadgold was also from Eugene, Oregon. I discovered after I had worked with him for several years that we had, several years apart of course, attended the same grade school, Thomas A. Edison Elementary in Eugene.

10. Don was an Anglo-Catholic. The one time I remember disagreeing with him on something even back then was when, one day over coffee, he declared his opposition to the ordination of women on the grounds that Jesus was a man. Frankly, I still don't get that one.

11. The Over Procurator of the Holy Synod was a government official not a churchman. Peter the Great had abolished the Moscow Patriarchate and placed the Russian Orthodox Church under the control of a Holy Synod, a collective leadership presided over by a government appointee, the Over Procurator, who became in effect a kind of Minister of Religious Affairs for the Empire.

ing of the faith was still rudimentary at best, and religion was far from the most important thing in my life. Several years later, back in the Seattle area, Francie and I became members of Richmond Beach Congregational UCC. It was there that something happened that would, a few years later, change my life.

In the early 1990s, Richmond Beach Congregational Church created an Open and Affirming Committee. I really had no idea what it was about. Francie volunteered to be on the committee. I did not, but when the time came for the committee's first meeting, Francie was home recovering from gall bladder surgery. She asked me to go to the meeting and let her know what happened. So I went. I don't think I missed a single meeting of the committee. I became the only male committee member to see the process all the way through.

At that time in my life I had had virtually no experience of homosexuality. As far as I knew, I knew no homosexual people.[12] I had no doubt that I myself was heterosexual. There seemed to be no personal reason why the cause of gay and lesbian people should become a major life concern of mine, but it did. I began to have a vague sense difficult to describe that God was calling me to work in the church for the equal rights and dignity of gay and lesbian people. It wasn't an ordinary sense perception, but it was definitely a real experience. I couldn't tell you how I knew this call. I just knew. It made no sense, but I couldn't deny it. I didn't try to deny it. I followed it. It led me beyond Richmond Beach Congregational UCC to work in what was then the Washington North Idaho Conference of the UCC and as the Conference's representative on the board of a state-wide, ecumenical organization called Simple Justice, the function of which was to work in the churches to support the equal civil rights of gay and lesbian people.[13] Perhaps God needed my legal skills for explaining the fallacy of the "special rights" argument the proponents of legalized discrimination were making in an effort to trick people into writing bigotry into the law. I don't know. All I know is that for the first time in my life I experienced a call from God, a call to use my passion and my skills to work for justice for all of God's people.

12. As is the case with so many straight people who think they don't know any gay people, I did know gay people—both inside the church and outside it. I just didn't know they were gay because at that time they did not feel safe coming out.

13. It was during this Conference work that I first met a woman named Jane Ostby, now the Rev. Jane Sorenson my wife, Francie having passed away in 2002 from breast cancer.

Introduction

At roughly the same time, in the early 1990s, I discovered a passion for good Christian theology. One day I bought a used copy of Paul Tillich's *Dynamics of Faith*. I didn't know what it was. I'm not sure I even knew who Paul Tillich was,[14] but that little book of his changed my life. I now describe it as the book that made it possible for me to call myself a Christian. In that book I discovered for the first time a philosophical approach to religion and a coherent, persuasive, and intellectually legitimate exposition of nonliteral faith. In that book I discovered symbol and myth. As my own book now demonstrates, those concepts remain central to my understanding of faith to this day. Tillich's understanding of God as the ground of being, of faith as ultimate concern, and especially of symbol and myth as the language of faith gave me a way to understand my own faith that has informed and enriched my thinking and my faith more than any other understanding I have ever discovered. Needless to say, much of what follows here, while not a mere regurgitation of Tillich's thought, is heavily influenced by it.

Perhaps not coincidentally in 1994, after I had been working on Open and Affirming matters and reading theology for a couple of years, I began to burn out on the practice of law. That burn out eventually developed into a moderately severe case of depression. I had a feeling that there was something else I was supposed to be doing with my life. I didn't know what that something else was; but no matter how hard I tried to suppress it through denial and the use of anti-depressants, that sense just wouldn't go away.

In 1994, a pivotal year for me, I was Moderator of the Richmond Beach church, and the Rev. Dr. Dennis Hughes was our interim pastor. Dennis is ordained in the Presbyterian Church U.S.A., and he is a Jungian analyst as well as a pastor. Dennis introduced me to Jungian psychology. One day in 1994, as I sat in my law office trying to figure out why I was having so much trouble making myself do the law work that I had to do, I did a Jungian psychological exercise that I had read about in a book that

---

14. My father did. Once, perhaps in the late 1950s or early 1960s, Tillich attended a conference at Oregon State University that Dad went to. Somehow he got assigned the task of driving Tillich back to the airport in Portland after the conference was over. Apparently at one point on that trip Dad narrowly avoided a head-on collision. So I am only two degrees of separation removed from Paul Tillich. I am sure I am more degrees than that removed from Kevin Bacon.

Introduction

Dennis had recommended.[15] In that exercise, as I recall, you clear your mind of distracting thoughts, then ask yourself questions and wait for answers to come. You write or type your questions and answers as they arise.[16] I asked: Why am I having so much trouble making myself do my work? Immediately, and I mean immediately, an answer came booming back from somewhere in the depths of my psyche: "You're not a lawyer!" I argued with the voice, but it kept saying the same thing. I decided to play along. I said: "OK. I'm not a lawyer. What then am I?" Immediately, with no time for me to have given the matter any conscious thought, the voice said: "You're a preacher." With that I ended the exercise.

I was stunned. A preacher? I had never once thought of becoming a preacher. Where had that word come from? Not from my conscious mind surely. Something in my unconscious was telling me that I'm a preacher (whatever that meant), not a lawyer. I thought there must be something to it, but I didn't know what; so I immediately dismissed the matter from my mind. Even if I wanted to become a preacher, which as far as I knew I didn't, I knew that I was too old (I had turned forty-eight in September, 1994) to change careers, and I certainly couldn't afford to go back to school. So I kept telling myself you're too old and you can't afford it, and I kept going through the motions of practicing law and taking antidepressants to keep the recurrent passive suicidal ideation at bay.

Also in 1994 Dennis Hughes, who knew of my spiritual struggle at the time, gave me the business card of a Jungian analyst colleague of his named Kimbrough Besheer (who is also an Episcopal priest) and recommended that I go see him. I didn't call Kimbrough at the time, but for some reason I kept his card in my wallet. In early 1997 I still had it. I truly can't recall why, but in February 1997 I did call and made an appointment to go see Kimbrough. I still see him regularly today. He helped me work through that nagging sense that I was supposed to be doing something else with my life. With his help I came to realize that although it was certainly true from a worldly perspective that I was too old and couldn't afford to change careers, that was useless information. It just didn't matter.

---

15. Johnson, Robert A., Inner Work, Using Dreams and Creative Imagination for Personal Growth and Integration, (HarperOne, San Francisco, 1989.)

16. Johnson warns his readers against doing this exercise without expert guidance because, he says, there is a danger one might enter deep into the unconscious and be unable to get oneself back out. I ignored that advice, but I repeat it here for any of my readers with a strong recommendation to heed it.

Introduction

Then, another serendipitous (or perhaps providential) thing happened. On July 1, 1997, Seattle University, a Jesuit school, created within its School of Theology and Ministry the Institute of Ecumenical Theological Studies (IETS). IETS was, and is, affiliated with nearly a dozen Protestant denominations, including all the major "mainline" ones. Protestants who felt a call to professional ministry but who had had nowhere to go anywhere near Seattle came out of the woodwork.[17] Over night, half of the students at the Seattle University School of Theology and Ministry were Protestants. I became one of them in September, 1997.[18] I closed my law office, took a part-time job as a staff attorney at The Legal Action Center, a legal services office providing free legal services to low income tenants in eviction cases, and began my formal theological and ministerial education.[19]

By the time I got to seminary, I had long been appalled by the popular face of American Christianity. I watched the rise of the televangelist phenomenon with dismay as charlatan after charlatan bilked gullible people out of their money while claiming to be doing the Lord's work only to be exposed as immoral hypocrites.[20] My work in the Open and Affirming movement in the UCC, and other work I had done around the issue of gay rights, had sensitized me to the way in which bigots use the Bible to justify their bigotry as the will of God. My study of theology, especially my read-

---

17. Fuller Seminary had a branch in Seattle at Seattle Pacific University, a Free Methodist school, but Fuller is not appealing to most liberal Christians. The nearest compatible seminary was the Vancouver School of Theology in Vancouver, Canada. The nearest denominational seminaries for mainline Protestants in this country were at the Graduate Theological Union in the San Francisco Bay area.

18. It turned out that at fifty-one, I was only a few years older than the average for STM students, which made me feel considerably better.

19. Whenever I doubt divine Providence I remember this job at the Legal Action Center. For the first time perhaps in my entire legal career I was doing law that felt worth doing. The job was part time, which enabled me to go to seminary part time. Because the Legal Action Center was a program of Catholic Community Services of Western Washington, a ministry of the Roman Catholic Archdiocese of Seattle, I got a 25 percent tuition break at STM. When I graduated from STM in December, 2000, the Legal Action Center made my job full time for me. When I got a part-time call to Monroe Congregational UCC in March, 2002, they let me cut back to four days a week. I left only when my call to Monroe became full time in February, 2003. That job at LAC was a blessing I will never forget.

20. Once when I was running my own law office I handled an estate in which the decedent had left a gift of money to Jimmy Swaggart Ministries. I remember nearly gagging as I wrote the check on estate funds to pay that bequest. Honoring the decedent's wishes was my legal and ethical duty, but it was almost more than I could force myself to do.

Introduction

ing of Tillich's *Dynamics of Faith*, had shown me that there was indeed a better Christian way than the unthinking literalism applied in support of cultural prejudices and in opposition to many of the findings of modern science that so characterized popular American Christianity at the end of the twentieth century. I was beginning to discern that opposing what I here call Biblicism, although I had as yet developed neither that term nor my current understanding of its nature and limitations, would be an important part of whatever ministry I ended up doing.

I completed my seminary education in December, 2000. I had my Master of Divinity degree, and I was approved for ordination pending call by the (then) Washington North Idaho Conference of the UCC. That was all good, but by then tragedy had struck my family. My wife Francie had had breast cancer surgery in the early 1990s. We thought we'd gotten it. We thought we were safe. We weren't. At the very beginning of the year 2000 we learned that the cancer had returned and had spread to her bones. That cancer should have been manageable with chemotherapy for many years, but at the very beginning of 2001, within a very few weeks of my graduation from seminary, we learned that the cancer had spread to her liver. We fought it with intensive chemotherapy. Francie battled bravely, but we knew that there was no cure and that we were just buying time. Like so many families in that situation we became more concerned with quality of life than with length of life. I recount some of my spiritual experiences during her illness and upon her death on July 31, 2002, in this book. Because of Francie's illness, I did not begin a search for a call to a church other than to keep my ears open for anything that might come up in the greater Seattle area. I continued my work at the Legal Action Center. My spiritual and emotional energies were taken up with caring for my wife as she approached the end of her life.

God does not cause bad things like Francie's illness and death. God suffers them with us. God can and does, however, use whatever happens in our lives, even the horrible tragedies and what seems like unbearable grief, as the occasion for new opportunities and new life. Because I had not left the Seattle area to take a church somewhere else, in March, 2002, I was called as pastor of Monroe Congregational United Church of Christ. Monroe is about 35 miles northeast of Seattle but only about 25 miles from where Francie and I were living in a northern Seattle suburb. The call was part time; but it was a call to parish ministry, so I accepted. If working to educate the people of the church in nonliteral, progressive

Introduction

Christianity, in what I here call liberated and liberating Christianity, is truly my call, a better place for my ministry than Monroe could hardly be imagined.

Monroe is a city of about 17,000 people. It has something like 26 churches. One is Roman Catholic, four are so-called mainline Protestant, and the rest are just about every variety of socially conservative, Biblicist church there is. They include Mormon, Seventh Day Adventist, Missouri Synod Lutheran, Church of Christ, conservative Baptist, Pentecostalist, and evangelical community churches. The Monroe Pastors Fellowship, to which all of the churches at least nominally belong, has a strong evangelical and socially conservative bent. Even the Episcopal, United Methodist, and ELCA Lutheran churches have strong conservative elements within them. The religious culture of Monroe is, if anything, more conservative than the religious culture of the country as a whole.

In the midst of this sea of Christian conservatism sits Monroe Congregational UCC. Monroe UCC has for some time been what has passed for a liberal, progressive congregation in Monroe, although until recent times it was never very vocal or visible about it. It called a woman as pastor in the 1930s who served into the 1950s, but, as far as I have been able to determine, the church otherwise did little truly to mark itself as a progressive church until early 2001. At its annual congregational meeting in February of that year the congregation unanimously adopted a "Mission Statement." That statement had been worked out over several months under the guidance of then pastor Diane Schmitz. It contains several theological statements of a progressive nature. The most striking one reads: "We honor God's commandment to love our neighbors as ourselves and welcome all people regardless of race, nationality, ability, age, gender, sexual orientation, or appearance."[21] Although it is buried in the Mission Statement and could easily go unnoticed, this provision in fact committed the church to an Open and Affirming stance. For that community, it was a radical, even revolutionary statement, although I'm not sure the people of the church really understood at the time how revolutionary it was.

It quickly became clear to me that Monroe Congregational Church's role in Monroe was precisely to be a progressive, Open and Affirming alternative to the religious conservatism that so pervaded the community. In the years since 2002, we have had some significant success in becom-

---

21. The full text of the church's Mission Statement is available at www.monroeucc.org.

Introduction

ing that progressive alternative. We have received a good deal of local publicity for our Open and Affirming stance. As a result we are growing and becoming a spiritual home for people, both straight and gay, who are not welcome in other churches or who reject the prejudices and social conservatism that go hand in hand with Biblicist theology. The church's positioning itself as the local progressive alternative is breathing new life into what was a stagnant and declining congregation.

As I provided the pastoral leadership for that renewal, I was becoming ever more aware of a need to develop and articulate a non-literal, progressive Christian theology. Sometimes the theological gap between me and most of the other pastors in town seemed so wide that I even questioned on occasion whether there was any meaningful sense in which they and I could both be called Christians. I began to feel the need to write something that would analyze and articulate the differences between their Christianity and mine. If we were going to be the odd church out in Monroe, we needed to have a solid theological foundation for our beliefs. I knew generally what that theological foundation was. My reading of Christian theology and my training at Seattle University had made me familiar with concepts like myth and symbol, with the higher Biblical criticisms, with contemporary hermeneutics, and with other matters that relate to the questions that were beginning to preoccupy me. I knew my Paul Tillich and my Douglas John Hall reasonably well. I had read Marcus Borg's *Reading the Bible Again for the First Time* and *The Heart of Christianity*. I had even had my weekly adult education forum at church read and discuss them, and I found them very helpful in introducing lay people to the idea of nonliteral Christianity. They really are very good tools for adult education in the church, but I sensed that something was missing. My academic training and my discussions with my father about empiricist philosophy had led me to the belief that as good as many of the popularizing materials on contemporary, nonliteral, progressive Christianity are, they remain ultimately superficial. They do not go to the level of the philosophical, to ontology and epistemology. They do not critique literalism at that most fundamental conceptual level. I began to toy with the idea of attempting to write a book that did what the others I have read do not, that attempts to go to that foundational philosophical level in its critique of Christian literalism. After kicking the idea around for a good couple of years, I finally decided to do it. This book is the result.

Introduction

This study is intended as a guide and resource for people both inside the churches and outside them who are spiritual seekers resisting Christianity or struggling with it because they find any spiritual worldview irrational or because the Christianity they know is unbelievable or morally repugnant to them. It is also appropriate for Christians who have never questioned the popular approach to the faith but who may be curious about or open to considering and understanding a different way of seeing the faith. It is not appropriate for everyone. For example, for some Christians, Biblicism is deeply ingrained and comes easily, without raising significant questions. Many of these Christians find great comfort in their Biblicistic faith. It is not my intent to deprive these Christians of their faith. I believe that in the long run their type of Christianity will not survive, but I have no desire to deprive people of a faith that gives them hope and meaning.

Whether or not I have succeeded in writing a book that is useful for lay people in the church (and outside it who are nonetheless interested in religious issues) is not for me to say. I readily acknowledge that perhaps what I have attempted to do here is not possible or, much more likely, that it is not possible for me. Still, I cling to the hope that some people, be they many or only a few, will find this contribution to the literature on the emerging progressive Christianity helpful. If even only a few people do, my work will not have been in vain.

The material presented here is digested from many years of study. I will cite some of my more important sources. Many of the ideas I advance here are such common currency among Christian theologians, however, that either I cannot identify a particular source or I find citing a particular source to be unnecessary. Nonetheless, three of the authors who have played a major role in shaping my own view of the faith deserve special mention here. The ideas I present in this study are distilled in significant part from the work of the original theologians Paul Tillich, his student Douglas John Hall, and the great popularizer Marcus Borg. Indeed, students of Christianity can benefit by reading Paul Tillich's *Dynamics of Faith*[22] and Marcus Borg's *The Heart of Christianity*.[23] I cannot recommend these two books too highly, and I encourage the readers of this study to read them as well. For a more thorough, systematic, and challenging re-

---

22. Paul Tillich, *Dynamics of Faith* (New York: Harper Torchbooks, 1957).

23. Marcus J. Borg, *The Heart of Christianity: Rediscovering a Life of Faith* (San Francisco: HarperSanFrancisco, 2003).

Introduction

thinking of Christian theology, Douglas John Hall's trilogy, each volume of which carries the subtitle "Christian Theology in a North American Context," is worth the effort for serious students of the faith.[24]

Some readers may find some of the material presented here challenging. Some may find it leading them to question their faith. If you find yourself doing so, just ask yourself: Have I experienced God and God's grace in my life? If you have, and I hope that you have, then trust that experience. Trust that experience and know that God is real and really present in your life. Trust your experience, and look at this book not as something that challenges that experience but as something that affirms and strengthens it in new and exciting ways. Approach this work as a tool for learning to understand the faith in a way that makes it far more true, far more powerful, far more real than it could ever be as mere fact. If you can do that, this book can deepen and strengthen your faith, not undo it. I pray for all of you that it will.

Finally, a note about language. I am committed to using inclusive language wherever possible, but I find the constructions "he or she," "he/she," "his or her," and "his/her" impossibly awkward. Therefore I have chosen instead to use "he" and "she" as generic pronouns interchangeably. I intend no specific gender reference unless the context makes it clear that the reference is to a specific male or female person.

I also decline ever to refer to God using masculine pronouns. God is not male. Neither, of course, is God female. God, as the ultimately transcendent, both includes and transcends human gender distinctions. I therefore most commonly refer to God simply as God.[25] The refusal to use masculine or feminine pronouns for God can lead to some awkward constructions when a noun is used where one would expect a pronoun, or where we must resort to neologisms like "Godself." I, however, prefer this awkwardness to gender exclusive language and therefore tolerate it despite its frequent lack of eloquence.

I do however on occasion retain the term "the Lord" to refer to God or to Christ, as the context determines. I know that many modern people object to "the Lord" because it is, historically, a masculine term and because it refers, again historically speaking, to an authoritarian social and

---

24. These volumes, all published by Fortress Press, Minneapolis are *Thinking the Faith*, 1991, *Professing the Faith*, 1993, and *Confessing the Faith*, 1996.

25. I make a kind of exception to this rule when mentioning the Persons of the Trinity for the reasons I explain when that usage first appears in the book.

Introduction

political structure. I retain the word, however, because in our current context it has no referent other than God or Christ. It hasn't been used as a term applied to social or political relationships among us for centuries, at least in the United States. To me the word means God, or it means Christ. I intend no exclusive masculine meaning nor any statement about the nature of our relationship with God when I use the term. It is simply a title for God or for Christ.

A few weeks before he suffered a debilitating stroke, my twin brother Pete read a draft of this book. He sent me an e-mail in response in which he said: "Your book has made Christianity possible for me." My fervent hope and prayer is that it may do the same for you.

Thomas C. Sorenson
Sultan, Washington
June, 2008

Questions for Reflection and Discussion

1. What have been the barriers to Christianity in your life, if any?
2. What do you think of when you hear the word "Christianity"?

   Are your associations primarily positive or negative? Why?
3. Do you consider yourself a Christian?

   If so, what do you mean by calling yourself a Christian?
4. Do you know people who will have nothing to do with Christianity, or are you such a person yourself?

   If so, what do you think others' primary objections to Christianity are?

   Can you think of any ways of overcoming those objections?

   What, if any, are your primary objections to Christianity?

   What would it take to make Christianity more acceptable to you?

Part One

Overcoming the Obstacle of Philosophical Materialism

ONE OF THE PRIMARY obstacles with which the Christian faith is faced in our context today is the prevalence of the materialist worldview. "Materialist" here does not have its popular meaning of desiring to acquire many material goods. It means something more fundamental than that. It means the belief that only the material, only the physical, is real. A great many people in our dominant North American context today reject Christianity, indeed they reject all faith traditions, because they cannot accept the reality of the spiritual. To these people the only reality is physical reality. If they can't see it, hear it, touch it, smell it, or taste it, it isn't real to them. Many of these philosophical materialists, for that is what they are, consider any belief in the reality of the spiritual to be naïve at best and insidious at worst. Yet philosophical materialism is a rather recent development in the history of human culture, in which it is decidedly a minority voice. In this Part One we will consider the materialist worldview and seek to demonstrate that belief in a spiritual dimension to reality, which is in fact the nearly universal experience of humanity, is both reasonable and intellectually defensible.

1

The Rise of the Materialist Worldview and Its Effect on Christianity

ALL OF US IN our dominant North American context today are children of the Enlightenment and of the Scientific Revolution that was such a big part of it. The Enlightenment was nothing less than a major revolution in human thinking. In European cultures before the Enlightenment, and indeed in human cultures universally, about which more will be said below, the reality of a spiritual dimension was simply assumed. In the European Enlightenment for the first time reason replaced faith as the primary source of human knowledge. Ultimately, the Enlightenment and its intellectual offspring came to deny the reality of the spiritual altogether. We need to take a very brief look at how this happened if we are to understand the task before us of reclaiming the reality of the spiritual.

The Enlightenment was in part an evolution of Christianity. Its secular humanist values are in essence Judeo-Christian values with the faith or religious element removed. The Enlightenment was, however, also a reaction against Christianity. Specifically, it was a reaction against the violence and destruction that the religious wars of the sixteenth and seventeenth centuries visited upon Europe in the wake of the Protestant Reformation. By the time the Treaty of Westphalia ended the worst of those wars, known as The Thirty Years' War, in 1648, much of Europe's intellectual elite was thoroughly disillusioned with religion, in whose name countless people had been killed and many of Europe's cities had been destroyed. The contradiction between what Christianity preached and how Christian powers (if by no means all individual Christian people) had acted led the European intelligentsia to look for another way.

The thinkers of the Enlightenment found that other way in human reason. They elevated human reason to the status of the arbiter of truth.

The Cartesian revolution in philosophy introduced a dualism in which a sharp distinction was drawn between the thinking subject and an objective world about which the thinking subject thought.[1] Isaac Newton (1643–1727) introduced to the world a mechanical universe in which objects moved not at the will of God but according to immutable physical and mathematical principles called the laws of nature. Reason became the standard by which all human activity was judged. Reason dominated the political philosophy of John Locke (1632–1704) and the economic philosophy of Adam Smith (1723–1790). Reason was sweeping the field in virtually every area of human endeavor.

As reason and science became the dominant ways in which people understood truth, God was pushed more and more to the margins. As early as 1616, when the Catholic Church condemned the astronomy theories of Copernicus which denied that the earth was the center of the universe, science and religion came to be more and more at odds. The Catholic Church's infamous condemnation of Galileo (1564–1642) for teaching a Copernican view of the universe that he had confirmed with his own astronomic observations simply made the growing gap between science and religion wider and more apparent.[2] The church may have tried to stop the advance of scientific knowledge, but it was unable to do so. The Catholic Church's opposition to the new science served only to make the church more and more irrelevant in the development of European culture.

It wasn't long before Europe's intellectuals, forced to choose between faith and science, began to abandon belief in God altogether. Isaac Newton may have considered himself still to be a Christian, but by the mid-eighteenth century the high intellectual culture of Europe had largely abandoned the faith and was moving toward a strictly materialist worldview. Deism was a sort of halfway house on that journey. A rationalistic product of the Enlightenment, Deism did not deny the existence of God altogether. Rather, it limited God's role to that of Creator. Deism saw God as The Great Clockmaker. God created the universe, charged it with energy, then let it go to run on its own according to those natural

---

1. The term Cartesian refers to René Descartes, 1596–1650, the French philosopher famous for the saying "I think, therefore I am," often rendered in its Latin form *cogito ergo sum*.

2. In 1633, the Catholic Church forced Galileo to recant his writings on astronomy and sentenced him to house arrest for the rest of his life. In 1992, the Catholic Church lifted its "edict of Inquisition" against Galileo.

laws that Newton and the other scientists of the Enlightenment were so busy discovering.[3]

A God as marginal as the God of Deism is unlikely to survive very long. Indeed, Deism did not much outlive the eighteenth century. By the nineteenth century European intellectuals had largely abandoned belief in God altogether. There certainly were great Christian theologians in the nineteenth century. The name Søren Kierkegaard comes readily to mind in this regard. Yet the worldview that was coming more and more to dominate the cultural landscape was philosophical materialism, or at least a philosophy that left little or no room for God. The German philosopher Georg Wilhelm Friedrich Hegel (1770–1831) undertook to create a philosophical system to explain all of human experience. One of his bywords was "the real is rational, and the rational real." The French philosopher Auguste Comte (1798–1857) developed the influential doctrine of Positivism, which denies the value of metaphysical speculation and holds that the objects of human perception are the only things we can know. There may still have been some room for God in Hegel's system, but Karl Marx (1818–1883), in many ways a disciple of Hegel and of Comte, took the final philosophical step to materialism. With Comte he taught that only the material is real, but with Hegel he accepted the validity of metaphysical speculation. He developed an entire philosophy of economics, politics, society, history, and culture on the basis of what he called "dialectical materialism," the belief, that truly is nothing more than metaphysical speculation, that matter, the only reality, has its own internal dynamic that produces the events of human history. In biology, Charles Darwin's great work *The Origin of Species* (1859) that introduced the concepts of evolution through adaptive genetic changes and the survival of the fittest seemed to challenge humans' supposedly privileged position in creation as the one creature made in God's image. It even challenged God's role as Creator, at least in the traditional Christian sense. Philosophical materialism, whether "dialectical" or not, became the dominant world view of the European and North American intelligentsia. God was denied, or at least

---

3. Deism was the belief of most of the "Founding Fathers" of the United States, including Thomas Jefferson, the author of the Declaration of Independence. Deism is only marginally Christian, denying as it does the active presence of God in the world after the initial act of creation. Jefferson went so far as to rewrite the Gospels, removing from them all miracles and any claim that Jesus was divine. The claim of Christian social conservatives that this country was founded as a "Christian nation" is therefore simply false as an historical matter.

displaced, in the dominant intellectual disciplines, including economics, sociology, and political science. The spiritual worldview became culturally marginalized, and, by the dawn of the twentieth century, religious belief was considered quaint and naïve in most Euro-American intellectual circles.

One form of philosophical materialism that is very widespread in our context today is what we can call scientism. Scientism starts with the scientific method, the method of observation of natural phenomena and the confirmation or rejection of hypotheses about those phenomena through experimentation. This method produces what are considered to be valid scientific truths. In scientism, all other ways of discerning truth are rejected. To put some fancy words on it, epistemology becomes ontology. A way of knowing certain truths (an epistemology) becomes the determiner of all reality (an ontology). Only that which can be established by the scientific method is accepted as real. Most people who believe in scientism probably don't recognize it as a belief system. To them it is simply how things are. People who believe in scientism (some but by no means all of whom are scientists) are not open to the spiritual truths of Christianity or of any other faith. Christianity will have nothing to say to them until they can see that scientism is in fact a very narrow understanding of truth that rejects a nearly universal human experience of the reality of the spiritual.

Philosophical materialism is an obstacle to faith in at least two ways. First, in the philosophical materialist worldview, truth consists only of facts. Especially in scientism, as we have seen, only that is true which can be established as true through the scientific method. The scientific method works very well for establishing facts about the physical world. Modern science has produced an explosion of human knowledge about the physical world. This knowledge consists of facts (or things we assume to be facts, which for our purposes here amounts to the same thing). When our understanding of reality is reduced to that which can be established by science, our understanding of reality is reduced to facts. What we take to be true has to be factual because for us only facts are true.

We will have much more to say about Christian literalism in the course of this study. The point we must make here is that Christian Fundamentalism and other forms of Christian literalism have been profoundly influenced by and indeed reflect this modern, materialist reduction of truth to facts. One example will illustrate this point. Christian literalists in our context insist that the creation account of Genesis 1:1–2:3

The Rise of the Materialist Worldview and Its Effect on Christianity

is "true." By this they mean that God's act of creation occurred literally in the way it is presented in that ancient story. By "literally" they mean factually. This is a philosophically materialist view of truth. For the true literalist, the Genesis creation story is not true if it is not factually true. The true literalist says that if we had been there we would have observed things happening exactly as the first creation story in Genesis describes them. For the literalist, the truth of Genesis 1 must be the same order of truth as the truths of science because that is the only kind of truth they recognize. Christian literalism has thus been profoundly influenced by philosophical materialism. Because Christianity must be liberated from literalism, philosophical materialism is also something from which Christianity must be liberated.

Philosophical materialism is, however, an obstacle to Christianity in an even more profound way. Like any tradition that can truly be called religious, Christianity is a spiritual worldview. It understands that reality consists of more than the material, more than the physical. Neither Christianity nor any other faith tradition will be an option for countless people in our context so long as they cling to the materialist view of reality. Overcoming the obstacles to faith in our context requires nothing short of a major paradigm shift in the way the most educated and sophisticated elements of our culture view reality. As Christian apologists[4] we must make the spiritual worldview reasonable to those of our contemporaries who today consider it to be an irrational superstition. It is to that task that we now turn as we consider the scope and nature of the human experience of the spiritual.

---

4. An apologist in this sense is not someone who says she's sorry about something. An apologist, as the term is used here, is one who practices apologetics. Apologetics is the branch of theology that attempts to present the faith to the world in meaningful ways which speak to the culture of the time and to those living in that culture. This book is an attempt at Christian apologetics for our contemporary North American context.

Questions for Reflection and Discussion

1. What is real for you?

    Is the physical world that you perceive with your senses real?

    How do you know?

    Is there any reality beyond the physical world that you perceive with your senses?

    How do you know?

2. What does our culture consider to be real?

    Is there any dimension of reality that our culture denies?

3. Recall anything you may have learned in school about the European Enlightenment and the role it assigned to reason in human life.

    What is reason?

    What is the proper role of reason in human thinking?

    Are there types of knowledge that transcend or at least are different from reason? What are they?

2

The Reality and Nature of the Spiritual

PHILOSOPHICAL MATERIALISM IS AN obstacle to faith. It is perhaps the most obvious obstacle to faith, since it is grounded precisely in a denial of the reality of all but the material, the physical. The defining characteristic of philosophical materialism is precisely that it denies the reality of the spiritual. The variety of philosophical materialism that we have here called scientism is the dominant worldview among educated people in our context today. Philosophical materialism can seem a natural position for humans to take because it is the ruling view of those who occupy the "commanding heights" of our culture.[1] We constantly hear members of the American intelligentsia belittle belief in spiritual reality. The astronomer Carl Sagan's name became virtually a household word among us with his captivating television shows about the wonders of the physical universe and his radical scientism. The biologist Edward O. Wilson has become famous promoting a biological reductionism that leaves no room for the spiritual. Authors like Sam Harris have critical success with books like his *The End of Faith: Religion, Terror, and the Future of Reason*.[2] The examples could go on and on. Culturally aware people in our context can easily get the idea that philosophical materialism is the only reasonable worldview. It is easy in our context to conclude that belief in the spiritual is nothing but an anachronistic superstition.

Yet philosophical materialism is a decidedly minority view in human experience. Every human culture has had an experience of the numinous. We know that this is true because every human culture has a mythology, that is, every human culture has its stories of the gods, or of

---

1. The term comes from the history of Soviet Marxism, where it referred to the dominant economic institutions of the country.

2. Sam Harris, *The End of Faith: Religion, Terror, and the Future of Reason* (New York: Norton, 2004).

God, and of how these divine beings, or divine being, relate to humanity and to the world at large. These stories are not mere flights of fancy. They are grounded in and reflect an experience of the spiritual dimension of reality. Their very universality shows that they reflect a universal human experience. Experiencing the spiritual, it seems, is part of what it means to be human.

This experience, of course, takes a great many forms. Some of them may seem a bit primitive to us, yet they all reflect an experience of the divine. You may have heard some of the myths of the Native American peoples. These stories of the gods reflect the experience of the people who created them. The myths speak of the divine using images from the experience of the people, the animals they knew and the places where they lived. In some of those myths, Raven is the instrument of creation, for example. We have all probably heard of the Native American concept of the Great Spirit. It is an expression of the people's sense that there is a transcendent spiritual reality with which they can relate in life and in death.

We all learned a little bit about the gods of the Greeks and Romans in school. We've all heard of Zeus, for example. These myths may seem primitive to us moderns. The gods and goddesses seem so human. They have human passions and can be every bit as deceitful as we humans can. Yet these myths too reflect a people's experience of the spiritual realm. Some of the myths are great simply as stories, yet in the culture that produced them they functioned as more than that. They were stories of how the spiritual forces in life relate to the people of the culture. That's what makes them myths and not mere stories. The same thing is true of the myths of other cultures you may have heard of. The Egyptians told stories of Isis and Osiris. The Norse told stories of Odin and Thor. The names and the stories were different. The gods they spoke about were different; yet these myths all reflect the experience of these diverse people that there is a reality beyond physical reality, that there is a numinous reality that we can experience and to which we can relate in different ways.[3]

The people who were the direct spiritual ancestors of contemporary Judaism, Christianity, and Islam also had experiences of the divine. They also reflected those experiences in their myths, that is, in their stories of

---

3. For brilliant treatments of myth in human culture see Joseph Campbell, *The Hero with a Thousand Faces* (Princeton: Princeton University Press, 1972), and *The Power of Myth* (New York: Doubleday, 1988). See also Carl Jung, *Man and His Symbols* (New York: Dell, 1964), and Paul Tillich, *The Dynamics of Faith* (New York: Harper Torchbooks, 1957).

The Reality and Nature of the Spiritual

the gods or, if you prefer, of God.[4] We have a great collection of those stories, some of the oldest spiritual literature that the world has today. We call it the Hebrew Bible or the Old Testament.[5] Unlike the myths of the Greeks, the Egyptians, and others, the Hebrew Bible also tells stories of the history of a people, the Hebrew people, from their legendary ancestor Abraham through triumph and tragedy, through nation building, conquest, exile, and restoration. Its focus on history and on God's presence and actions in history make it one of the most revolutionary documents in human history and one of the most foundational for our modern conceptions of the nature of God and of reality.

Yet the Hebrew Bible also tells myths, and indeed its historical stories often have mythical elements in them. It tells stories of the gods and their interactions with the people. It tells the story of one particular god, most commonly named Yahweh. In its magnificent stories, Yahweh evolves in the people's conceptions from a primitive tribal war god to the Creator God of the entire universe, the ruler of all creation, and the only true God.[6] The Hebrew Bible presents a magnificent panorama of the numinous experiences of the Hebrew people. It is truly one of the great spiritual documents that humanity has produced.[7]

For Christians, of course, there is more to the Bible than the Old Testament. We have the collection of early Christian writings that we call the New Testament. Whatever else the New Testament may be, it is at its

---

4. It might be helpful here to point out that the earlier writings in the Hebrew Bible (which are not necessarily the ones that come first in the Bible as we now have it) do not deny the reality of other gods in addition to Yahweh. The Ten Commandments, for example, begin by saying: "I am Yahweh, your God.... You shall have no other gods before (or besides) me." Exod 20:2–3, NRSV adapted. This statement so far from denying the reality of other gods besides Yahweh clearly assumes them. The First Commandment is not a statement of monotheism. It is rather a statement of henotheism, a belief that there are many gods but that a particular people is to worship only one god in particular. It is a command that the Hebrew people shall worship only Yahweh and shall not worship the gods of other peoples.

5. The literature of Hinduism is older, but this statement still stands.

6. This evolution is chronological but it is not reflected in the traditional order of the books of the Hebrew Bible. Those books do not appear in the order in which they are written, and many of them contain materials written at different times.

7. Jews, Christians, and, to some extent, Muslims, usually see the Hebrew Bible as fundamentally different from and superior to the myths of other ancient cultures. Whether it is in fact different in the ways our faith tradition has usually asserted is a subject we will take up in part two.

core a collection of myths, that is, a collection of stories about the numinous, about God, and about how God relates to creation. The stories of the New Testament see God relating to creation primarily through the figure of Jesus of Nazareth. That focus on Jesus, whom Christians call the Christ, is what makes the New Testament specifically Christian. It reflects the spiritual experience of the people of the early Christian communities of God seen in and known through Jesus.[8]

The other great world religions function in the same way. Muslims tell stories of Allah (simply a contraction of the Arabic for "the God") and of Muhammad, whom they consider to be God's Messenger. They see God relating to the world through the teachings of Muhammad and through the Quran, the words of God that Muhammad conveyed to them. Like other religions, Islam reflects a people's experience of the divine and uses myth to talk about that experience. Hinduism is the oldest of the world's great religions. It tells stories of numerous gods and goddesses, or of numerous male and female manifestations of the divine, stories which once more reflect the people's experience of the divine. Hinduism's spiritual descendant Buddhism is somewhat harder to fit into this scheme because it represents less a system of stories about the gods than a philosophy of living. Yet Buddhism too has an understanding of the nature of ultimate reality, although it doesn't call that reality God. It too is a system in which people live their spiritual lives, in which people live their relationship to the numinous, envisioned in Buddhism not as personal but ultimately as Nothingness or the Oneness of all Being.

All human cultures have had an experience of the spiritual. From the tribal religions of Africa, Australia, and the Americas to the great theological systems of Scholasticism,[9] from the ziggurats of ancient Sumer to the rural church on the American prairie and the great mosques of

---

8. At this point I say nothing about the literal truth of those stories or the lack thereof. We will take up that prickly issue soon enough. The point here is only that the New Testament is, perhaps among other things, a collection of stories that reflect a people's experience of God and that it thus reflects a universal human experience in a particular form for a particular people.

9. Scholasticism is the school of Christian theology that flourished in the High Middle Ages in the twelfth and thirteenth centuries, when theologians like Thomas Aquinas (c. 1225–1274) developed great theological systems that were heavily influenced by the philosophy of Aristotle, who was just then becoming known in Western Europe, having been re-introduced into Europe by the Moors who ruled Spain and who had preserved the work of that great ancient Greek philosopher.

The Reality and Nature of the Spiritual

Istanbul, people of all times and all cultures have experienced the reality of the spiritual. As they have sought to express that experience and to give it structure and content, they have told stories of the gods. They still do.

The exception is the culture of the European Enlightenment and the philosophical materialism that it produced. That culture makes the conscious decision to deny the reality of the spiritual. Evidence of the reality of the spiritual is all around us, but Western secular culture sets itself above all other cultures and claims that only it has the truth about the nature of reality. It dismisses humanity's experience of the spiritual as primitive and unworthy of sophisticated people. That dismissal is an act of the will. It is itself a kind of faith because it is a decision about the ultimate nature of reality. In his great television series with Bill Moyers, Joseph Campbell explains this phenomenon using the metaphor of scales. In refusing to see the reality of the spiritual, we put scales over our eyes. All that is necessary for us to open ourselves to spiritual reality is for us to remove the scales, to allow ourselves to see what is really there. That our contemporary secular culture refuses to do, all the while proclaiming that it alone has discovered the true nature of reality.

Human experience of the spiritual is universal; but that, of course, does not mean that every individual human has an experience of the spiritual. Some people never have an experience that they identify with a spiritual reality, especially in the context of our dominant culture in North America. The prevalence of the materialist worldview among us may predispose many of us to deny spiritual experience. The dominant voices of our culture tell us it isn't real, so many of us do not believe in the reality of the spiritual. We explain away any experience that transcends what we experience as physical reality because we are told that what we experience as physical reality is the only reality. Or we never have any such experience at all because our minds are closed to the reality of spirit by a pervasive philosophical materialism and a rationalism that denies the reality of the mystical. Many of our compatriots in fact do not experience the reality of the spiritual.

Yet some of us still do. I have, and perhaps the best way for me to illustrate for you the way in which personal experience of the spiritual makes the spiritual real for us is to describe for you the most powerful spiritual experience of my life. I've had others, but this is the one that cinches it for me. It happened on the morning of Saturday, August 3, 2002. I had graduated from seminary some twenty months earlier. I was serving part-time as pastor of the congregation I still serve. Three days earlier, on July 31, my wife of thirty years had died of breast cancer. Although we had known for many months that her death was coming, I was devastated. I felt an emotional and spiritual anguish I didn't know I was capable of feeling. On the morning of August 3, as I stood in the shower weeping, I began to sink to my knees in grief. It was simply too much to bear. As I was dropping to my knees, without thinking about it, I uttered the prayer "Lift me up, Lord." Immediately I felt myself physically lifted up onto my feet. All I can tell you is how I experienced it. I didn't do it. I didn't stand myself up. I couldn't have. A force that I did not control grasped me and lifted me up upright. I can't explain it. All I know is that I felt it. I experienced it. When I did the thought that immediately flashed through my mind was: "Oh! All that stuff I'm always talking about really is real!" That was my experience. A spiritual reality had broken into my life and put me back on my feet. Many, many times since then, when I have felt depressed or disillusioned with the world, slouching in care or emotional pain, I have lifted myself upright to remind myself of that experience. Doing so has always made me feel better. Beyond that, a few times, I have felt a reprise of that original experience, not as strong as it was the first time but nonetheless real. I have felt myself once more lifted up, and when I have I've said: "Oh, yeah. That's right. God really is real."

Perhaps you haven't had a spiritual experience as dramatic as the one I just described. Not everyone does, yet many people have other types of experiences of the spiritual. Have you ever stood in awe at a glorious sunrise and been filled with a sense of wonder and wellbeing? That's an experience of the spiritual. Have you ever given birth to a child, or been present as your life partner has done so? Were you filled with joy and amazement at the appearance of precious new life? Have you been moved to tears that you can't really explain? That's an experience of the spiritual. Have you felt the power of the Bach B Minor Mass? That's an experience of the spiritual. Have you been so moved by great worship that you've leapt up and shouted for joy? That's an experience of the spiritual. Have you held a dying loved one in your arms and comforted them, and yourself, as your loved one passed from this life to whatever lies beyond this life and felt not only grief but also a kind of peace that you can't explain? That's an experience of the spiritual. Maybe you've had experiences like these, and maybe you haven't. Maybe you've had other experiences that had about them something extraordinary, something transcendent, something both

The Reality and Nature of the Spiritual

higher and deeper than ordinary, everyday experiences. Or maybe in your ordinary, everyday experiences you've experienced love, and satisfaction, and fulfillment. Maybe you've felt anger at all the violence and injustice in the world and been moved to join a demonstration against war or a march for civil rights. Maybe your sense of compassion has moved you to adopt a child through an international relief agency or even just to send money to help the victims of a natural disaster in some distant part of the world you've never seen and never will. All of these experiences, and so many, many others, are experiences of the spiritual. They are experiences of the transcendent, of ultimate mystery, and they are very real.

A philosophical materialist would dismiss our experiences. He would say they're all psychological or even biological, not metaphysical. She would say we attribute more to our experiences out of a desperate desire to believe in God. Can I prove the philosophical materialist wrong? No, I can't. All I can really say is that that's not how I have lived the spiritual experiences in my life. That's not what those experiences mean to me. Perhaps it is not what your experiences of the spiritual mean to you.

You may be saying: "Well, if that's all it is, there's no reason for me to take it seriously. All that is just his subjective experience talking. It isn't objective reality." If that's what you're saying, please consider this. As human beings we all exist within ourselves. We are centered selves. It is how we are constituted as human beings. From the center of our selves we perceive a world outside ourselves. If we have all of the normal human senses, we see a world of people and objects. We hear sounds that seem to come from outside ourselves. We touch things and feel them. We taste and smell things. Even if we lack some of those senses, we perceive a world outside of ourselves. Maybe we can't see it, but our hearing and our touch convey it to us. Maybe we can't hear it, but we see and we feel. From the center of our selves we perceive a world, and because we perceive that world, it is real to us. Our perception is what makes the world real. Our *experience* of a world outside ourselves makes that world real for us. The great Scottish philosopher David Hume (1711–1776) had the profound insight that our perception of the world is in fact all that we know or can know. Perception is all we humans have or can have. We experience our perceptions, and our experience makes our perceptions real.

As humans we necessarily live in subjectivity. This conclusion flows from the analysis in the Philosophical Appendix to this book, but because subjectivity is such an important concept in this study let me say a bit more about it here. By subjectivity I do not mean bias. We often use the word subjective to mean that a person is responding to something out of the person's biases, prejudices, or pre-conceived notions, but that is not the term's meaning here. Here, subjectivity means only that from the center of our selves we as subjects perceive a world through our senses. We as subjects experience a world that we perceive to be external to ourselves. Our experience of that perceived world makes it real for us. We relate to that world as a subject who perceives it. That is the only way we can relate to it. It is real to us not because we can absolutely know that it exists apart from our perception of it, but because we perceive it, because we experience it, because we relate to it as a perceiving, experiencing subject. In other words, we interpret the world we perceive as real precisely because we perceive it and experience it.

Beyond that, we accept the world we perceive and experience as real because doing so facilitates our existence. It works. Accepting the world of our perceptions as real, most of the time, facilitates our existence. The world is real to me because I perceive it from the center of my self, and that perception facilitates my existence. That perception and the existential benefit that flows from it are what make the world real.

We accept the physical world as real because we perceive it as real and because accepting it as real facilitates our existence. It works. My spiritual experience in the shower that Saturday morning in August is real to me in the same way. I experienced it. I experienced it as a force outside of myself acting on me quite apart from my own volition, my own voluntary actions. Interpreting that experience as spiritual makes sense of it for me. It gives me strength and hope. It got me through a time of grief I don't know how I would otherwise have survived. That spiritual experience is as real to me as a speeding car bearing down on me as I cross the street, and for all the same reasons.

Yet there is one more issue we need to consider. Accepting what we perceive and experience as real does not in fact always facilitate our existence. Our perception may in fact work to diminish or even to end our lives. The delusory perceptions of mental illness are an extreme example of this phenomenon, but most of us have at one time or another believed in the reality of some fact, or of some attitude toward us by another person, that turned out not to correspond with further experience but to be contradicted by it. Maybe my experience of the reality of the spiritual in the shower that morning was that kind of hallucination. How can I know?

The Reality and Nature of the Spiritual

There are, I think, two responses to that question. The first is that my accepting the reality of the spiritual in my experience has had no negative consequences. To refer here to an example from the Philosophical Appendix at the back of the book, it hasn't caused me to run in front of a bus I didn't see coming while fleeing a car I thought was there but wasn't. Instead it has facilitated my existence by giving me that strength and hope I just mentioned. Beyond that, one of the things that we humans perceive, experience, and accept as real is other humans. Other humans share their perceptions and their experiences with us. When a great many other humans report experiences similar to ours that also facilitate their existence, that help them make sense of their lives and that give them hope, courage, strength, peace, and the other things we think of as fruits of the spirit, it helps me to know that my experience is not an aberration, that it is not idiosyncratic.

This is why the universality of the human experience of the spiritual is so important. It tells us that countless other humans, in all times and places and from all human cultures, have had spiritual experiences like ours; or, if we haven't had an experience that we can identify as spiritual, it tells us that nonetheless an experience of the spiritual is a human possibility. It can, if we will let it, open us up to that possibility. Our openness to the possibility of a spiritual experience actually makes our having a spiritual experience more likely, since we are unlikely to experience that to which we are closed. If I don't accept the possibility that another person could love me, I am unlikely to experience another person loving me. If I don't accept the possibility of the spiritual, I am unlikely to experience the spiritual.

The point is this: The universal human experience of the reality of the spiritual, and our own personal experiences of the reality of the spiritual, if we have had them, tell us that the spiritual is real. It is not less real for us than physical reality because both physical and spiritual reality are real because we perceive them, we experience them, and accepting them as real facilitates our existence. I know that that is true because I have experienced it. Perhaps you have too.

The reality of the spiritual is a universal human experience in the sense that it has been part of every human culture. It is also for at least some of us part of our personal experience. But there is one more important question we must consider here. What do we mean by the term "the spiritual" or by its synonyms the numinous or the divine? How are we to understand the reality which human culture universally experiences and that we have been calling the spiritual? How am I to understand that force that grasped me in the shower that morning, lifting me up in my grief? At this point I am asking these questions at the most basic level. I am not yet asking "who is God?" Not all human cultures name the spiritual "God," so we have to start at a more basic level. Human experience of the spiritual is extremely diverse. People in different times and in different places have experienced the spiritual in different ways. They have experienced it as consisting of one God and of many gods. They have experienced it as gracious and loving and as malevolent and threatening. They have experienced it as personal and as nothingness. The question before us here is: What is there about those experiences that allow us to say of them all that they are experiences of the spiritual?

At the most general level, what all of those experiences have in common is that they are experiences of a reality beyond the reality that we humans perceive with our ordinary senses. They are experiences of a reality that is not apparent to most of us most of the time. When we experience this reality, we experience it differently than the way we experience what we perceive as physical reality. On rare occasions some of us may have a vision—something we see—or an audition—something we hear—that we experience as being a sight or a sound of the spiritual; but for most of us who have had what we experience as an encounter with the spiritual, our perception of the spiritual has been of a different nature. We experience a feeling. We experience a pull in a certain direction. We experience an emotion that seems to transcend the ordinary. We have a dream that is particularly powerful, meaningful, or moving. Science doesn't tell us we have spirituality as a sixth sense, but people who are particularly sensitive to the spiritual often speak of having a sixth sense, of having some faculty with which they experience a different order of reality. So one way of understanding the spiritual is that it is that reality which we definitely experience but which we experience in a different way.

Because the experience of the spiritual is an experience of something that seems to us to be beyond our ordinary experiences and perceptions, we can call that experience an experience of the depth dimension of reality. At its most basic level, the spiritual is the more in everything that is. It is the reality that transcends physical reality and yet is present within physical reality. It is the realm of that which is other and beyond but that is also immanent in everything we perceive and experience. Tillich called

The Reality and Nature of the Spiritual

it "the ground of being," which points to its role as the reality upon which all other reality is founded and by which all other reality is sustained.[10]

Because the spiritual lies beyond the world that we perceive with our ordinary senses it always has and retains the character of mystery. We can experience it, but what it actually is remains always unknown. In his great hymn "Bring Many Names," Brian Wren calls it the "joyful darkness far beyond our seeing."[11] The spiritual is mystery not in the sense of a mystery novel where we try to resolve the mystery and where all is revealed in the end. It remains always ultimately unknown. It remains always mystery. It is that which we can experience but that is ultimately unknown and unknowable.

You have no doubt detected by now that there is an inherent problem in any effort to describe the spiritual and much more of a problem with any effort to define it. Language fails us. It *must* fail us because language is part of the world of ordinary physical perception and experience, yet we are trying to use it precisely to describe something that transcends ordinary physical perception and experience. There is indeed a major and unavoidable problem of language when we seek to talk about the spiritual. It is to that question of how we are to talk about the spiritual that we now turn in part two.

Questions for Reflection and Discussion

1. Recall anything you may have learned in your life about the mythology of other cultures.

    Are those myths more than ordinary stories?

    Do they tell us anything about the human experience of reality? If so, what do they tell us?

2. Have you ever had a spiritual experience?

    What was it?

    What does it mean to you to call the experience spiritual?

---

10. See, for example, Paul Tillich, *Systematic Theology*, Vol. 1, (Chicago: University of Chicago Press, 1951), p. 156. "The ground of being" is Tillich's basic term for God.

11. Being a good theologian, Wren expresses the paradoxical nature of the spiritual mystery when he also calls it "closer yet than breathing."

Part Two

Overcoming the Obstacle of Biblicism

In Part One, we saw that philosophical materialism, which denies the reality of the spiritual, is a rather recent development in human culture and that it represents a distinct minority viewpoint. We explored another way of understanding reality, the way of subjective perception and experience. We saw that that worldview accepts and validates the human experience of the spiritual. Yet while philosophical materialism is a prevalent worldview in our context, it is by no means universally held among us. A great many people today say that they are "spiritual" people, yet a great many of these people who accept the reality of the spiritual reject Christianity as a valid expression of our relationship to the spiritual. One major reason why so many people among us who are open to experiencing the spiritual in their lives reject Christianity is Biblicism, the concept that we introduced in the Introduction to this work. In Part Two we will explore Biblicism more deeply. We will examine the nature of the language of faith generally and introduce the concepts myth and symbol. We will explore some of the ways in which literalism rests upon philosophical fallacies. We will explore the Bible as myth and take a closer look at Biblicism's claim that the Bible is God's word because God wrote it or at least inspired it. We will look at the ways in which seeing the Bible not as divine but as a human product opens it up as a source and guide for our own spiritual lives.

3

The Language of Faith: Symbol and Myth

At the end of Part One we saw that there is an inherent problem in any attempt to use human language to talk about the nature of the spiritual. By "the spiritual" we mean something that we experience in a different way than we experience the ordinary world of our sense perceptions. The spiritual, or the numinous which is another common word for what we mean here, both inheres in and transcends that world of ordinary perception. Humans, however, create language out of and in response to those ordinary perceptions. Language originates as a way to help us live in and understand that world of sights, sounds, smells, tastes, and tactile sensations. It is very good at coming up with words to designate perceived objects. It can also come up with words to describe human thought processes, words like idea for example. It creates words for concepts which the human brain constructs but which do not refer to material objects, words like freedom and love. Human language works very well to describe and communicate these ordinary perceptions and the human thought processes that derive from them.

Although we do perceive and experience the spiritual, we do not perceive or experience it with the usual human senses, and it is not merely a human thought process that derives from those perceptions. Human language, therefore, cannot truly grasp what the spiritual is. In its characteristic of transcendence, the spiritual transcends human language. Therefore, any attempt to name it or describe it in human language involves the use of a tool that is incommensurate with the task to which we apply the tool. The tool, our language, simply isn't up to the job at hand, namely, the job of naming or adequately describing the spiritual dimension of reality.

Yet we humans have within us a drive to communicate our experiences of the spiritual, to share them with others, to hear of others' experiences, and to try to make sense of these experiences, our own and those of other people. The only tool we have for this job is human language, inadequate as it may be. And so we use it. We talk about our experience of the spiritual. We give the spiritual, or various aspects of it, names. We tell of our experiences in human words. We tell stories about our experiences, or we tell stories that are like our experiences and that we hope will convey the essence of our experiences to other people. Sometimes we use images to go along with our stories, images of things that we know from our ordinary perception of the physical world. In other words, we use myth and symbol. Myth and symbol are the language of faith. They are the use of finite, limited human words, concepts, and images in an attempt to communicate something of the truth we have experienced of that which is infinite and which infinitely transcends our finite, limited words, concepts and images.

To understand the nature of myth and symbol, we will begin with the concept of the symbol. Specifically, we will begin with the concept of the symbol as the great twentieth century theologian Paul Tillich explains it in his book *Dynamics of Faith*.[1] In Chapter Three of that work, "Symbols of Faith," Tillich gives a concise, insightful, and powerful (albeit too brief) explanation of the nature and function of symbol, and we can do no better than to borrow and to some extent to amplify his discussion here.[2]

Tillich defines symbols as having six characteristics. The first is that they point beyond themselves to something else.[3] To illustrate this first characteristic of symbols, Tillich uses not symbols themselves but what he calls signs, because signs, like symbols, point beyond themselves to something else. "The red sign at the street corner points to the order to stop the movement of cars at certain intervals."[4] A red sign and an order to stop have no relationship to each other except that which people create through agreed upon conventions. A symbol, like a sign, points beyond itself to something else with which it has no necessary relationship but only one given it by human convention.

---

1. Paul Tillich, *Dynamics of Faith* (New York: Harper Torchbooks, 1957).

2. Tillich properly notes that not all symbols are religious. The flag, for example, functions as a symbol for a nation in the same way that a religious symbol functions for the spiritual. Our focus here, however, is on religious symbols. We will not consider non-religious symbols further in this work.

3. Ibid., 41.

4. Ibid.

The Language of Faith: Symbol and Myth

Unlike a sign, however, a symbol has several other necessary characteristics. The first is that a symbol participates in that to which it points.[5] "Participation" is an important concept in Tillich's overall philosophy and theology. It means that a symbol has a presence in ordinary, physical reality, but that it also has a presence in the transcendent spiritual reality to which it points. It exists in two planes of reality at once. If it did not, it would be merely an ordinary physical object. It is the symbol's "participation" in the greater reality to which it points that makes it a symbol and not merely a sign, not merely another physical object to which humans ascribe a certain meaning.

Tillich's third characteristic of a symbol is that it "opens up levels of reality which otherwise are closed for us."[6] This is another way of saying that symbols are the only tools we have for accessing the spiritual. A true symbol connects us with transcendent reality without itself actually being transcendent reality. Symbols are our windows into a plane of reality that would otherwise be closed to us because it transcends our usual sense perceptions and experiences. This third characteristic of the symbol is closely related to the fourth characteristic. A symbol not only opens for us a dimension of reality that otherwise remains closed to us, it "also unlocks dimensions and elements of our soul which correspond to the dimensions and elements of reality."[7] Tillich doesn't use this concept here, but what he's getting at is that a true symbol mediates between the transcendent spiritual reality and the corresponding parts of the human soul that strive for connection with the transcendent. It mediates, that is, it communicates and conveys something of the transcendent spiritual to those parts of the human soul where, through symbols, we connect to that transcendent spiritual. Put more simply, a symbol is something that connects us to that which transcends us but that is also immanent within us, that is, to the spiritual dimension of reality.

Tillich's fifth characteristic of symbols is that they cannot be produced intentionally.[8] Tillich says that they "grow out of the individual or collective unconscious and cannot function without being accepted by

---

5. Ibid., 42.
6. Ibid.
7. Ibid.
8. Ibid., 43.

the unconscious dimension of our being."[9] Symbols come to be symbols because they resonate with something deep within the individual human psyche and the collective unconscious of humanity. They touch and satisfy some deep human psychological and spiritual need. That is one of the things that makes them symbols, and without doing it they aren't symbols at all.

The sixth and last characteristic of symbols is a consequence of the fact that we can't just make them up, we can't just invent a symbol. They grow. Symbols arise as symbols "when the situation is ripe for them...."[10] This means that new symbols come into existence when they correspond to the psychic and spiritual needs of a group of people and produce within those people a response to the symbol as symbol.[11]

Perhaps this concept of the symbol will become clearer if we take a familiar Christian symbol, the cross, and see how it corresponds to each of Tillich's six characteristics. The cross points beyond itself to something else. As a mere physical object, a cross is simply two pieces of wood, a vertical upright and a crossbeam. Historically, it was an instrument of torture and execution, yet for Christians it points to something else. It points to Jesus Christ. It is our symbol for Jesus Christ. It does more than point to Jesus, however. In a real sense, it *is* Jesus present among us. In the terminology of Tillich's second characteristic of a symbol, it participates in the spiritual reality of Jesus. And beyond that, it satisfies the third and fourth characteristics as well. It mediates Jesus to us. It conveys to us the transcendent reality of Jesus and touches our souls, which respond to that touch. To put the matter again more simply, the cross as a symbol connects us to Jesus and Jesus to us.

---

9. Ibid. Tillich takes this characteristic of symbols from the depth psychology of Carl Jung, and it may be hard for students unfamiliar with Jung's psychology to understand. I cannot possibly explain Jungian psychology here. Suffice it to say that Jung believed that there is not only an unconscious dimension to the individual human psyche but that humanity has a collective unconscious that connects all humans and from which human symbols and myths emerge. The similarity of religious symbols and myths from unrelated cultures across the globe led Jung to this conclusion.

10. Ibid.

11. Tillich also says here that symbols die as symbols when "they can no longer produce response in the group where they originally found expression" (43). The task of liberated Christianity is nothing less than to prevent the death of the symbols and myths of the Christian faith.

The Language of Faith: Symbol and Myth

The cross also satisfies Tillich's fifth and sixth criteria for a symbol, which are closely related and which to some extent say the same thing in different words. No one sat down and invented the cross as the primary Christian symbol for Jesus Christ. It wasn't the earliest Christian symbol. The earliest Christians used the fish, not the cross, to identify themselves as followers of Christ. Yet over time the cross displaced the fish as the primary Christian symbol. Its function as symbol grew out of the collective unconscious of the Christian community. It touched a part of the Christian soul and resonated there. It still does. That's why it is still a true symbol and not merely an identifying mark or, worse, an item of decoration or adornment.

The cross is a physical object, but not all symbols are physical objects. Words can also be symbols. The word God, for example, is a symbol. Tillich calls it "the fundamental symbol of our ultimate concern."[12] To stick with the terminology we're using here, the word *God* is Christianity's fundamental symbol for the spiritual. God is not a name. There is no one named God. God is the word that we apply to that ultimate transcendent reality that we call the spiritual. It is a word that mediates that ultimate spiritual reality to us. The word *God* connects us with that reality. It finds resonance in our souls, which cling to it as their connection with ultimate spiritual reality. It is a word that bridges the gap between us and the spiritual. Through that word we connect with the spiritual, and the spiritual connects with us. In other words, the word *God* is a symbol.

Because symbols are not literal but point beyond themselves to a transcendent reality in which they participate and with which they connect us, they necessarily contain their own negation. This characteristic of symbols may be a bit harder to grasp than their other characteristics that we have discussed so far. An illustration will perhaps help. It is very common in the Christian tradition to call God Father. Jesus called God Abba, Father. Most Christians begin their prayers by saying "Heavenly Father," or some other phrase that includes the word *Father*. The prayer we say Jesus taught us, the Lord's Prayer, begins "Our Father." When used this way the word *Father* is a symbol. It is a word from ordinary human experience. All humans have at least biological fathers, and most of us were blessed with having actual fathers who are, or were, an important part of our lives. A father in human terms is one who begets another person and, ideally,

---

12. Ibid., 45.

nurtures, guides, and cares for the person he has begotten. We apply the word to God because we understand God as Creator and as One who nurtures, guides, and cares for us the way a human father should care for his children. Yet God is not literally our father. God did not beget us biologically. God did not physically or directly raise us. Our human fathers, or others who filled the same role whatever their gender, did that. A father is a human person. God is not a human person. When we call God Father we use the word symbolically. There are ways in which God is a Father to us, and there are ways in which God is not our father as well. The symbol of God the Father, precisely because it is a symbol, contains within it its own negation. The same is true of all symbols. Because they are things from created existence applied to that which transcends created existence, they are always both true and not true. Symbols necessarily contain their own negation. They contain a yes, and they contain a no.

Symbols connect us with the spiritual, but religions do not consist only of symbols. They have their symbols—a cross, a Star of David, a crescent—but they also have their myths. As we noted briefly in Chapter Two, myth here does not have its popular meaning as something that is believed to be true but that is not in fact true. We must now explain the proper meaning of the word myth more fully. A myth is a story that functions as a symbol. A myth is a story that connects us to the spiritual. A myth mediates the spiritual to us in the same way that a symbol does. To return to our example of the cross, the cross is a symbol that comes out of a myth. It comes out of the story of Jesus' crucifixion. That story, like the cross, connects us to Jesus; that is, it connects us to the spiritual reality that we call Jesus Christ.[13] That story is, in other words, a myth.

Our calling the story of Christ's crucifixion a myth raises the question of whether a myth must have or must be grounded in historical, factual truth. I will discuss the issue of the historical factualness of the Bible in greater detail later in this work. Suffice it to say for now that the spiritual truth of a true myth is independent of any historical truth there may be in the myth. It seems to be true as an historical matter that the Romans crucified a man called Jesus of Nazareth sometime around the year 30 CE. The spiritual truth of the Christian myth of the crucifixion of Jesus Christ, however, is not dependent upon that historical truth. The story's spiritual truth is dependent upon the story's function as true myth,

---

13. It should be clear by now that "Jesus Christ" is also a symbol. I will not, however, pause to explain that fact every time I use this symbol.

The Language of Faith: Symbol and Myth

that is, its function of connecting us to the spiritual and the spiritual to us. The myth of the crucifixion is "true" not because the crucifixion happened but because the Christian story of the crucifixion mediates to us truth about the nature of the spiritual and about the spiritual's relationship to the world and to us.[14]

You may at this point be saying: Well, if Christianity is mere symbol and myth, why should I have anything to do with it? Let me begin to answer this question by quoting Tillich again on symbols. Tillich says that anyone who says "only a symbol" has not understood "the power of symbolic language, which surpasses in quality and strength the power of any non-symbolic language. One should never say 'only a symbol,' but one should say 'not less than a symbol.'"[15] We can substitute myth for symbol in Tillich's statement, and it will be equally true. Historical fact is just that, fact (or what we take to be fact based upon the available sources). The historical facts upon which Christianity is based are nothing more than things that happened to other people a long time ago in a place far away. Facts are external to us; they are not part of us. Symbols and myths operate at a much deeper level than mere facts. They touch ultimate spiritual reality both beyond us and within us. They connect us to that reality. They thus have a power that mere fact can never have. Mere symbol and myth? No. Nothing less than true symbol and myth. That's what gives our faith its saving power.

Questions for Reflection and Discussion

1. What does the word "symbol" mean to you?
2. Can you think of some common symbols used in American culture today?

    What makes these things symbols and not mere objects?
3. Can you think of some common Christian symbols?

    What makes these things symbols and not mere objects?

---

14. We will discuss the mythic significance of Christ's crucifixion in detail in chapter nine.
15. Tillich, *Dynamics of Faith* 45.

4. What does the word "myth" mean to you

> in common usage?
>
> in the word "mythology"?

5. Using the understanding of myth explained in Chapter Three, can you think of any Christian myths?

> What makes them myths?
>
> How do you react to calling them myths?

6. Chapter Three calls the Crucifixion of Jesus an historical myth:

> What, if anything, about the Crucifixion do you understand as historical?
>
> What, if anything, about the Crucifixion do you understand as mythic?
>
> Does understanding the Crucifixion as historical myth make it less significant to you? Why?
>
> Does understanding the Crucifixion as historical myth make it more significant to you? Why?

4

The Nature of Religious Truth

IN CHAPTER THREE, WE saw that symbol and myth are the language of faith. Symbol and myth are images and stories taken from the world of ordinary sense perception and experience and applied to the spiritual, to which they point and in which they participate but cannot fully capture and cannot ultimately define. Symbol and myth connect us to the spiritual and the spiritual to us, but because they come from the world of ordinary sense perception and experience while the spiritual utterly transcends that world (while nonetheless being immanent in it), they cannot convey absolute truth about the spiritual; they can only point beyond themselves to that in which they participate and with which they work to connect us.

Because religious language is symbolic and mythic, it necessarily follows that religious truth is symbolic and mythic. If a symbol is not itself the spiritual but rather acts to connect us with the spiritual, the truth of the symbol must be symbolic truth. If a myth is a story that is not itself the spiritual but which rather acts to connect us to the spiritual, the truth of the myth must be mythic truth. The truth of a symbol or of a myth must be a truth that is commensurate with the nature of the symbol or the myth. Symbol and myth cannot convey truth that is inconsistent with their nature as symbol and myth.

This means that the truth of a symbol or a myth cannot be literal truth. The function of a myth or a symbol is to point beyond itself to that transcendent reality in which it participates. That's where truth lies, but the myth can only point to that truth; it cannot be that truth. When we take the myth rather than the spiritual reality to which it points and in which it participates as the truth, we divert our attention from the spiritual reality with which the myth seeks to connect us onto the myth itself. We take the myth's story as the truth rather than take the spiritual reality with which the myth seeks to connect us as the truth. In other words, we literalize the story. We make it literally rather than mythically true. When we do that we deny its character as myth. When we deny a story's character as myth, we weaken its power to connect us with spiritual reality.

Another way of saying the same thing is to say that when we take myths or symbols rather than the spiritual reality to which they point as the truth, we turn them into idols. An idol is a symbol or a myth that claims to be or to point to an ultimate reality that is in fact not ultimate reality. In religious language, an idol is something that people take to be God or that functions as God for them that is not truly God. When we turn the myths of a religious tradition into literal truth, we make them and not the spiritual reality to which they point when they function as myths our "ultimate concern," to use Paul Tillich's famous phrase.[1]

Perhaps the best way to explain this point is to give an illustration familiar to all of us from contemporary American Christianity. A great many churches that approach the faith in a literalistic fashion call themselves Bible churches. They may use "Bible Church" as part of their name, or they may define and promote themselves as Bible-believing churches. Many Christians define and describe themselves as Bible-believing Christians. When I hear that claim I always want to say, "That's interesting. You believe in a book. I believe in the God that I know in and through Jesus Christ." The "Bible-believing" Christian has made the Bible the object of his belief. For this Christian, the Bible and the stories in the Bible have ceased to function as myth. Rather than being a collection of stories pointing beyond itself to God, for this Christian the Bible has become God. Faith has ceased to be faith in God and has become faith in the Bible. To say the same thing another way, the Bible has ceased to be symbol and myth and has become an idol.

Another way of putting the point is that for Biblicism the truth of the Bible has ceased to be symbolic and mythic and has become literal. The truth of faith understood literally is always idolatrous. It must be idolatrous because a claim that a religious myth or symbol is literally true is a claim that something taken from the world of ordinary sense perception and experience conveys absolute truth about something that transcends ordinary sense perception and experience. It is a claim that the myth or symbol is true in a way in which it cannot by its nature be true. To claim that a symbol or myth is literally true is to claim that it has captured the infinite in the finite, which is impossible.

---

1. Paul Tillich, *Dynamics of Faith* (New York: Harper Torchbooks, 1957) 1.

The Nature of Religious Truth

We must therefore always cling to, preserve, and defend that mythic and symbolic nature of religious truth. A religious symbol or myth may connect us with religious truth. It may mediate that truth to us in a way that our finite minds can grasp. Yet because the religious symbol or myth is not itself that truth but is mediating that truth to us in finite words and images, it cannot be literal truth. To literalize religious truth is to turn the infinite into the finite (God becomes the Bible) and the finite into the infinite (the Bible becomes God). Religious truth, if it is to retain its character as truly religious and not become idolatrous, cannot be literal truth.

It follows that religious truth, because it is necessarily symbolic and mythic, is necessarily subjective. Objective truth is factual truth. To say that something is objective truth is to say that it exists as truth outside of and apart from the subject who perceives or experiences it as truth. Yet, as we have seen, all human knowledge and all human truth begin with perception by a perceiving subject, who experiences that perception and whose mind shapes that perception and that experience into meaningful forms, that in effect uses them to create a world. All human knowledge and all human truth are therefore subjective. We cannot get outside of our centered selves to see anything objectively. We cannot transcend the subjective process of perception, experience, and meaning making to gain objective knowledge or even to know that such a thing as objective knowledge exists. Our experience of the spiritual is subjective in the same way. It is our internal experience. It is something of which our minds seek to make sense. They do that using symbols and myths. That process is necessarily subjective. Religious truth is therefore necessarily subjective.

Which begs the question: If religious truth cannot be literal truth, and if religious truth is necessarily subjective truth, what does it mean to say that a religion or a religious proposition is true? Paul Tillich teaches that a religion is true if it adequately expresses an ultimate concern and if its content is really the ultimate.[2] In the terminology we have been using in this study, we would say that a religion is true if it adequately connects us to the spiritual and if that to which it connects us is really the spiritual. The function of religion is not to express objective truth. As we have seen, that is impossible. The function of religion is to connect us to the spiritual. A religion, or any religious proposition, is true, therefore, to the extent that it does that.

2. Ibid., 96.

Let me make it personal. I am a Christian. Christianity is true for me because it is within that faith tradition's symbols and myths that I find my connection to the spiritual dimension of reality. To use another word for the same thing, it is within that faith tradition's symbols and myths that I find my connection to God. When I read the stories of the faith, when I contemplate the symbols of the cross and of bread and wine, when I pray in the name of Jesus, I experience connection with the divine, with the spiritual dimension. Those symbols and myths work for me. They connect me with the numinous, with transcendent reality, with God. They are therefore true for me. Christianity is true for me. It is not true because the stories and doctrines of the faith are literally, objectively true. It is true for me because it functions the way a religion is supposed to function. It connects me with the spiritual and the spiritual with me. It participates in that transcendent reality and mediates it to me. That is why it is true. That is how it is true.

There is another implication of this understanding of symbol and myth as the language of faith that we need to draw out here. Because the truth of religion understood in this way is necessarily subjective, it is not and cannot be exclusive truth. Many religious traditions, including especially Christianity and Islam, have throughout their existence claimed to have the exclusive truth about God. They have denied that there is truth in other faith traditions. Christianity is even guiltier of this sin than is Islam. Islam at least recognizes Christians as "People of the Book," who once knew the truth and who have not completely lost that truth. Christianity, on the other hand, has always denied that there is any truth in Islam because, among other reasons, that faith does not accept the doctrines of the Christian church about the divine nature of Jesus and the Triune nature of God. These exclusivist claims have led to massive bloodshed and are part of the difficult world dynamic today.

When the subjective nature of religion understood as a system of symbols and myths that function to connect us with the spiritual and that are true to the extent that they truly connect us to the spiritual is understood, exclusivist claims for any religion are ruled out. Truth understood objectively can be absolute and exclusive. If truth is a particular fact, then any other fact is false to the extent that it contradicts the fact that is the truth. When we understand, however, that truth for us humans cannot be objective fact, that it is necessarily and unavoidably subjective, then the very possibility of truth being exclusive and absolute disappears. When we say that a religion is true to the extent that it connects us with the spiritual

The Nature of Religious Truth

and to the extent that that to which it connects us is really the spiritual, we acknowledge that *any* religion is true to the extent that it satisfies that test. Christianity is true for me because that faith, understood as I understand it, satisfies that test for me. I must however admit that Islam, for example, is true for those who follow it to the extent that it connects those people to the spiritual and to the extent that that to which it connects them is really the spiritual.[3] Some Christians may respond that Islam cannot truly connect a person to the spiritual because Jesus is the only true way to God. That response, however, betrays a failure to understand the nature of religious truth.[4] The claim that Jesus is the only way to God turns religious truth back into a claimed objective truth, and we have seen that objective truth is a conceptual impossibility. A Christian cannot deny the experience of a devout Muslim that the stories, symbols, and practices of Islam connect him to the spiritual and that that with which they connect him is truly the spiritual any more than the Muslim can deny the same claim by the Christian about her faith tradition. Both traditions are true for those who find their connection to God within them, and for the same reason.

This is not to say that there is no ground for us to question religious claims by our co-religionists or by the followers of other faiths. Indeed, this entire study constitutes a criticism of the claims of Christian Biblicism. I could make the same criticism of the Islamic belief that the Quran is the literal, revealed Word of God. I believe that claim to be idolatrous, but not because it isn't Christian. I believe it to be idolatrous for the same reason that I believe comparable Christian claims about the Bible to be idolatrous. The Quran and the Bible are books. They are therefore perceived objects from the realm of ordinary sense perception and experience. As such, they may function as symbols that mediate the spiritual to us, and both the Quran and the Bible do function in that way for hundreds of millions of people; but they cannot be immediate objects of absolute, exclusive, divine truth. They consist of human language, and human language cannot by its very nature capture the fullness of the reality of God. According to orthodox Islamic teaching, Muhammad received the Quran in a series of visionary experiences. He memorized the words he was given during those experiences. He recited those words to his associates,

---

3. I use Islam only as an example. You can substitute any other faith tradition, and this analysis will work equally well.

4. For a more detailed discussion of the exclusivist passages in the New Testament see chapter ten.

who later wrote them down. The Quran, therefore, originated in a subjective experience of Muhammad. He gave that experience the meaning that it came directly from God. That can be, and I'm quite prepared to believe that it was, Muhammad's subjective experience. It cannot, however, be more than that. Belief in the divine origin of the Quran (or of any other sacred text) can be truth for those who accept it to the extent that accepting that truth connects those who accept it with the spiritual. There is no basis, however, for claiming that that truth is absolute or exclusive, that it is somehow objectively true for all people.

My point is only this: The understanding of religious truth that I advocate here allows us to critique any religious belief on the ground that its adherents claim absolute, exclusive status for their truth. The understanding of religious truth that I advocate here does not deprive us of all ground for critiquing religious claims, but it does change the basis on which we can make that critique. In this understanding, that someone's religious belief differs from ours is no basis for calling that belief false. That belief is not false if it connects the person who holds it to the spiritual and if that to which it connects that person is truly the spiritual. We can, however, and we must, critique any claim that any person's religious truth is the only religious truth, that it has absolute, exclusive validity for all people. Such a claim cannot be true. It is necessarily false.[5]

The power of symbol and myth is precisely that they allow us to live in relationship with the spiritual *without* having to make untenable and destructive claims about the absolute nature of our truth, but at this point you may well be thinking that this subjectivist view of religion and religious truth diminishes religion. You may think that religion understood as myth and symbol, as subjective, and as relative is minimal religion, that it lacks the power and grandeur of religion understood as absolute, exclusive truth. There is a way in which this impression is correct. The claims this understanding makes for religious truth are modest claims compared to the grandiose claims that some religions, especially Christianity, have traditionally made for their truth. I do not claim that Christianity is true

---

5. I was once teaching an adult education course at my church on other Christian traditions. I had made some poorly considered, flippant remark dismissing one of those traditions with which I have profound disagreements. One of my church people called me on it. She said that all religions are OK. I recovered from my irreverent mood quickly enough to say no, all religions are OK up to the point that they claim that other religions are not OK. That, put colloquially, is the point I'm making here.

for all people. I certainly do not claim that it is the only religious truth. I make only the modest claim that it is true for me, that it is true for a lot of other people, and that it can be true for anyone who finds a connection with the spiritual in its stories and symbols, its rituals and sacraments. Before you decide that a religion that makes such a modest claim for its truth isn't worth devoting your life to, please consider the following.

The world today desperately needs to understand religion, and indeed all truth, in this modest way. It is when people decide that they have absolute truth that they start killing each other. When people believe that they have the only truth and that all people need that truth, they quickly conclude that they have not only the right but the duty to impose their absolute truth on the benighted souls who lack it. They quickly conclude that because they have God's exclusive truth they have not only the right but the duty to impose their way on all people. They have the right and the duty to rule other people. History amply proves this point, the history of Christianity more than any other. Christian claims of exclusive truth led to the Crusades, those ultimately unsuccessful attempts to impose European rule and Christianity on the Muslim people of the Middle East under a claim of divine right. Christian claims of exclusive truth led to the persecution and often the slaughter of Jewish people in Europe. Catholic claims of exclusive truth led to wars against supposed heretics. Catholic and Protestant claims of exclusive truth led to the Thirty Years' War that we mentioned earlier in this work. The list could go on and on.

Today, Muslim claims of exclusive truth lead a fanatic fringe in Islam to use terrorist tactics against non-Muslims and against Muslims with whom they disagree. Religious exclusivism has even infected Hinduism, that traditionally most tolerant of faiths, and has led to Hindu-on-Muslim violence in India. The absolute, exclusivist claims by Jewish extremists that God gave certain land in Israel/Palestine to the Jews, and competing absolute, exclusivist claims by Arab Palestinians, have led to decades of violence in that land that is holy to all three Abrahamic faiths. That religious claims to absolute, exclusive truth are one of the most destructive forces in the world today is beyond question. Certainly there are other destructive forces at work in the world today. Nationalism and claims of national prerogatives are every bit as destructive as claims to exclusive religious truth. Nonetheless, overcoming religious exclusivism will do as much as anything else, or more, to ease tensions and end violence in our world.

The necessity of overcoming religious exclusivism, however, does not address the question of whether religion understood as myth and symbol, with all of the implications of that understanding, can be as spiritually powerful for individual people as the traditional exclusivist, absolutist understandings. I am convinced that it can be if we will just let it. The definition we've used here of religious truth as that which truly connects us to the truly spiritual isn't just an abstract, intellectual assertion. Connecting us with the spiritual has always been what religion is truly about. Finding our connection with the spiritual is a universal striving of human beings. It is part of what it means to be human. The understanding of religion advocated here focuses on that legitimate function of religion. The only functions of religion that it denies are functions that were never legitimate to begin with. So embrace your religion. Open yourself to its legitimate power. Live into it. Pray into it. Let it do its work in your life. Let it connect you with God. Don't deny that other people find connection with the spiritual dimension of reality through other faith traditions. Rejoice in that fact. Celebrate the myriad ways in which we humans find that connection. Give thanks that God has many ways to connect with people and cannot be limited to any one way, not even to our way.

Maybe it will help to share an experience I had recently. I was leading worship at the church of which I am the pastor, and we were celebrating Communion that day. During the Communion service, as our lay servers were serving the people, I looked at the bread and at the wine (grape juice actually, but that doesn't matter) that were still on the Communion table. At first I just saw bread and wine, but then, as I contemplated them sitting there on that little table, I experienced them not as mere bread and wine but as true symbols of the real presence of Jesus Christ among us as we worshipped. Jesus became real for me in those symbols. They connected me with Him and Him with me. My understanding of the bread and wine as symbols didn't rob them of power; it gave them their power. I didn't reject the bread and wine as "mere" symbols. I let them be *true* symbols, and they did their symbolic work in my soul. They connected me to God. It didn't matter to me that other people around the world find that connection not in Jesus Christ but in the Five Pillars of Islam, or in the Torah, or in the prayers and rituals of the Hindu faith, or in so many other ways. Why should it? I didn't need what operated as true symbol for me to be true symbol for them. That is the power of symbol. That is the power of the subjective understanding of faith.

The Nature of Religious Truth

Yet the objectivist, factual understanding of truth is so deeply ingrained in most of us that you may still find it difficult to accept the myths and symbols of the Christian faith as symbols and myths and not as objective facts. You may find it awkward to keep referring to Bible stories as myths, or to the cross, the bread, the wine, and the water of baptism as symbols. That, after all, is not the language of corporate worship or of private devotion, and indeed it doesn't have to be. When I was presiding at that Communion service I just mentioned, where I had such a powerful experience of the symbolic power of the elements, I didn't call them symbols. When I'm preaching from a Bible story, I don't call it a myth. If you heard me preach, most of the time, you wouldn't know that I wasn't operating from an objectivist, factual understanding of the stories and of the symbols of the faith. It is a legitimate question to ask how I can, with integrity, advocate a mythic, symbolic understanding of the faith and still speak in worship and in private prayer the same way persons with a factual understanding do.

Answering that question requires us take another step in our understanding of symbols and myths and how they function in religion beyond the point we have reached so far. Paul Tillich explains that step by saying that it is not necessary that we remove or discard a myth that is understood as a myth. He calls a myth understood as a myth but not removed or replaced a "broken myth."[6] He doesn't mean that it is broken in the sense that it no longer works. He means that its nature as myth has been understood and broken open to reveal its mythic power. We must retain our "broken" myths, he says, because "there is no substitute for the use of symbols and myths: they are the language of faith."[7] We continue to use them. We continue to tell the stories. We continue to use the symbols. The difference is not so much what we say in worship or private devotion as it is how we understand the words we use. We use them in much the same way a literalist uses them. We just understand them differently.

Marcus Borg replaces Tillich's concept of the "broken" myth with the concepts of "pre-critical naiveté" and "post-critical naiveté."[8] In the state of pre-critical naiveté, people understand the myths of religion literally. They understand them literally because they have no reason not to. Pre-critical naiveté is the state in which most people have lived throughout most of

---

6. Tillich, *Dynamics of Faith*, 50.

7. Ibid., 51.

8. Marcus Borg, *Reading the Bible Again for the First Time* (San Francisco: Harper, 2002), 49–50.

human history. Most people throughout most of human history have had no scientific understanding of the earth or of the universe. Most people lived before the advent of modern critical methods of studying scripture. In Biblical times, for example, people had no reason not to believe in a three-tiered universe, with the earth in the middle, heaven literally above (and not very far above at that), and hell below. The science that demonstrates that the universe is, in fact, a very different place than that did not exist. In Biblical times, people had no reason not to believe the story of Adam and Eve in Genesis literally. There was no science of paleontology, no science of anthropology, no concept of evolution, to tell them otherwise. The literalism of Biblical times, and indeed of all times before the modern era, was pre-critical literalism. People operated in a state of pre-critical naiveté.

The advent of modern critical approaches to human understanding has made pre-critical naiveté impossible for anyone who has been exposed to them or who even knows of their existence. We know, or at least have available to us, the findings of modern astronomy, physics, biology, and anthropology. We have available to us the tools and the conclusions of the higher modern criticisms of the Bible, historical criticism, literary criticism, form criticism, and canonical criticism to mention a few of them. We know, or can learn, of the source theories of the books of the Torah and of the Gospels, for example. We, unlike most people who have ever lived, live in the age of criticism.

Because we live in the age of criticism, all literalism today is what Tillich calls "conscious literalism."[9] Literalism, or what I have here called the objectivist, factual understanding of the myths and symbols of the faith, today requires an act of the will to deny or overlook the findings of modern science and all of the critical disciplines. Perhaps a story from my own ministry will help explain this point. A pastor of a large, literalist community church in the same town as the church which I serve as pastor once challenged me on our church's "Open and Affirming" position, that is, our acceptance of the full and equal dignity of God's gay and lesbian children. He, of course, considers homosexuality inherently sinful and demands celibacy or a change of sexual orientation from gay and lesbian people (the latter being an impossibility for most, something this pastor, of course, denies). He relies on the few Bible passages that condemn homosexual acts, especially Leviticus 18:22. I explained that when Leviticus

---

9. Tillich, *Dynamics of Faith*, 53.

was written the modern scientific understanding of homosexuality as a naturally occurring variety of human sexuality did not exist. He replied: "Yes, but the problem with applying your sociological understandings [sic] to the Bible is that then you don't know what to take literally." His solution to that perceived problem is to take everything literally.[10] It is clear that he makes a conscious decision, the conscious effort to reject or to ignore the findings of modern critical study. Unlike the people of Biblical times, he is aware of them, but he chooses to ignore them when it comes to his understanding of the Bible and of the Christian faith. His is a conscious literalism. For people like this pastor who know about modern understandings, conscious literalism is the only possible type of literalism. Conscious literalism is a decision to live as if in a state of pre-critical naiveté despite one's knowledge of the findings of modern critical study.

Post-critical naiveté, to return to Borg's terminology, is an alternative to conscious literalism. It fully accepts and values modern critical understandings. It refuses to close the mind to the wonders of human intellectual pursuits the way conscious literalism does. It refuses to close the mind to the awesome, wondrous discoveries of modern science. Yet it does not reject or seek to replace the myths and symbols that in the modern world are the object of so much critical scrutiny. Rather, it acknowledges them as myths and symbols. It sees them not as factual truth but as spiritual truth. Beyond that, it discovers a spiritual power in them as myth and symbol that far exceeds the power of any mere fact. It discovers that as myth and symbol they truly can connect us to God. So it uses them. It delights in them. It immerses itself in them and opens itself to their gracious, saving work. It tells the mythic stories, and it uses the symbols; but it doesn't stop to point out that they are myths and symbols. It doesn't have to. That's the naiveté part of post-critical naiveté.

That's why I and others with this understanding of the nature of faith can speak in much the same way as the literalists with integrity and authenticity. We know about modern science. We know about the higher Biblical criticisms. We know that the stories we tell are myths and that the objects we use are symbols. Yet, entering into a state of post-critical naiveté, we speak the language and perform the rituals of the faith without

---

10. No one, not even the most convinced Fundamentalist, truly takes everything in the Bible literally, but that is a subject for another day. As should be clear by now, my solution is to take nothing literally, although in the interest of full disclosure I must admit that I didn't say that to this pastor. I simply acknowledged that yes that was an issue, and moved on.

always stopping to explain. Worship and prayer are, after all, not primarily intellectual activities. They are spiritual activities. They operate not only at the level of the mind but at the level of the soul. Telling the myths and manipulating the symbols without necessarily making the mind's understanding explicit allows them to be what they are— powerful mediators between the spiritual dimension of reality and our own souls. So I urge you too: Let the myths be myths. Let the symbols be symbols. If you will open your heart to them, they will bring you to God and God to you.

There is one caveat we need to discuss. You might have concluded from our discussion this far that people who live at the level of pre-critical naiveté, and even more people who live in conscious literalism, the stage of a conscious denial of all human knowledge that contradicts a literalist understanding of a faith, have no connection with the spiritual because they do not understand faith as myth and symbol. We must make clear that this is not the case. Most religious people who have ever lived have lived at the level of pre-critical naiveté, and a great many people in the world today still do. Pre-critical naiveté clearly can connect people with the spiritual. Every religion, including Christianity, originated, developed, and grew in cultures that functioned at that level. The great religions of the world all arose and developed long before the Enlightenment, long before the rise of modern science and the higher critical disciplines. Pre-critical naiveté was the only approach to religion that existed in those times. Those religions developed and grew in a pre-critical world precisely because they connected the people among whom they originated with the spiritual. If they had not, they would not have survived to become the religions that we know today. The people who follow religions in a state of pre-critical naiveté clearly find a connection with the spiritual in their pre-critical understanding of faith.

People who operate at the level of conscious literalism present a different issue. These people, like the literalist pastor I mentioned above who challenged me on gay and lesbian issues, know about modern science. They know about the findings of the higher Biblical criticisms, or at least they know that such criticisms exist. They make a conscious decision to disregard that modern human knowledge. By an act of will, they hold to a literalism that they can maintain only by denying the validity of much of modern science and virtually all modern Biblical criticism. Pre-critical naiveté does not understand the mythic and symbolic nature of religion because it has no way to understand it and no reason not to accept the stories and symbols as fact. Conscious literalism, on the other hand, denies the mythic and symbolic nature of religion despite having the mythic and symbolic understanding fully available to it and, to a certain extent at least, with knowledge of that other understanding. Do these conscious literalists find a connection with the spiritual despite their act of will in denying the true nature of faith and so many accomplishments of the human mind?

The answer, I think, has to be yes, a great many of them truly do find a genuine connection with the spiritual in their conscious literalism. The popularity of literalist religion among us today makes any other conclusion impossible. Many people in Biblicist churches may eventually find the Biblicist faith unsatisfactory; but even these find a true connection with God in that faith at least for a time, and others may stay in it for a lifetime. Biblicist, consciously literalist faith touches the souls of millions of people. Those of us who find that kind of faith unsatisfactory are well advised not to deny or overlook that fact.

What does the fact that conscious literalism can connect people with the spiritual, with God, mean for our analysis here? It means that symbols and myths can work as symbol and myth even in a person who consciously denies their character as symbol and myth. The Bible stories truly are myth. The cross, the bread and wine, and the water of baptism truly are symbols. They do not lose their character as myth and symbol simply because a particular believer, or an entire church, denies that character. They still work in the believer's soul. They still mediate the spiritual dimension of reality; that is, they still mediate God to the believer who practices the religion, who hears the stories and participates in the symbols. The dynamic is the same with people in a state of pre-critical naiveté. Symbols and myths do not need us to recognize them as symbols and myths for them to do their work. They therefore do their work in people regardless of which of these types of spiritual awareness the people have. There are nonetheless serious problems with a faith lived in a state of conscious literalism. We have already seen some of those problems. Others are the subject of a subsequent chapter.

Symbol and myth are the language of faith. Religious truth is, therefore, symbolic and mythic. With this understanding we can live the life of faith without denying the accomplishments of the human mind. With this understanding we can live our relationship with the spiritual without insisting that our truth is the only truth and without the need to impose our truth on other people. Understanding Christianity as a system of symbol and myth can indeed liberate our faith and in the process liberate us as well.

Questions for Reflection and Discussion

1. What is truth?

    Are there different kinds of truth?

    What are they, and how do they differ?

2. Have you experienced Christianity as true?

    What does it mean to you to say that Christianity is true?

    Have you experienced truth in any other religious tradition?

    If so, how does the truth that you experienced in that tradition differ, if at all, from the truth you experienced in Christianity?

3. Is there such a thing as objective, absolute truth?

    If so, how do we know what it is?

    If not, how do we live without it?

4. Consider how, if at all, claims by some people to have absolute, exclusive religious truth have had destructive consequences in our world today.

    How, if at all, would the relative nature of religious truth advocated here help alleviate or avoid those negative consequences?

    Is the way in which absolute, exclusive claims of religious truth leads to violence an argument against such claims? Or must we learn to live with the negative consequences of absolute religious claims because there is in fact an absolute religious truth?

5. Where would you place your own understanding in the scheme presented in Chapter 4 of pre-critical naiveté, conscious literalism, and post-critical naiveté?

    Why?

6. Have you had an experience of God truly coming alive for you in the symbols of the Christian faith or of some other faith?

    Describe that experience.

    How did the symbolic nature of religious objects work in that experience for you?

5

The Limits of Literalism

IN OUR STUDY so far we have seen that myth and symbol are the language of faith, the language that connects us with the spiritual and the spiritual with us. We have given a critique of literalism that addresses some of its limitations; but because literalism is so prominent and prevalent in our context, more needs to be said. We have seen that literalizing symbol and myth is inconsistent with their mythic and symbolic nature. We have also seen, however, that symbols and myths can and do connect people with the spiritual even when those people do not understand them as symbol and myth either because they are living in a state of pre-critical naiveté or because they are living in a state of conscious literalism. In this chapter we take up other limitations of literalism. Before we turn to those limitations, however, let us recall the most fundamental fallacy of literalism, which we have already considered in the previous discussions. Literal truth is factual truth. As factual truth, it assumes that there is an objective, external reality that we can know and that exists independently of the perception of it by a perceiving subject. This assumption is, as we have seen, false. Because all knowledge is subjective knowledge, all truth is subjective truth. It cannot, therefore, be factual truth. It can only be true in the subjective experience of the subject who experiences it.

We have seen, moreover, that religion is true to the extent that it connects us with the spiritual and that with which it connects us is truly the spiritual. Given that understanding of religious truth, literalist religion necessarily entails a degree of falsehood. Literalist religion can and does connect people with the spiritual, as we have already recognized. However, it does that in spite of the fact that it also necessarily connects people with something that is not the spiritual. Literalism takes myth as fact, as we have also already seen. A literal understanding of the faith connects the people who hold it with truths understood as objective fact, but objective fact is not and cannot truly be the spiritual. Therefore, literalism connects people with something that is not the spiritual, that is less than the spiritual. It, therefore, tends toward idolatry. Christians become "Bible-believing" Christians, with the Bible understood literally rather than as symbol and myth. Literalism focuses the attention of the faithful on the symbol rather than on that to which the symbol points, namely, the spiritual or God. It, therefore, has an inherent fallacy that weakens its spiritual power.

Although literalism does not destroy the spiritual power of myth and symbol altogether, it does weaken that power. We must now consider why this is so. To do that, let us consider a famous story about Jesus from the Gospel of Mark, the story of Jesus stilling the storm on the Sea of Galilee from Mark 4:35–41. It seems such a simple little story—and such a miraculous one. Jesus and his friends get in a boat and set off across the Sea of Galilee, headed for the distant, opposite shore. As they sail across this large lake—the Bible usually calls it a sea, but we'd call it a large lake—a great storm comes up. Even a large lake can get dangerously rough when the wind blows hard enough. The boat is being swamped, and Jesus and his friends are in mortal danger. Jesus rebukes the wind and the waves, and the storm subsides. Then his Disciples wonder: "Who then is this, that even the wind and the sea obey him?"[1] I'm sure Mark meant the question to be rhetorical. The only possible answer is: God or, at least, someone endowed with the power of God. The meaning of this story taken literally is that one day a long time ago in a place far away a man known as Jesus demonstrated divine power over the elements, over the wind and the water of the Sea of Galilee. If we limit our understanding of the story to the literal plane, that is all the meaning the story has or can have.

Like all great Bible stories, however, this story comes to life and gains the power to change our lives when we see that it isn't just about something that happened a long time ago to other people in a place far away. The story comes to life and gains the power to change our lives when we see that it is also about us, right here, right now. In other words, the story comes to life and gains the power to change our lives when we see it as myth, as a story about God and God's relationship not just to Jesus but to us. Let's take a closer look.[2]

1. Mark 4:41.

2. The interpretation of Mark 4:35–41 is from the author's sermon "Be Still My Soul," given June 25, 2005, at Monroe Congregational United Church of Christ, Monroe,

The Limits of Literalism

This journey begins where all journeys begin—at the beginning. Jesus initiates the journey. He says to the Disciples, "let's go." Let's leave the place where we are and move across an open expanse to another place on the distant shore. That's how it is with our life journeys too. Our life journeys begin with God, who in the story Jesus clearly represents. God starts us and sends us out across the open expanse of our lives, headed toward the far shore of return to God.

So the Disciples start out. Jesus initiates the journey, and the Disciples agree to go with him. So you'd think the story would say that Jesus took them with him, but it doesn't. It says: "They took him with them." And that's how it is with us too. God sets us out on our life's journey; but if we want Jesus to go with us, we need to bring him along. It's also true that God comes with us whether we knowingly bring God along or not; but if we want Jesus to come along, that is, if we want to *know* that God comes with us, we need to do something to make that happen. We need to bring God's presence with us into our consciousness. We need to think about God's presence, to turn to God, to invite God to join us. We do that mostly by praying and worshipping. That, I think, is what it means for us when the story says, "They took him with them," not "he took them with him." This is a mutual journey. God sends us out, but what happens after that is at least partly up to us. God's grace is unconditional, but we can either be aware that we live in that grace or not.[3] We can invite God to be our conscious companion or not.

Moving on, we come to the crucial part of the story. Once Jesus and the Disciples are out in the open water, they run into big trouble. Mark tells the story with his characteristic sparseness of detail: "A great windstorm arose, and the waves beat into the boat, so that the boat was already being swamped." Perhaps like me, many of you have been in a small boat out on some body of water roughly comparable to the Sea of Galilee when the weather turned nasty. It can be pretty frightening. Yet in Jesus' day it must have been a lot more frightening than it is for us. They didn't have our safety equipment and gasoline engines, after all. When that great windstorm came up, and the waves began beating into the boat, and the boat was being swamped, Jesus and his friends were in serious trouble. Their lives were definitely in immediate danger.

Washington. The complete text of the original sermon can be found at the Sermon Archive link at www.monroeucc.org.

3. This idea is more fully developed in chapter ten.

That's how it is with our souls on our life journeys too. Life is easy when all is well, when metaphorically speaking the sea is calm and the winds are gentle. Like a sailboat ride on a quiet lake on a peaceful, sunny day, life can be very pleasant. We can relax, do what we want to do, and go where we want to go. We may be aware of the potential for trouble. We may know at some level that there are always threats to our lovely tranquility lurking somewhere, but we don't think about them much. When things are good in our lives and with our souls, we just enjoy the peace and quiet. We may go to church. We may pray occasionally, out of habit, or because we think we should, or maybe even because we want to; but basically in these times we don't feel like we need Jesus much. We're quite content to let him sleep in the back of the boat.

The problem is that those threats to our peaceful lives don't stay lurking in the background forever. We all get hit with great windstorms at times. We've all experienced them. Maybe they're things that happen to us in our lives. We lose a job or lose a loved one. We become seriously ill, or a loved one does. We suffer financial reversals and discover we can no longer keep on living as we like. Or maybe the storm is inside our psyches, inside our souls. We lose hope. We feel powerless and meaningless. We get depressed or suffer anxiety attacks. We lose our faith and our ability to see the good in a world full of so much evil. Storms like these, and so many others, can and do make us feel like our boats are being swamped. We feel despair and just want to give up trying. It feels very much like Jesus is asleep in the back of boat, offering no help at all.

Which is exactly what he was doing when the storm came up in Mark's little miracle story. He seemed quite unconcerned about the storm. He was sleeping through it. On those nights when I can't sleep at all, I envy him that ability to sleep through trouble, but his friends in that sinking boat sure didn't. They were mad at him. I think Mark understates their reaction when he only has them say, "Teacher, do you not care that we are perishing?"[4] My reaction would have been quite a bit more vociferous. I might even have used language that it wouldn't be appropriate for me to use here. There they were, trying to keep the boat as head up into the wind as possible and bailing with all their might, fearing for their lives. And there Jesus was, calmly sleeping through it all.

---

4. Mark 4:38.

The Limits of Literalism

I imagine that they were more than a little irate, but I also think that Mark is making an important point with that detail of Jesus being asleep until his companions woke him up. That's how it is with us too. Jesus may be coming along for the ride on our life's journey, but if we want to get the help he has to offer us, we have to wake him up. He's not going to step in and calm the storm just because he can. That's not how it works. Mark knew that too almost two thousand years ago. So in this myth, this metaphor for our lives' psychological and spiritual journeys and how God in Christ relates to those journeys, he has Jesus asleep until the Disciples wake him up.

When they did, the miracle occurred. He "rebuked the wind, and said to the sea, 'Peace! Be Still!'"[5] And the storm subsided: "Then the wind ceased, and there was a dead calm."[6] The point is made. When we turn to Jesus in those times of trouble in our lives, he can and will calm the storm. The Disciples in the boat received the gift he had to offer when they talked to him to wake him up. It works that way for us too. We can receive the gift of peace that Jesus has to offer when we talk to him, when we wake him up in our souls and turn to him for help. The only difference is that the Disciples could talk to him directly as a living physical person in their midst. We do it by praying to him directly as a living spiritual person in our midst, and it works the same way.

That mythic interpretation of Mark's story of Jesus calming the storm illustrates the power of Scripture understood as myth. It changes the story from being a story about something that happened to other people a long time ago in a place far away into a story about us and about our relationship to the spiritual understood and accessed through the symbol of Jesus Christ. Moving beyond the literal breaks the story open and reveals its meaning for our lives. We still need, however, to inquire into the relationship of the story to factual truth if we are fully to understand the limitations of the literal interpretation.

The literal understanding of the story of Jesus calming the storm requires us to accept as a matter of fact that on a certain day, at a certain hour Jesus in fact made the wind to cease blowing and the waves to subside. Many people today have great difficulty accepting the literal truth of this and many of the other miracle stories about Jesus. The mythic un-

5. Mark 4:39.
6. Ibid.

derstanding of Mark's miracle story does not require us to accept that the story actually happened as a matter of fact. It doesn't require us to deny that it did either, but its mythic meaning is independent of its factual truth. We can discover a mythic, symbolic meaning to the story without concerning ourselves with the question of whether it ever happened or not. The mythic meaning is there, the mythic meaning is true, either way. If we insist, however, that the story must be understood literally, we never get to the mythic meaning; or we get so hung up on defending the factual accuracy of the story that we never get to live fully into the story's mythic truth.

A more serious objection to an insistence on the factual truth of this story or of any Bible story, however, has to do not with how Christians read the story but with what the popular literalist understanding of Christianity means for the future of the faith in our context. Literalism acts as a barrier that keeps a great many people from even considering Christianity (or any other faith, since our popular culture understands them all literally) as a spiritual alternative for them. Literalism makes the faith absurd for most thoughtful, sensitive, intelligent people among us. Nowhere is this fact more apparent than in the rejection by the most vocal and visible elements of Christianity in our culture of the science of evolution and their insistence on the literal truth of the first creation story in the Book of Genesis.[7]

The creation story of Genesis 1 is well known, at least in general outline, to most people in our culture. It is the story of the six days of creation. It begins on the first day with the earth as a formless void. The void is apparently a watery expanse, for the text says that "darkness covered the face of the deep, while a wind from God swept over the waters." God creates light through the divine word: "Let there be light." God separates the light from the darkness and calls the light day and the dark night. "And there was evening and there was morning, the first day."[8] Creation continues through successive days. On the second day, God creates a "dome" in the midst of the waters to "separate the waters from the waters." God names the dome Sky, and the second day ends.[9] On the third day, God separates the waters so that dry land appears, and God creates plants on the dry

---

7. Gen 1:1—2:3, often simply called the Genesis 1 creation story despite the fact that it spills over into chapter two. I will follow that convention here for the sake of brevity.

8. Gen 1:1–5.

9. Gen 1:6–8.

The Limits of Literalism

land, and the third day ends.[10] On the fourth day, God creates lights in the sky, the sun, the moon, and the stars. The sun is ordained to rule the day and the moon is ordained to rule the night, and the fourth day ends.[11] On the fifth day, God creates "swarms of living creatures," birds, and the creatures of the sea. And the fifth day ends.[12] On the sixth day, God first creates the land animals. Then God creates humans, both male and female, in the image and likeness of God. God gives the humans dominion over creation and makes them vegetarians. Then the sixth day ends.[13] On the seventh day God rests from the divine labor of creation and blesses the seventh day.[14] The work of creation is finished.

The creation story of Genesis 1 is a magnificent myth. It makes God the creator of all that is. It declares God's conviction that God's creation is good and not evil. It creates men and women as equals.[15] The story declares the majesty, power, and goodness of God. It sets humans at the apex of God's creation and echoes the high anthropology of much of Scripture.[16] As poetry, as myth, the creation story of Genesis 1 is one of the great creations of the human spirit.

As literal truth, however, it is utter nonsense. It is such nonsense that it is hard to imagine how anyone could take it literally, or how anyone could believe that its author ever intended that it be taken literally. We don't need to resort to the findings of evolutionary science to reach this conclusion. Two aspects of the story itself make the point. The first has to do with the creation of light, day and night, and the sun. In the story, God creates light on the first day. On that first day, God separates the light from the darkness and calls the light day and the darkness night. On earth, the light of day comes from the sun. We have darkness when the sun sets below the horizon. The concepts day and night are meaningless apart from the sun. Yet in Genesis 1, God creates day and night on the first day but doesn't create the sun until the fourth day. The story doesn't explain what

---

10. Gen 1:9–13.
11. Gen 1:14–19.
12. Gen 1:20–23.
13. Gen 1:24–31. It seems that most people who insist on taking this story literally overlook the fact that in it God creates people as vegetarians when God gives them the plants to eat but not the animals.
14. Gen 2:1–3.
15. Gen 1:27.
16. See, for example, Ps 8.

gave the light on the first day, when there was no sun. It doesn't explain what day and night mean in the absence of the sun. It is not and cannot be a literal scientific or historical account of creation.

The second aspect of the story that shows that it cannot be a literal scientific or historical account of creation has to do with the account of the second and third days. On the first day of creation the earth is still a formless void consisting of water. There is as yet no dry land. On the second day, God creates through the divine word a "dome in the midst of the waters," the function of which is to "separate the waters from the waters."[17] God calls the "dome" Sky.[18] The result is that God has created a giant bubble in an earth consisting of water. The text says that there were waters under the dome and waters above the dome. On the third day, God gathers the waters that are under the dome together so that dry land appears.[19] God calls the dry land earth and the waters sea.[20] The literal meaning of this story is that earth appeared in a giant bubble. The dry land is surrounded above and below by water.

We can perhaps understand how a writer in ancient times without a modern, scientific cosmology could reach such a conclusion. Water falls from above as rain. Generally speaking, you travel down when you're going from the land to the sea.[21] Before the advent of modern science, it was not completely unreasonable to believe that dry land existed in a bubble surrounded by water. Today, however, no one, not even the most ardent literalist, believes this to be the case. Not even those literalists who insist that Genesis 1 gives an accurate scientific and historical account of creation believe that the earth's dry land is surrounded by water above and below. We know where rain comes from, and it doesn't come from holes in a dome that holds back the deluge. We know that above earth's atmosphere there is not more ocean but the vast emptiness of space. We know that the account of the second and third days in the Genesis 1 creation story is not a factually accurate description of the cosmos. The story of the

---

17. Gen 1:6–7.
18. Gen 1:8.
19. Gen 1:9.
20. Gen 1:10.
21. It is true that the Dead Sea, something the author of Genesis was presumably familiar with, lies more than 1,000 feet below sea level. People in ancient times, however, may not have been aware of that fact.

dome amid the waters is further proof that Genesis 1 is not and cannot be a literal scientific or historical account of creation.

If we read Genesis 1 as poetry, the fact that it is not and cannot be a literal scientific or historical account of creation doesn't matter. If we insist on reading it as science or as history, however, it matters a great deal. The creation account in Genesis 1 is mythically, spiritually true and powerful. As science or history it is simply impossible. People today can take Genesis 1 as a literal account of the origins of the earth only through an act of will that denies the findings of modern science. Believing Genesis 1 to be literally true requires an intentional blindness to the reality of the world as modern people know it. It is not too extreme to say that literalism requires people to turn off their minds or, as we sometimes say, to check their minds at the church door.

That is something most people among us will not do. Certainly most educated people will not do it. Many of us value the life of the mind. Many of us treasure the vast expansion of human knowledge that has occurred in the past few centuries. We are not prepared to turn our backs on that knowledge simply because a story written almost 2,500 years ago in a pre-scientific age appears on the surface to say something different. Many people in our context, faced with a choice between a literalist understanding of religion and the knowledge that modern science makes available, will choose science every time. Literalism asks them to deny a great deal of what they know and to accept as factual something that they know cannot be factually true. Yet because those who insist on the literal truth of Genesis 1 are so vocal among us, and because relatively few people among us know of any way of approaching religion except the literalist way, these people who value the life of the mind and accept the findings of science reject Christianity altogether. Literalism rules Christianity out as a spiritual alternative for these people. That, briefly stated, is why literalism is so damaging to Christianity in our world today

Literalist Christians appear to be aware at some level of this problem with their approach to the faith. In an effort to overcome it, they undertake efforts to make literalism more intellectually respectable. The result is the grossly misnamed "creation science." This is not the place for an in-depth analysis of creation science, or creationism as it is often called. In brief, creation science seeks to demonstrate the literal correctness of Genesis 1 by using scientific evidence to posit supposedly scientific conclusions that differ from those of mainstream science. The academic scientific community is virtually unanimous in their rejection of these alternative conclusions. More importantly, creation science simply is not science. Science is above all a method. It is a method that, at its most basic level, observes natural phenomena, formulates hypotheses that may explain those phenomena, then tests the hypotheses by experimentation. If the results of the experiments confirm the hypothesis, the hypothesis is taken as established. If the results of the experiments contradict the hypothesis, the hypothesis is rejected and other hypotheses are formulated that better explain the observed data from the experiments. In theory, science makes no a priori assumptions. Moreover, no statement can be scientifically true if it is not subject to being proved or disproved by the scientific method.

Creation science does not satisfy these requirements for scientific truth. It begins with an a priori assumption, or with several of them. It assumes the reality of a Creator God. Science does not. The reality or unreality of a Creator God is not a scientific proposition, for it can neither be proved nor disproved through scientific method. Creation science also assumes the literal truth of the story of Genesis 1. Creation science is not a neutral attempt to prove or disprove the account in that story. It is a committed attempt to prove that the story is factually true. Creation science is therefore not science. It cannot and does not render a belief in the literal, factual truth of Genesis 1 intellectually acceptable.

Yet the advent of creation science, and the zeal with which its advocates advance it, reveals something important about literalist religion. Creation science clings with immense energy to the literal truth of something that, as we have seen, is not and cannot be literal truth. Why? The answer has to be, I believe, that literal religion is brittle religion. Because the only truth it knows is literal truth, every religious truth must be literal truth. For literalist Christianity, everything in the Bible must be literally true, or it is not true at all. If anything stated in the Bible can be shown not to be literal truth, the entire structure of literalist Christianity collapses. If Genesis 1, which appears to the literalist to be literal truth, is not literally true, how can we know that anything else in the Bible that appears to be literal truth is in fact literally true? The answer, of course, is that we cannot. This fact generates great fear in the hearts of Christians who have no understanding of Christianity other than the literal one. It forces them to take untenable positions about the literal truth of the Bible and to defend those positions with irrational ardor against all criticism. It forces them to try to impose creation science on the public schools, not only or even so much because they think creation science is better science than mainstream science but because they cannot allow mainstream science to be true. They cannot allow it to be true because, if it is true, their literal understanding of Genesis 1 is not true, and if their literal understanding of Genesis 1 is not true, their entire faith is at risk. So, being unaware of any other alternative, they cling tenaciously to an untenable belief rather than lose their faith altogether.

The mythic and symbolic understanding of the faith therefore has not only the potential to save the faith for non-Christians, it has the potential to save the faith even for a great many Christians. It can allow those Christians to give up untenable literalist positions without giving up their faith.

Questions for Reflection and Discussion

1. Pick a favorite bible story, one that is presented as historically, factually true. Examples include the exodus of the Hebrews from Egypt, the Babylonian exile of the Jews in the sixth century BCE, the accounts of Jesus' birth in Matthew and Luke, the story of the Transfiguration, any of Jesus' miracles, or Jesus' crucifixion and/or resurrection. Almost any Bible story will do, but, for this exercise, do not use one of Jesus' parables or any other passage that is clearly not to be understood literally. Try creating a mythic, symbolic, nonliteral interpretation of the story's meaning. Considering the following questions about the story you have chosen may help:

    Does the story remind you of any personal experience you have had?

    Does the story suggest any general, universal human experience?

    Is the story making a moral or ethical point?

    Is a major purpose of the story to make a point about one of the people in the story?

    Why might the author be telling this story?

    Can you see more than one meaning in the story?

2. Does it matter for your interpretation whether the story ever actually happened or not?
3. Does your interpretation of the story make the story more meaningful for you than understanding it merely literally does?

6

Relationship and Decision: The Nature of Spirituality and Faith

WE HAVE SAID THAT religion is true to the extent that it connects a person with the spiritual and that with which it connects the person is truly the spiritual. By religion we have meant a particular spiritual tradition. A religion is a system of symbols and myths that seeks to connect people with the spiritual and to convey to the adherents of the religion an understanding of the nature of the spiritual. There are, however, two other concepts that require our attention. They are the concepts of spirituality and of faith. What is spirituality? What is faith? How do the concepts of spirituality and of faith fit with our definition of religion? How do spirituality and faith relate to our understanding of spiritual truth as that in a religion that connects us to the spiritual? Many nonreligious people today consider themselves to be spiritual people, and the term faith is very widely used among us. In the political sphere, we talk about "faith-based organizations." We call religions "faith traditions." Indeed, I have done so in this work. We speak of "people of faith" and distinguish them from people who lack faith. If we are to avoid confusion and understand how our connection to the spiritual actually functions, we must gain a clearer understanding of what we mean by faith. That effort will lead us to a consideration of spirituality and of the difference between spirituality and faith.

Marcus Borg gives a very helpful (although as we shall see ultimately not definitive) discussion of the nature of faith in his book *The Heart of Christianity*, and reviewing Borg's presentation will be a helpful starting point for our own examination of the meaning of faith and of spirituality. Borg discusses four possible meanings of faith, giving them each fancy Latin names. The first is *assensus*. *Assensus* is closely related to the English

Relationship and Decision: The Nature of Spirituality and Faith

word assent. It is "faith as belief—that is, as giving one's mental assent to a proposition, as believing that a claim or statement is true."[1] Borg points out that *assensus* is the dominant understanding of faith in our context today. Someone has said somewhere that faith understood this way is taking as true facts for which there is little or no evidence. It is saying: I can't prove that a certain proposition is true, but "I take it on faith." To return to Borg's discussion, faith understood this way is "what you turn to when knowledge runs out."[2] As Borg so correctly points out, faith as belief in the truth of problematic propositions is, despite its popularity, a strange concept. It "suggests that what God really cares about is the beliefs in our heads... as if having 'correct beliefs' is what will save us."[3] As Borg says, it is strange to think that God cares so much about the ideas in our heads.

Before we move on to Borg's other three meanings of faith, we need to say a bit more about faith as belief. It should by now be clear that faith as belief, as assensus, is inconsistent with the understanding of religion and of our relationship to the spiritual that we have developed this far in our study. Whatever faith may be, it is not giving intellectual assent to factual propositions that cannot otherwise be proven. Yet popular Christianity among us today consists primarily of doing precisely that. Accepting Jesus Christ as our personal Lord and Savior, the principal emphasis of popular American Christianity, has come to mean accepting as true the supposedly objective fact that that is who and what Jesus Christ is. It devolves to believing as factually true the doctrine of Jesus as Savior.[4]

The understanding of faith as belief in the truth of alleged facts for which there is little or no evidence is a powerful obstacle to faith in our context. Understood as mere facts, the central myths of Christianity make very little sense. People quite understandably say incredulously, "God became human in a particular person something like two thousand years ago in a backwater province of the Roman Empire, and that 'fact' is supposed to mean that I'm saved?" "Nonsense," most of the people of our context reply, and they're right so long as that claim is understood as fact

---

1. Marcus J. Borg, *The Heart of Christianity: Rediscovering a Life of Faith*, 28.
2. Ibid., 29.
3. Ibid., 30.
4. It also has come to mean understanding that doctrine in a particular way. It has come to mean believing as factually true, as something that once "really" happened objectively, the claims of the doctrine of substitutionary sacrificial atonement, a subject we discuss in detail—and reject—in part three.

and not as the myth that it truly is. Even worse, the understanding of faith as the acceptance of facts for which there is little or no evidence, or acceptance of alleged facts against the weight of evidence to the contrary, makes Christianity seem absurd. The classic example is, of course, "creationism," an acceptance as fact of the myth of Genesis 1 that we discussed at length in Chapter Five. The frequent attempts of Christians to force public schools to teach "creation science" as though it were in fact science (and sometimes succeeding) make Christianity appear superstitious, obscurantist, and intellectually indefensible. They are grounded in this understanding of faith as the acceptance of alleged facts as objectively true. Overcoming faith as intellectual acceptance of the factual truth of certain alleged facts and propositions is a major task of Christianity in our context today.

Now let us return to Borg's discussion of various understandings of faith. After his consideration of faith as *assensus,* Borg next discusses faith as *fiducia,* which is, he says, faith as trust, "as radical trust in God." It is not trusting the truth of a set of propositions but trusting in God.[5] Borg uses the opposite of faith as trust to highlight its meaning. The opposite of faith as trust is not doubt or disbelief but mistrust. It is, therefore, anxiety. Faith as trust "casts out anxiety."[6] Faith as trust works better in the understanding we are developing here than does faith as belief, but, as we will see, even faith as trust does not really capture the meaning of faith for this understanding. Borg's third meaning of faith is *fidelitas. Fidelitas* is faith as fidelity. It is "loyalty, allegiance, the commitment of the self at its deepest level, the commitment of the heart."[7] It is a "radical centering on God."[8] This meaning comes closest of any of Borg's four understandings of faith to the meaning of faith in the system we are developing here. Finally, Borg discusses faith as *visio. Visio* is faith as vision. It refers to a way of seeing "the whole." We can choose how we see life and how we react to it. We can react to the whole of our existence as threatening, as indifferent, or as, in Borg's words, life-giving and nourishing.[9] Faith as seeing ultimate reality

---

5. Ibid., 31.
6. Ibid., 32.
7. Ibid.
8. Ibid., 33.
9. Ibid., 34–35.

Relationship and Decision: The Nature of Spirituality and Faith

as life-giving and nourishing can be one part of the proper understanding of faith, but I am convinced that there is more to it than that.

Another understanding of the meaning of faith, and a very famous one, comes from Paul Tillich, on whose work we have relied so heavily for our understanding of myth and symbol as the language of faith. Tillich famously said that faith is the state of being "ultimately concerned."[10] In this understanding, to have faith is to be ultimately concerned about something or someone. The dynamics of faith, then, are the dynamics of being ultimately concerned. This understanding has the virtue of making it clear that everyone has a faith. Tillich taught that the two most prominent ultimate concerns, and the two most destructive, in our context are nationalism and success. In nationalism, the nation is the person's ultimate concern. He will sacrifice everything to the nation, and he expects ultimate reward from the nation. He puts his hope and trust in the nation as his ultimate concern and counts on the nation for what amounts to salvation, for happiness, security, prosperity, and so on. When success is a person's ultimate concern, she will sacrifice everything to the pursuit of success. Most commonly in our context that means material success. The person grasped by an ultimate concern with success puts her hope and trust in success and counts on success for what amounts to salvation, for happiness, security, prosperity, and so on. These are, of course, idolatrous ultimate concerns. In Tillich's analysis, they are idolatrous because what functions as an ultimate concern is not truly ultimate. In the terms we are using here they are idolatrous because that to which they connect people is not the spiritual.

All of these understandings of faith have some truth in them, even *assensus*. Faith does involve accepting as true some things for which the evidence may be abundant but for which the evidence is of a different nature than the evidence for factual propositions, at least on a superficial level. Faith involves trust in God, our main symbol for the spiritual. It involves fidelity to that in which we have faith, and it is a vision, a way of seeing the world. In non-idolatrous faith, the spiritual (which Tillich calls the truly ultimate) does become our ultimate concern. Yet none of these understandings fully captures the meaning of faith for our understanding that religion is true to the extent that it connects us with the spiritual and that with which it connects us is truly the spiritual. To get at the meaning

10. See, for example, Tillich *Dynamics of Faith*, 1.

of faith we must go deeper than any of the understandings of faith that we have mentioned so far. We must in fact go deeper than faith and first consider a more fundamental concept, the concept of spirituality.

Our understanding that religion is true to the extent that it connects us with the spiritual assumes that religion is about our relationship with the spiritual. That assumption in turn posits that we do indeed have a relationship with the spiritual. It says that we may be connected with the spiritual, or we may not be. Either way we have a relationship with the spiritual. Either way we live in a relationship with the spiritual. That relationship is our spirituality. Spirituality is the way we live our relationship with the spiritual.[11] Spirituality may be positive or negative. It is positive to the extent that we experience a connection with the spiritual. It is negative to the extent that we do not experience a connection with the spiritual. Negative here does not have a pejorative meaning. It is merely descriptive. It simply means that a person does not herself experience the reality of the spiritual. Negative spirituality is nonetheless still spirituality because it is a way of living one's relationship with the spiritual, the way of unawareness or denial.

It follows from this understanding of spirituality that everyone has a spirituality. That people who live within a religious tradition have a spirituality is obvious. The purpose of religion is to connect people with the spiritual. Religion is, therefore, a way of living one's relationship with the spiritual. Thus, a religion is by definition a spirituality.[12] It may be less obvious that atheism, that is, the denial of the reality of the spiritual, is also a spirituality. Many people who adamantly deny the reality of the spiritual may indeed be offended when told that they nonetheless have a spirituality. Be that as it may, a negative relationship to the spiritual is still a relationship to the spiritual, the relationship of negation or denial. We have a relationship to everything that we deny. For example, I deny that beets taste good. I deny the reality of good taste in beets. That does not

---

11. I once heard Father Stephen Sundborg, S. J., President of Seattle University, define spirituality as "our lived relationship with mystery." He meant by mystery much the same as I mean here by the spiritual. The spiritual, being ultimately beyond the realm of our ordinary sense perceptions, remains ultimately mystery.

12. It is very common in our context for people to make a sharp distinction between religion and spirituality. A great many people say they are spiritual but not religious. That may be true, but this contention often rests upon an assumption that religion is not a spirituality. That assumption is false. As a way of living one's relationship with the spiritual religion is necessarily a spirituality.

Relationship and Decision: The Nature of Spirituality and Faith

mean that I have no relationship to the good taste of beets. It means that I have a negative relationship to the good taste of beets, a relationship of denial. For me, the good taste of beets is not a reality. As hard as I find it to comprehend, other people apparently have a positive relationship to the good taste of beets. They experience beets as tasting good. For them the good taste of beets is therefore a reality. That is a trivial example, of course, but I trust it makes the point. One who accepts the reality of the spiritual has a positive relationship to the spiritual. One who denies the reality of the spiritual has a negative relationship to the spiritual. Nonetheless, they both have a relationship with the spiritual. One who accepts the reality of the spiritual has a positive spirituality. One who denies the reality of the spiritual has a negative spirituality. Nonetheless, they both have a spirituality.

There is another possible relationship to the spiritual, that is, another possible spirituality which we must consider before we move from a consideration of the nature of spirituality to a further consideration of the nature of faith. This other possible spirituality, which is quite common among us, lies between the positive spirituality of connection with the spiritual and the negative spirituality of atheism. It is the spirituality of the seeker. Many people today describe themselves as spiritual seekers. The seeker longs for a connection with the spiritual. He is on a quest for an experience of the spiritual. He does not deny the reality of the spiritual the way the atheist does, but he cannot fully accept it either, perhaps because he has never identified any experience in his life as an experience of the spiritual. Or, as is the case with some people I know, she may have had what she identifies as an experience of the spiritual at one point in her life but has lost it and is seeking to find it again. Seeking the spiritual is a profound type of spirituality. The decision of faith, which I discuss below, does not mean an end to one's seeking a relationship with the spiritual. Those profound experiences of the spiritual, those so-called peak experiences in which one perceives oneself to be in the immediate presence of the spiritual, are so rare, so elusive, even for people of faith, that the quest for them continues after the decision of faith has been made. For many people in our context today seeking is a life-long spirituality. Their relationship with the spiritual consists of living in the quest for the spiritual. They may live that spirituality within or outside of a faith tradition. Either way, their experience is that the spiritual is something for which they long, not something that they have found.

If spirituality, then, is the way in which we live our relationship with the spiritual, whether that relationship be positive, negative, or one of seeking, what are the meaning and function of faith within our understanding of the function of religion as connecting us with the spiritual? There is, in fact, a meaning of faith that works very well within that understanding. That meaning has its roots in the work of the great nineteenth century Danish existential theologian Søren Kierkegaard. It is the notion of faith as decision. Often characterized by the famous phrase "leap of faith," faith as decision is not a decision to believe in the truth of a set of propositions or alleged facts. Faith understood in this way is a decision to live one's spiritual life within a certain religion, within and using the myths and symbols of a particular spiritual tradition. It is not a decision to accept as factually true the doctrines and stories of that faith tradition. As we have seen, religious truth consists of subjective, mythic truth not supposedly objective factual truth. Therefore, faith is not intellectual assent to the factual truth of propositions; it is a decision to immerse oneself in a system of symbols and myths and to live one's connection with the spiritual within that system.

It should be clear, then, that faith as a decision to live one's relationship with the spiritual, that is, one's spirituality, within a particular faith tradition can be a characteristic both of positive spirituality and of seeking spirituality as I have outlined those concepts here. One may find and experience the spiritual in and through the myths, symbols, and sacraments of a particular faith tradition. Or one may only decide to seek an experience of the spiritual within that tradition. Indeed, a decision to seek a connection with the spiritual within a particular faith tradition may well precede actually finding that connection within that tradition. This is especially true in our context today, when most people do not automatically live within a particular faith tradition the way most Americans did in previous generations. One cannot have an experience of the spiritual in a faith tradition from outside that tradition. Therefore, faith as a decision to seek the spiritual within a religion almost certainly precedes an actual experience of the spiritual within that tradition. A person may indeed persist in her decision to seek a connection with the spiritual within a particular faith tradition even when the only connection she actually finds is the seeking itself.

Faith in this sense is a decision, but it is also a commitment. One could, in theory, decide for a particular religion, and then do nothing to follow up on that decision. That decision would not constitute faith. It would be an idle intellectual exercise that would do nothing to connect the person making the decision with the spiritual or even make possible a quest for the spiritual within the religion for which one has supposedly decided. The decision of faith is precisely a decision *to live* one's spiritual life, whether positive or seeking, within a particular religion. It is a decision to commit oneself to the religion, to enter into it, to practice it. Practicing it has a double meaning. It means participating in the religion's rituals, but it also means practicing the religion as one practices any art or skill that one wishes to master. It means being diligent in one's use of the religion. It means learning about the religion through study and guidance from an experienced practitioner. The decision of faith is a commitment of one's whole self to enter into a religious tradition and let it do its saving work of connecting the whole self to God, or at least to give it a chance to do so.

Because the decision of faith involves a commitment of the whole person, it is not an uncritical decision or an uncritical commitment. A decision to enter into a particular religious tradition does not require us to abandon our critical facilities and merely accept the religious tradition we are entering as we find it. Commitment is not blindness. As we enter a religious tradition, we consider what it offers us critically, examining it for things that work to connect us to the spiritual or to facilitate our quest for the spiritual and things that do not. We examine the tradition critically to see if it is true to its own professed ideals. We examine it to see where it is in need of reformation and renewal, for all religious traditions are constantly in need of reformation and renewal. The decision of faith is a commitment to let a religion's myths and symbols work their magic in our souls. It is not a commitment to check our minds at the door of the church, synagogue, mosque, or temple.

Faith as the decision and commitment to live our spiritual lives within a particular religious tradition is what enables a religious tradition to fulfill its purpose of connecting us to the spiritual. It is quite possible to participate in the worship or other rites of a religion without being connected to the spiritual at all. If we attend church without having made a true decision for Christianity, without having made a commitment to enter into it, to open ourselves to it, and to let it do its work in us, nothing will happen. Without our decision, our commitment, a religion will never become more than a curiosity to us. We will never experience its truth.

The decision for a particular religion is not necessarily a once for all thing. Some Evangelical Christians in our context teach that one must have a "born again" experience for one to be a Christian. The born again experience is a one-time experience of conversion to faith in Jesus Christ. It is a valid and legitimate variety of religious experience, to use William James' famous term.[13] It is, however, not the only one. Many people come to religious faith gradually, over a long period of time. Their path to faith may not be a direct one. Many of us who grew up in the Christian religion have at some point in our lives wandered away from it. Some of us have come back. Setbacks on the road to a connection with the spiritual and reversals of course are not matters for concern. They are a normal part of the religious experience for most people. Those of us who have made a decision for Christianity, who have committed our lives to it, must not demand conversion from the seekers in our midst. We must seek with them. We must walk with them on their spiritual path insofar as they invite us to do so. We must offer support and guidance. We must share our experience of the faith and any wisdom we have gleaned from it. In this way a seeker may in time find that connection with the spiritual for which he is seeking. Or not. Either way we will have helped the seeker along his spiritual path. We will have done our part to help him live his own connection with the divine.

Finally, we note that because faith is the decision and commitment to live one's spiritual life within a particular faith tradition, the truth of a religion can only be fully understood from the inside. We can study a religion from the outside, treating it as an object of examination and explanation. The study of religions is a useful and beneficial activity. It can further interfaith understanding and promote peace and cooperation between people of different religions. Yet the study of a religion cannot reveal the religion's spiritual truth. The truth of any religion lies in its ability to connect its followers with the spiritual and the extent to which that with which it connects them is truly the spiritual. The truth is in the connection, and the connection can occur only from inside the religion, not from outside it.

It is, therefore, illegitimate for the follower of any religion to say that any other religion is false for that religion's adherents who in fact find a genuine connection to the spiritual within it.[14] It is legitimate for a person

---

13. William James, *The Varieties of Religious Experience* (New York: Random House, 1902; Boston: Harvard University Press, 1985).

14. Because I find it to be such a barrier to faith among us, I am constantly tempted

Relationship and Decision: The Nature of Spirituality and Faith

who is not a follower of a particular religion, or of a particular type of a particular religion, to critique the ways in which that religion or that type of it seem to her to have harmful consequences, to include barriers to faith, or to connect people with something that is not truly the spiritual, that is, to critique the idolatry inherent within a particular religion or type of it. It is legitimate for an outsider to call a religion on its hypocrisy and to criticize it when it leads to violence or to other results that are harmful to God's people or to God's creation. All that is quite different from calling the religion false for those for whom it is in fact true in the sense that it truly connects them with the spiritual. At its best, such outside criticism calls a religion to its own better nature, calls it to be truer to itself and to the spiritual reality with which it seeks to connect its adherents.

We should be neither surprised nor discouraged when people outside the Christian religion criticize it as irrational or otherwise unconvincing. They have not made the decision for Christianity. They have not experienced it from the inside. Or perhaps they have been exposed to a particular type of Christianity that they found intellectually or morally repellant. Perhaps they have experienced Christianity rejecting them because of some inherent human characteristic of theirs, such as their sexual orientation, or because of something else about them or their lives. Or perhaps they do not even know of any Christianity other than a Biblicist Christianity that they, like many of us Christians, find unattractive and unconvincing. Or perhaps for whatever reason Christianity will never appeal to them. Perhaps they will never be moved to make the decision for that particular faith. No religion is for everyone. All we can do, all we should do, is to invite people to try Christianity as we understand it. If, in that religion, they find their connection to God, that is a very good thing. If, in that religion, they find even a way to keep seeking for God, that is a very good thing too. If not, then we can still pray for them that they will find that connection somewhere else.

---

to call Biblicistic religion false. I consider it to be a great obstacle to faith in our context. I consider it ontologically unsound and intellectually indefensible; yet I know, and I have acknowledged in this work, that Biblicistic Christianity can and does connect a great many people with the spiritual. To that extent, using the definition of religious truth I have developed in this work, it is true for them. If I have not completely succeeded in avoiding the temptation to call Biblicistic Christianity false even for those people for whom it is clearly true, please forgive me. This acknowledgement, however, does not require us to relate to any religion or any version of a religion uncritically within the limits outlined here.

Questions for Reflection and Discussion

1. Do you consider yourself a person of faith?
    If so, what do you mean by calling yourself a person of faith?
2. Do you consider yourself a spiritual person?
    If so, what to you mean by calling yourself a spiritual person?
3. What is the relationship between religion and faith?
4. What is the relationship between religion and spirituality?
5. Describe your relationship to the spiritual, or if you prefer, to God.
    Is that relationship one of
    Belief?
    Trust?
    Fidelity?
    Vision?
    Ultimate concern?
    Decision and commitment?
    Some combination of these, or something else altogether?

7

The Bible: Myth and Spiritual Experience

IN CHAPTER FIVE, WE saw how the spiritual power of a Bible story, the story of Jesus calming the storm on the Sea of Galilee, is unlocked when we see it as myth and not merely as a literal story of something that happened once a long time ago in a place far away. We also saw how a literalist understanding of one Bible story, the creation account in Genesis 1, forces people to reject the findings and conclusions of the human mind in a way that most people today simply are not willing to do. In this Chapter, we will take a closer look at the Bible as myth and as expressions of the spiritual experiences of its human authors. Properly understanding the Bible is, of course, crucial for liberating Christianity. Whatever else the Bible may or may not be, it is our book. It is the church's book. It is the book that all Christians share.[1] It is the book we use in worship and in personal devotion. Protestants say that it contains all that is necessary for salvation, and, while the Roman Catholic Church disagrees with that claim to some extent, the Bible nonetheless plays a central role in Catholic teaching and piety as well. Obviously we cannot undertake anything more than a cursory look at the Bible in this study. My purpose here is merely to suggest how understanding the entire Bible as myth and as a human creation, that is, as a collection of stories by human beings about God and God's relationship to creation rather than as a literal history having its origins in God, opens up a universe of meaning that we might otherwise miss.

---

1. At least they share all of it that is in Protestant Bibles. All of the books of the Protestant Bible are in Catholic and Orthodox Bibles. The Catholic and Orthodox Bibles, however, contain books that are not in Protestant Bibles. All references to the Bible here are to the sixty-six books of the Protestant Bible.

1. THE BIBLE AS MYTH

We established in Chapter Two that myth and symbol are the necessary language of faith. To explore what it means to understand the Bible as myth, let us begin with the Hebrew Scriptures, those books originally written in Hebrew (I'm referring again to Protestant Bibles) that Christians usually call the Old Testament. It consists of three parts: the Torah or the Law, the Prophets, and the Writings. It is an extremely rich and diverse collection of ancient writings. Scholars tell us that those writings span nearly one thousand years. The oldest fragment in the Hebrew Scriptures is the "Song of Miriam." Found in the Book of Exodus, it reads, "Sing to the LORD, for he has triumphed gloriously; horse and rider he has thrown into the sea."[2] Dating from well over one thousand years before the Common Era, this ancient fragment depicts Yahweh, rendered in the NRSV and many other English translations as "the LORD," as a tribal war god who has brought his people military victory by destroying the pursuing Egyptian army. The newest book is Daniel, which sets its story in the time of the Babylonian exile but which dates from the third century BCE. In between those two writings, the books of the Hebrew Scripture tell the epic story of the people of Israel, from their origins with Abraham and the other patriarchs through captivity in Egypt, liberation, the conquest of a land their god had promised them, through faithfulness and idolatry, justice and empire building, conquest, exile, and restoration. Along the way, the people's understanding of God evolves from that tribal war god of Miriam's song to the true ethical monotheism of 2 Isaiah.[3] The Hebrew Scriptures are the greatest collection of writings from the ancient Middle East that we have and are among the greatest collections of ancient writings known to us from any culture anywhere in the world.

One of the things that make the Hebrew Bible unique in the annals of world religions is its view of history and of God's role in history. The

---

2. Exod 15:20. See also Exod 15:1, where virtually the same song is attributed to Moses and all the Israelites.

3. Scholars divide the Book of Isaiah into three parts. The first part, or 1 Isaiah, consists of chapters one to thirty-nine and was written in the eighth century BCE. The second part, or 2 Isaiah, consists of chapters forty to fifty-five. It was written by a different, otherwise unknown prophet, during the Babylonian exile in the sixth century BCE. The third part, or 3 Isaiah, consists of chapters fifty-six to sixty-six and was written either by the same prophet as 2 Isaiah or by a disciple of his following the restoration of the Jews to Judah by the Persians late in the sixth century.

The Bible: Myth and Spiritual Experience

books of the Hebrew Bible are holy books. They are the books that form the foundation of the Jewish faith, yet they contain not just stories about God nor even just books of the Law that is so central to Judaism. They contain the history of a people. Some of the books—Joshua, Judges, 1 and 2 Samuel, and 1 and 2 Kings--known collectively as the Deuteronomic history—are explicitly historical, but many of the other books, including Exodus among others, contain history as well.

The history books of Hebrew Scripture are among the oldest writings recognizable as history, yet they are not history in the modern sense. As part of the rationalizing of all areas of human endeavor in the Enlightenment and the centuries that followed, scholars, especially German scholars, developed the modern intellectual discipline of history. They named as the goal of historical study the determination of what actually happened in the past. The byword for this modern understanding of history is the German phrase *"wie es eigentlich gewesen,"* how it actually was, a phrase attributed to the great German historian Leopold von Ranke (1795–1886), considered the founder of modern historical science. The goal was to eliminate the personal beliefs and biases of the historian to the greatest extent possible from the study and writing of history.

The history in the Hebrew Bible predates that understanding of the historian's task by over two thousand years. It was not written to show *"wie es eigentlich gewesen,"* how it actually was. Rather, it was written as much for theological purposes as for what we would call historical ones. It was also written for what we would call political purposes, and scholars have detected different political voices woven through it. The Deuteronomic history in the form in which we have it, for example, includes both pro-monarchy and anti-monarchy voices. More importantly for our purposes, God is the central player in the Bible's account of the history of the people of Israel. God cannot be a player in history the way we understand history today because, as we have seen, God is a symbol for the spiritual and is a subjective reality. God doesn't leave tracks through time that the historian can uncover and study the way she does an ancient manuscript or account records impressed on clay tablets from ancient Sumer. A modern historian might believe that he sees the hand of God at work in a certain set of historical developments, but his training would tell him he can't say that in scholarly, historical writing. Yet the historians of the Hebrew Bible talk about the role of God in the history of the people without reservations. They describe both historical facts and the actions of God in those facts without making any distinction between the two phenomena. This practice presents the modern reader with a dilemma: how much of what we read in the Hebrew Bible is actual historical fact and how much of it is theological belief or political agenda? Hebrew Bible scholars have lots of opinions on that subject.

Fortunately we don't have to examine those opinions here. The important point for our purposes is only that in the Hebrew Bible, history often functions also as myth. To illustrate the point let us take the story of the captivity of the Hebrews in Egypt and their escape from that captivity as it is presented in the book of Exodus. The story is a familiar one. In broad outline it says that the Hebrew people fled to Egypt to avoid famine and became enslaved there. After a time, the God of the Hebrews declared God's intention that the people should be freed from their bondage in Egypt. God seeks to soften the heart of Pharaoh so that he will let the people go, but nothing works. God raises up a leader of the people, Moses, and tells Moses to tell Pharaoh to let the people go. Pharaoh says no. God sends plague after plague on the Egyptians, essentially trying to terrorize them into letting the people go. Several times Pharaoh agrees, but he always changes his mind. Finally, when Pharaoh agrees one last time, Moses leads the people out of Egypt, but Pharaoh changes his mind again and comes after the people with all the might of his empire. When all appears lost, God intervenes again, parts the Red (or Reed) Sea so that the fleeing Hebrews can pass through, then closes the waters over the pursuing Egyptians and destroys them. God's people then escape into Sinai and are freed from their bondage in Egypt.

Taken literally, the story of the Exodus paints a picture of a brutal, destructive god who cares nothing for the Egyptians but only for the Hebrews. Taken literally, the Exodus is a story of a God who will even massacre children in an attempt to get God's way. It is also a story of a God who is powerless to soften the hearts of the dominant people. All in all, taken literally, the story isn't very appealing, unless I suppose you have no problem with the way God treats the Egyptians in the story.

Yet the story of the Exodus has been a powerfully true story for Jewish people for something like three thousand years. It is the foundational story of their faith. They celebrate it every year during the holy festival of the Passover. The Hebrew Scriptures are full of admonitions to the people to treat the slave and the alien justly, because they were once slaves in Egypt. The story of the Exodus was also vitally important to another

The Bible: Myth and Spiritual Experience

enslaved people in more recent times. It gave hope to African Americans through generations of slavery. God's leading the Hebrew people out of slavery in Egypt became their central metaphor for the end of their own slavery in America. Their spirituals sang the story: "Go down, Moses, way down in Egypt land. Tell ol' Pharaoh to let my people go" was for them not a song about other people a long time ago in a place far away. It was a song about them and their own yearning for freedom.

The story of the Exodus has that power for the Jews, and it had that power for enslaved African-Americans, because it is a myth. It is a story about God and about God's will for God's people. It is a story that says: God wants all people to be free. It is a story that says God hates oppression and exploitation and wills that all people be free from it. It speaks to people in all times and places who experience oppression and promises them freedom one day.

Beyond that, the story of the Exodus is a myth that speaks to each of us individually. We all have our own personal experiences of bondage. Perhaps we are in bondage to an addiction to alcohol, drugs, gambling, or some other addictive behavior. Perhaps we are enslaved to a need for money, power, or social prestige. The story of the Exodus tells us that God wants to lead us out of our addiction, out of our slavery, into a new life of freedom and wholeness.

The story of the Exodus is a myth, but it sounds like history to us. It purports to tell us of events that actually happened once upon a time in the history of Israel. The Bible presents the Exodus as fact, but those of us who live in the age of Biblical criticism naturally ask: Is it history? Did it happen the way the Bible says it did? We know that the stories of Scripture were written in pre-modern times. We know that they were written as much for political and theological purposes as for what we would call historical ones. Therefore, we don't automatically assume that a Bible story happened the way it is told in the Bible simply because it is told that way in the Bible. We want corroboration before we will accept the story as fact. In the case of the Exodus, it turns out, there is little or no corroborative historical evidence to back up the Bible's account. So we can accept that the story is a foundational part of the self-identity of the Jewish people. We can accept that it has great mythic meaning. We can perhaps accept that there may be some kernel of historical fact buried in the story so deep that it is no longer possible to determine just what the historical fact is. We cannot, however, accept the story as historically true.

Our inability to accept the story as history teaches us something important about the Bible. Many of the great stories of the Bible are probably grounded in some historical truth. Perhaps the Hebrews did somehow migrate from Egypt to Canaan. We know that they did develop a state in Canaan that became a regional power under King David and King Solomon. We know that that state split in two after the reign of Solomon, that the northern kingdom of Israel was eventually conquered and destroyed by the Assyrians and that the southern kingdom was eventually conquered and destroyed by the Babylonians. We know that after the Persians conquered the Babylonians there was a partial restoration of the southern kingdom as a Persian vassal state. We know that there is this much history in the Hebrew Scriptures.

We also know, however, that the real truth of Hebrew Scripture for us does not lie in the history. It lies in the myth. The Hebrew Bible consists not so much of history as it does of historical myth. A historical myth is a story grounded at least to some degree in history that uses that kernel of historical truth as the basis for a story that tells us something about God and God's relationship to the people. The great writing prophets of the eighth century BCE—including Isaiah, Micah, Hosea, and Amos—tell us that the destruction of the northern kingdom is God's punishment for the failure of the people to live lives of justice for the widows, orphans, and aliens. The history is that the Assyrians destroyed the northern kingdom. The myth is the meaning the prophets gave to that destruction. That's why those books are more than books of ancient history. When Amos thunders "let justice roll down like waters, and righteousness like an ever-flowing stream"[4] he speaks God's truth not only for his time but for ours. When he says that God is going to destroy Israel because they have not heeded God's demand for justice, he speaks not a historical truth but a mythic one. He expresses in mythic terms God's displeasure at human oppression and injustice. His words, and the words of all of the prophets, are historical myth. They are grounded in history, but they speak mythic truth.

It is relatively easy for Christians to see Hebrew Scripture as historical myth. Only the true literalists among us are particularly upset by the idea that perhaps the Exodus didn't really happen the way the Hebrew Bible says it did. Except for the true literalists among us, we aren't upset by questions like, was there really a person called Abraham who did the

---

4. Amos 5:24.

things Genesis says he did? Did someone named Jacob really wrestle with an angel of God so that his name was changed to Israel, which means "struggles with God"? Did someone named Jonah really get swallowed by a great fish and then vomited up on the beach? Most of us are even comfortable with questions like did God really destroy the world with a great flood, saving only Noah and some animals in a great boat called an ark? Did God really destroy wicked cities called Sodom and Gomorrah and turn Lot's wife into a pillar of salt? All but the true literalists among us are probably willing to see those stories either as pure myth (i.e., Jonah in the great fish) or as historical myth containing perhaps a kernel of historical truth but important mainly for their mythic meaning.

It gets a lot harder for a great many Christians when we turn to the New Testament and make the same assertion, when we assert that the stories about Jesus contained in the Gospels and other writings have a similar character to the stories of the Hebrew Scriptures, namely, that they are historical myth. Yet that is surely what they are. Like the stories of the Hebrew Bible, they were written in pre-modern times. They were written in a time when it was conventional and perfectly acceptable to make theological points not by writing theological essays but by telling stories. They were written in a culture that considered it perfectly appropriate to make a point by attributing words to a person who never actually said those words. That culture had no problem at all with making a point about a person by telling a story about the person that never actually happened. Indeed, people in those days would have been baffled that anyone should have a problem with doing such things. That's what writing was. That's what an author did. The ancient literature of the Mediterranean world is filled with speeches attributed to emperors and great generals that they never actually made, for example. The speeches were attributed to them not to show what actually happened but to glorify a hero and to celebrate his heroic deeds, his great feats of conquest. This literary technique was in no way considered dishonest. It was how things were done.

Perhaps we have no trouble understanding that this is how it worked in the secular literature of the ancient world. It's fine for Cicero, but for Matthew? That probably strikes us as a different matter. Yet the writings of the New Testament all come from the Greco-Roman world of the first century CE. They all reflect the cultural norms and expectations of the time and place in which they were produced. It should, therefore, neither surprise nor shock us that they too are largely historical myth, that is, stories grounded in a bit of historical truth that are told not to convey mere historical truth but to make a theological point. And like the stories of the Hebrew Bible, the real importance of the stories of the New Testament to us is not their historicity but their mythic meaning.

An examination of two central Christian myths will help explain the point. The first is the myth of Jesus' virgin birth. The Gospels of Matthew and Luke both say that Mary was a virgin when she conceived and gave birth to Jesus. The virgin birth is a staple of Christian orthodoxy. A literal belief in it is one of the five "Fundamentals" of Christian Fundamentalism. In most Christian circles, to deny its literal truth is to be guilty of a grave heresy or even of apostasy. Yet within the Christian Scriptures themselves there are grounds for doubting its literal truth. The Gospels of Mark and John and the Apostle Paul know nothing of a virgin birth of Jesus. They make no mention of it at all. Moreover, the word "virgin" in Matthew and Luke is almost certainly the result of a mistranslation into Greek of a Hebrew word from Isaiah that actually means young woman, not virgin in the sense of a woman who has not had sexual intercourse. These facts suggest that Matthew and Luke speak of a virgin birth not because that's what happened physically but because they want to make a theological point.

What might a mythic meaning of the story of a virgin birth be? A person conceived not by the usual biological means but by the intervention of the Holy Spirit would have to be a very special person indeed. Such a person's origins would be as much divine as they would be human. The early Christian communities experienced Jesus as something more than human. They called him the Son of God. By the time Matthew and Luke were written, perhaps five or six decades after Jesus' death, some of those communities had come to express the experience of Jesus as in some way divine by speaking of his virgin birth. The virgin birth of Jesus is a myth. That doesn't mean it isn't true. It means that it isn't necessarily factually true. It isn't important whether it is factually true or not. What is important is the statement it makes about who Jesus was for those communities, not about the mechanics of his conception and birth. It says: This one is different. This one is special. In this one we see God so clearly that his origins must lie with God in some unique way. That is the mythic meaning of the virgin birth. This understanding doesn't rule out the possibility that Jesus actually was born to a virgin, although most people today find that hard to believe as a factual matter. The point is that we don't have

The Bible: Myth and Spiritual Experience

to believe it as a factual matter. It isn't about fact. It's a myth, a powerful, truthful myth about the presence of God in Jesus.

Another Christian story that most Christians have even more trouble seeing as myth is the story of Jesus' Resurrection. From very, very early in the Christian tradition people told stories of Jesus being resurrected from death and appearing to his Disciples. Belief in the physical resurrection of Christ became the cornerstone of Christian faith. St. Paul even wrote, "If Christ has not been raised, then our proclamation has been in vain and your faith has been in vain."[5] Nearly two thousand years later, literal belief in the physical resurrection of Christ has become another one of the five Fundamentals of Fundamentalism. Every Easter, Christians of every variety all around the world proclaim: "Christ is risen! He is risen indeed!"

Yet there is good reason to see the Resurrection as another historical myth, that is, as story grounded in a kernel of historical truth that is told less to convey historical truth than to make a theological point. How much do we know as a matter of history? We know that there was a person called Jesus of Nazareth who the Romans crucified when Pontius Pilate ruled the Roman province of Judea. We know that he had a following during his lifetime, and we know that his followers did not disband and disappear after his death as had the followers of so many other would-be Messiahs in Judea under the Romans. We know that not later than twenty years after Jesus' death, and probably even earlier than that, his followers claimed that he had been resurrected, that some of them had seen him risen from the grave. That much we know as history and nothing more.

As with the myth of Jesus' virgin birth, we find in the New Testament itself reason to treat the stories of the Resurrection as historical myth. The Gospels themselves are inconsistent on the question. In its original form, the Gospel of Mark ended with chapter sixteen, verse eight, which has the women who went to Jesus' tomb fleeing an empty tomb in terror. Mark, the oldest of the Gospels, originally had no Resurrection appearances of the risen Jesus. The appearances described in verses nine to nineteen of chapter sixteen are clearly later additions that express a theology quite different from that of Mark himself. The three Gospels that do have stories of Resurrection appearances by the risen Christ do not have the same stories. In Matthew, Jesus appears to the women and then meets the Disciples in Galilee, where he gives them the Great Commission to

---

5. 1 Cor. 15:14.

baptize all nations in the name of the Father, the Son, and the Holy Spirit. Luke has, among other things, the wonderful story of the Disciples on the road to Emmaus and the mysterious stranger who opens the Scriptures (the Hebrew Scriptures of course) to them and whom they recognize as the risen Christ in the breaking of the bread. John has, among others, the profound and puzzling story of "doubting Thomas," in which Jesus appears twice through a locked door to the frightened Disciples and says to them "Peace." No Resurrection appearance story is included in more than one Gospel.[6]

What are we to conclude from what we know of history and what we see in the Gospel accounts of the Resurrection? The conclusion is unavoidable, I think, that as a historical matter Jesus' Disciples had some kind of powerful experience of his continuing presence with them after his crucifixion. Such an experience explains why they didn't disperse and disappear from the pages of history after their leader's execution. Exactly what that experience was, we cannot know. In accordance with the literary customs of their time, the Disciples spoke of their experience in stories. They didn't write modern newspaper accounts. They wrote stories that became myths. They wrote stories that say with Jesus, death is not the end. They wrote stories that say that with God, death is not the end, not for Jesus and not for us. They wrote myths, stories about God, that say that God wills to, can, and does bring new life out of death. They say that the tombs of our lives can be empty too if we will open ourselves to God and let God lead us out of them. And they say, this was the one. Jesus was indeed the Christ, the one anointed by God to reveal God to the fullest extent we humans are capable of receiving and to teach us God's ways. As is always the case with the great Bible stories, as factual accounts they are merely about something that happened to someone else a long time ago in a place far away. As myth they are about us and about our relationship to God. As fact, they are ancient history, of interest only to historians. As myth, they are life-giving stories that connect us to God and God to us. As fact, they are dead. As myth, they are alive, mediating God to us in ways our finite minds can grasp and our spirits can embrace.

---

6. What they all have in common is that the first witnesses to the Resurrection are the women. In all of them either Christ himself or an angel tells them to go to the men and bring them the news that Christ is risen. Thus, in all four Gospels, the first Apostles are women, since an Apostle is one who is sent and, in the Christian setting, specifically one who is sent with the good news of the Resurrection.

The Bible: Myth and Spiritual Experience

The Bible then is a collection of myths. It is a collection of the stories certain ancient people told about God, about their experience of God in their lives. Marcus Borg says that the Bible is the stories about God of two ancient communities, ancient Israel and the earliest Christians.[7] We need to modify that statement a bit. The Bible is the stories about God of many more communities than two. They come from different times and different stages of the religious development of the Jewish people. They come from diverse Christian communities with different views of Jesus Christ. Mark's Jesus falling to his knees in agony in the Garden of Gethsemane, for example, is very different from John's Jesus, at whose word even those come to arrest him fall to *their* knees. Yet Borg is right that the Bible consists of the stories of ancient communities about their experience and understanding of God. It is, in other words, myth.

2. THE BIBLE AS HUMAN PRODUCT

Another important point about the Bible that we must now consider is implied in our understanding of the Bible as myth. When we said, with Marcus Borg, that the Bible is the stories of ancient communities about their spiritual experience, we are saying that the Bible is a human document not a divine one. This position, too, is a revision of long-held Christian beliefs about the origins of the Bible. It certainly differs from the nearly universal understanding in popular American Christianity. The first Fundamental of Fundamentalism, and the one that all the others rest on, is the literal inspiration and inerrancy of the Bible. Most Christians in our context today believe that the Bible derives its authority from its origins; that is, it is authoritative for Christian belief and practice because it comes from God.

The belief in the divine origin of the Bible comes in two basic forms.[8] We can call them a hard form and a soft form. The hard form of the belief in the Divine origin of the Bible is very similar to orthodox Muslim belief about the origin of the Quran. Islam teaches that the Quran, in the original Arabic, is the literal words of God transmitted to Muhammad through the Archangel Gabriel. The words of the holy book are not Muhammad's words; they are God's words. Some Christians, especially true Fundamentalist Christians, believe essentially the same thing about

---

7. Borg, *The Heart of Christianity*, 45.
8. Borg has a similar discussion in *The Heart of Christianity*.

the Bible. God didn't write it exactly, but God gave the words to men who faithfully recorded them. This belief minimizes the human element in the production of the Bible, making humans responsible for any errors in the texts as we have them but not for the texts themselves. This hard version of the divine origin of the Bible is summed up in the bumper sticker you may have seen: "God said it. I believe it. That settles it."

The soft version of the divine origin of the Bible is probably more common among us. This belief holds that while the Bible was indeed written by men, those men (they're always men, not women) were writing under the direct inspiration of the Holy Spirit. The soft form of belief in the divine origin of the Bible allows for a greater human element in the writing of the holy books while preserving a belief in their divine origin. This belief has it that the books were written by men under divine inspiration, but, because they were men, they made mistakes. Some of their own thoughts crept in along with the divinely inspired truth. This softer version of the divine origin of the Bible allows for human error more than does the hard version of divine origin because it allows for more human input into the Bible's creation.

It is important to understand that a belief in the divine origin of the Bible is a faith position. One can make the decision to believe it. One can perhaps experience the Bible as so spiritually powerful and as so "true" that one believes it must come from God, either directly or somewhat indirectly. One cannot prove this contention, however. There are no indicators external to the Bible itself to support a belief in its divine origin. All of the original manuscripts of the various books are lost. The ancient manuscripts that we do have are just that, ancient manuscripts. They are products of a human hand. There is nothing obviously divine about them. Biblicists sometimes cite 2 Timothy 3:16a in support of their belief in divine inspiration of the Bible. It reads: "All scripture is inspired by God...." It should be obvious that the reference here can only be to the Hebrew scriptures, since there was no such thing as the New Testament when 1 Timothy was written. More importantly, it is obviously circular reasoning to try to prove the divine inspiration of the Bible by citing a verse in the Bible. Citing this verse to prove the divine inspiration of scripture is citing as authority for a proposition something that has authority only if one already accepts the proposition the citation is attempting to prove, a logical error of major proportions. The citation may reassure those who already believe in divine inspiration. It will mean nothing to anyone who does not. Thus belief in the divine origin of the Bible is just that—belief. It is a decision that one makes or declines to make. It is not something that can be proven or demonstrated in any scientific way.

Beyond that, both the hard and soft versions of the belief in the divine origin of the Bible present insurmountable problems. We will start with the hard version. If God literally crafted every word in the Bible, and if God is infallible as Biblicists always assume, then every word in the Bible must be literally true. There can be nothing in it that is demonstrably false, and it can contain no contradictions. God doesn't make mistakes, and God doesn't contradict Godself. Biblicists therefore assert that there are indeed not only no errors in the Bible; there are no contradictions. Years ago, I heard a Biblicist preacher on the radio—I've long since forgotten his name—say, "People are always telling me that there are contradictions in the Bible, but I can assure you that there are absolutely no contradictions in God's holy word," or words much to that effect. I couldn't help but mutter the question to myself, "Has he ever *read* it?"

The Bible is, in fact, full of things that are demonstrably false, and it is full of contradictions. We have already seen how the creation account of Genesis 1 cannot be literally true. Taken literally, its account of creation is demonstrably false, but the famous creation stories of Genesis 1 and 2 illustrate our point in other ways as well. The creation story of Genesis 1 contradicts the creation story of Genesis 2. In Genesis 1 God creates men and women on the sixth day as we have seen. In Genesis 2, most of creation occurs in one day not six, as Genesis 2:4 begins: "In the day that the Lord God made the earth and the heavens...." That obviously and undeniably contradicts Genesis 1's six days of creation. There are other contradictions as well. In Genesis 1 God creates men and women simultaneously. In Genesis 2, God first creates Adam. Only later does God create the woman Eve.[9] Genesis 1 and Genesis 2 cannot both be literally correct. Since they contradict each other, they cannot have come from God but must be of human origin.

9. This story is almost universally taken to mean that God created man first and woman second. It has been used for millennia to justify the subordinate position of women in society. Feminist theologians, however, have pointed out that "Adam" actually means not "man" but "earth creature," or a creature made from earth. Since "man" has meaning only when juxtaposed to "woman," one can argue that even in Genesis 2 man and woman are created at the same time because "Adam" didn't become man until there was woman. I heard this exegesis from Elizabeth A. Johnson in a class at Seattle University in the summer of 1998.

Examples of contradictions in the Bible could fill an entire large book. I will mention just two more that I think illustrate the human origins of the Bible quite clearly. The first is the story of Noah. Almost everyone in our context knows the story of Noah and the Ark. Most of us know that Noah took all of the animals two by two into the ark to rescue them from the flood.[10] How many of us, however, know that the story of Noah and the flood in Genesis actually combines two different stories in a contradictory way? In Genesis 6:19, Yahweh says to Noah, "And of every living thing, of all flesh, you shall bring two of every kind into the ark, to keep them alive with you." Yet in Genesis 7:2, just a very few verses later, Yahweh says to Noah, "Take with you seven pairs of all clean animals, the male and its mate, and a pair of the animals that are not clean, the male and its mate...." Which is it? Two of every kind of animal or seven pairs of clean animals and one pair of unclean animals? It can't be both. God wouldn't make a mistake like that if God were writing the Bible. The only explanation for this contradiction is that a human editor has combined two different, contradictory stories, and done so not all that skillfully.[11]

---

10. I have long been puzzled by how the story of the flood could be turned into a cute story for children about a kindly old man and a bunch of animals sailing around in a great big boat. When I see the story in illustrated children's books I always want to ask, "where are all the floating corpses of the people and animals who were drowned?"

11. Recurrences of stories like this in slightly different form are common in Genesis. They are among the evidence that has led scholars to the "four source theory" of the origins of the books of the Torah. We need not consider the matter in detail here, but in brief that theory holds that a later editor put those books together in the form in which we have them from four sources. The sources are known as "J" (because the stories from this source generally refer to God as "Yahweh," which in German begins with J), "E" (because the stories from this source generally refer to God as "Elohim), "P" (because the material from this source reflects priestly concerns with purity and the Law), and "D" (which consists mostly of the Book of Deuteronomy). In our example of the Noah story, the two pairs version is probably an "E" story, because it begins by calling God, in most English translations, "God," i.e., not Yahweh, which according to custom is usually translated as "the LORD." The seven pairs of clean animals is probably from "P" because it reflects a priestly concern with the distinction between clean and unclean animals. The priests would insist on more clean animals than unclean ones because clean animals were needed for food and for sacrifice. Unclean animals were used for neither. This ability of scholars to tease out different sources for the books of the Torah, and their similar work in decoding the sources of the Gospels of Matthew and Luke (i.e., the Gospel of Mark and the hypothetical source "Q"), along with a great many other accomplishments of the higher Biblical criticisms, strongly support our understanding of the Bible as being of human origin.

The Bible: Myth and Spiritual Experience

That contradiction may be a bit trivial, but there is one in the New Testament that is not trivial at all. I have already mentioned it briefly. It is the difference between the two garden scenes in the story of Christ's Passion in Mark and in John. In the fourteenth chapter of Mark, after they have eaten the Passover meal, Jesus and the Disciples go out to the Mount of Olives, to a place called Gethsemane. Jesus leaves the Disciples behind and goes off by himself. Mark then writes that Jesus tells the Disciples, "I am deeply grieved, even to death. . . ."[12] Mark continues: "And going a little farther, he threw himself on the ground and prayed, that if it were possible, the hour might pass from him. He said, 'Abba, Father, for you all things are possible; remove this cup from me; yet, not what I want, but what you want.'"[13] Mark's account is a poignant, moving tale of a very human Jesus in agony over what he knows is coming and praying that it might not have to be.

Contrast that picture to the one we see in the Gospel of John. Again after a meal scene (although one that does not include the institution of the Sacrament of the Eucharist), Jesus and the Disciples go out, this time across the Kidron Valley to an unnamed garden, which they enter. Judas leads "a detachment of soldiers together with police from the chief priests and Pharisees" into the garden carrying lanterns, torches and weapons.[14] Jesus takes charge. He asks the men who have come, "Whom are you looking for?"[15] They answer "Jesus of Nazareth."[16] He replies, "I am he."[17] John continues: "When Jesus said to them, 'I am he,' they stepped back and fell to the ground."[18]

The contrast with the Garden of Gethsemane scene in Mark could hardly be more stark. In Mark a very human Jesus is on his knees begging God not to make him go through the suffering and death that were in store for him. In John, a divine Jesus commands the action with such di-

---

12. Mark 14:34.
13. Mark 14:35–36.
14. John 18:3.
15. John 18:4.
16. John 18:5.

17. The New Revised Standard Version has a translators' note at this point that reads "Gk *I am*." "I am," of course, echoes the meaning of the Hebrew name of God "Yahweh." In saying "I am," Jesus is essentially claiming to be God, something that is perfectly consistent with John's theology but not with Mark's.

18. John 18:6.

vine power that even the armed band that came to arrest him fall to their knees in awe before his divine presence. Which is it? Understood literally it can't be both. God wouldn't make that mistake. These two accounts are clearly the work of two human authors making very different theological points through the way they tell the story of Jesus' arrest.

We could look at many more examples of contradictions in the Bible, but the point is made. The Bible is full of things that cannot be literally true, and it is full of contradictions. These undeniable facts establish beyond any reasonable doubt that the Bible is a human product not a divine one or at least that fallible human beings played a major role in its production. The possibility still remains, however, that the mistakes and contradictions might be the result of error by human authors who were nonetheless divinely inspired as to the broader content and the meaning of their work. This is the softer version of belief in the divine origin of the Bible, and it is very widely held in both conservative evangelical and Pentecostalist churches, in the so-called mainline Protestant denominations, and in the Roman Catholic tradition. It is surely the most common understanding about the origin of the Bible among Christians in our context today. Yet it too presents insurmountable problems.

The major problem with the soft version of belief in the divine origin of the Bible is that as soon as you say that the Bible contains divinely inspired truth as well as human error you are faced with the necessity of distinguishing between the two. If we are going to accept some things in the Bible as divine, infallible truth and dismiss other things as human error, we have somehow to determine which things in the Bible fall into which category. It is perhaps this necessity that drives some people into the hard version of belief in divine origin. That belief, hard as it is to maintain in the face of all the evidence to the contrary, at least has the virtue of not forcing one to make distinctions between different parts of the Bible. The soft version does, and that means that we must formulate some criteria for making the distinctions if those distinctions are not to be totally arbitrary.

It is certainly possible to formulate such criteria. Many of us, for example, might be tempted to adopt the criterion of love. According to this criterion, those parts of the Bible are divinely inspired that speak of God's love and that call us to love one another. Those parts of the Bible are human error that speak of hate and call for conflict among people. Or we might adopt the criterion of grace. According to this criterion, those parts of the Bible are divinely inspired that speak of God's free and unmerited grace for sinful humanity. Those parts of the Bible are human error which make God's grace conditional upon some action or belief by individual men and women. Others might adopt the criterion of divine law. According to this criterion, the parts of the Bible that speak of God's law are divinely inspired. Those parts of the Bible are human error which appear to overturn or supercede any of the laws stated elsewhere in the Bible. Each one of these criteria for sorting out the divine inspiration from the human error is certainly possible, as I suppose are many others.

The fallacy in this approach, however, is that it is necessarily subjective while claiming to have some objective validity as a tool for determining which parts of the Bible are, objectively speaking, divinely inspired. It moves the level of arbitrariness from the distinctions between parts of the Bible themselves to the level of the criteria for making the distinctions. Bible verses can be cited in support of each of the possible criteria mentioned above, but the selection of which verses to cite must itself of necessity be arbitrary and based upon the subjective preferences of the person making the selection. There simply is no objective basis for making the distinctions or for selecting the criteria upon which to make distinctions.

It is, of course, a thesis of this book that everything is subjective, so you may be asking, "what's so wrong with a subjective selection of criteria for deciding which parts of the Bible are divinely inspired and which are not?" The answer is that this approach necessarily switches from the subjective to the objective in an impermissible way. As soon as we say that these verses are divinely inspired we have made an objective claim, but that claim is necessarily based upon a subjective decision about the criteria for our selection. We are, therefore, attempting to avoid subjectivity when in fact we are not avoiding subjectivity. Consistency and simple honesty require us to reject this approach to the question of how we determine which parts of the Bible are divinely inspired and which are not.

So what are we left with? There remain two possibilities. One is to discard any claim to objectivity about certain parts of the Bible being divinely inspired. In this approach we would say that we experience certain parts of the Bible as divinely inspired *for us*. We experience them as divinely inspired because they correspond to our own experience of God in our lives. We experience them as divinely inspired because for us they bring the fruits of the Spirit: peace, joy, comfort, courage, and all the rest.

We experience them as divinely inspired because they lead us to wholeness of life. This solution to the problem is honest and consistent. It rules out, however, any claim that any Bible passage that we experience as divinely inspired is necessarily divinely inspired for anyone else. It changes the claim of divine inspiration from an external, objective claim (which is in any event indefensible on philosophical grounds as we have seen) into a personal, subjective experience that can be true for the person who experiences it but which that person cannot in any way universalize.

The other honest and consistent solution to the problem of determining which parts of the Bible are divinely inspired and which are not is to give up the idea of divine inspiration altogether. This is the solution Marcus Borg advocates in his books *Reading the Bible Again for the First Time*,[19] and *The Heart of Christianity*.[20] Borg finds the problem of determining which parts of the Bible are divinely inspired and which are not insurmountable and so rejects such a determination altogether. It is the solution that most appeals to the historian, to the scholar. Borg does not expressly recognize the subjectivist solution we just examined, so he advocates a thorough rejection of the notion of divine inspiration.

Yet Borg offers an understanding that is substantially similar to the subjectivist understanding advocated here. He introduces the notion of the Bible as sacrament. Obviously neither the Protestant tradition with its two sacraments nor the Catholic tradition with its seven has historically considered the Bible to be a sacrament. Borg, however, explains that the Bible functions as a sacrament in that it is "a finite, physical, visible mediator of the sacred, a means whereby the sacred becomes present to us."[21] I take him to mean much the same thing as what I said above about a subjectivist understanding of divine inspiration. The Bible mediates to us the presence of God and brings us the fruits of the Spirit as we read it, meditate on it, and pray over it. We can also understand Borg's idea of the Bible as sacrament as another way of expressing the idea advanced here that the Bible functions primarily as myth despite Borg's consistent refusal to use that word, myth being precisely something that mediates the presence of God to us.

---

19. Borg, *Reading the Bible Again for the First Time*. 22.
20. Borg, *The Heart of Christianity*, 46.
21. Ibid., 57.

The Bible: Myth and Spiritual Experience

Our conclusion that the Bible is a human product that functions for us as myth raises another issue that we must address. It is the issue of revelation. Christianity has always held that its knowledge of God is the result of divine revelation, that God has revealed truth about Godself both in the Bible and most fully in the person of Jesus Christ. Our rejection of the notion of the divine origin of the Bible, in either its hard or its softer forms, combined with our contention that religious truth is symbolic and mythic, amounts to a rejection of the traditional Christian understanding of revelation. Humans wrote the Bible as an expression of their experience of God. Myth and symbol are human stories and objects that connect with the deep levels of the human psyche and connect us to God. It may seem that there is no place in this system for any action on God's part to reveal Godself to people.

Yet spiritual people have always understood that not only do we have an inherent desire and drive to connect with God, God also strives to connect with us. Christians have always understood that God is self-revealing. God does not remain entirely self-contained in the spiritual dimension of reality but seeks to make Godself known to us in ways that we can comprehend. In Chapter Nine of this work I will contend that the cross of Christ is to be understood precisely as the supreme act of divine self-revelation, with the understanding of course that that statement is mythic not literal. We, therefore, cannot simply jettison the concept of revelation. Rather, we must try to understand how that concept fits with the other understandings we develop here. We have seen that myth and symbol are the necessary and indispensable language of faith. We have seen that religious truth is necessarily symbolic and mythic truth. All religious concepts must be understood mythically and symbolically. Revelation is a religious concept. Therefore, there must be a mythic understanding of revelation. What might such a mythic understanding of revelation be?

When we enter into a true myth, when we properly contemplate a true symbol, we experience ourselves connecting with God and God connecting with us. As I have said before in this book, the function of myth and symbol is both to connect us to God and to connect God to us. We experience the movement in symbol and myth as two-sided. We experience ourselves as moving to encounter God, and we experience God as moving to encounter us. The spiritual experience is one of meeting. It is the experience of God coming to us across all that separates us and of us moving beyond ourselves to meet the God who comes to meet us.[22]

Revelation mythically understood refers to God's side of the dual spiritual movement that connects us with God and God with us. When we say that something is divine revelation, we are saying that we have experienced God coming to us and making Godself known to us in that thing. Or, for Christians, in that person, since we experience God most fully coming to us and revealing Godself to us in Jesus Christ. The claim that a book or a person represents divine revelation can no more be a claim of objective fact than can any other religious claim. Rather, the term describes a part of the human spiritual experience, the part of that experience that we experience as coming from God.[23]

The Bible, then, is a human product that functions for us as myth in that we experience the presence of the spiritual in and through it. It is divine revelation for us to the extent that we experience God coming to us and making Godself known to us through its various texts. These experiences are purely subjective, as in reality is all human experience. As the Bible functions as myth for us, we may experience it as being divinely inspired or as being divine revelation. That experience is, however, purely

---

22. Karl Barth, that giant of twentieth century Protestant theology, believed that the movement came entirely from God's side. His view of human nature was so negative that he did not believe that anything we humans could do could contribute to our connection with God. That connection had to come entirely from God's side. This view sharply distinguished Bart from Tillich and also from that giant of twentieth century Catholic theology, Karl Rahner. Clearly my thought is in the tradition of Paul Tillich on this point, as on many others.

23. The issue of revelation suggests for many the New Testament book The Revelation to John, often mistakenly called "Revelations." Biblicists have always taken this book as a prediction of events to happen in the future. They continue to do so. For two millennia now they have looked for signs that the events of their time are the events they believe are predicted in Revelation. False prophets have repeatedly predicted the coming of the end times they believe Revelation discloses, and they have always been wrong. They still make those predictions today, and they are still wrong. They are wrong because Revelation is not and cannot be a divine disclosure of factual events that will occur in the future. Our understanding of the Bible as myth and as human product rules out that understanding. Indeed, scholars have long known that Revelation is in fact not about future events but about the situation in the Roman Empire in the late first century CE. When Revelation says Babylon, it means Rome. When it says the number of the beast is 666, it is referring to the Roman Emperor Nero. For a good discussion of the proper understanding of Revelation see Wes Howard-Brook and Anthony Gwyther, *Unveiling Empire: Reading Revelation Then and Now* (Maryknoll, NY: Orbis Books, 1999).

The Bible: Myth and Spiritual Experience

subjective. We can share our experience with others, and we can invite them to share that experience. We cannot, however, contend that the Bible is the Word of God for anyone who does not experience it as such. The Bible is a human product. It tells stories about God and about the experiences of God of certain ancient communities. In it we may experience divine truth. That divine truth however comes not from anything objective about the Bible itself but solely from our experience of the truth of the Bible as divine. It is our experience of the Bible that gives it its authority, that makes it (or better, parts of it) divine for us. More we cannot claim. More we do not need to claim.

Questions for Reflection and Discussion

1. What, if anything, did you learn about the Bible as a child?

    Who did you think wrote the Bible?

    Did you think of the Bible's stories as:

    Fact?

    History?

    Biography?

    Myth?

    Did you think of the Bible's stories as "true?"

    If so, what did you understand "true" to mean?

2. Do you believe that the Bible contains "divine truth?"

    If so, does it contain only divine truth?

    Or does it contain both divine truth and human error?

    If the Bible contains both divine truth and human error, how do you separate the divine truth from the human error?

    What criteria would you use to make that distinction?

    On what basis did you choose those criteria?

    Are the criteria for separating divine truth from human error the same for everyone?

Part Three

Overcoming the Obstacle of the Denial of Grace

IN PART ONE, WE considered the reality of the spiritual dimension of life. In Part Two, we considered the nature and limitations of Biblicism. There are, however, other obstacles to Christian faith in our context which remain even when the culture's materialist assumptions about reality and the Biblicistic nature of Christianity are cleared away. We will consider some of those obstacles in Part Three of this work. They fall into two broad categories. The first is the understanding of the nature of Christ's saving work in the world. We will consider the nearly universal understanding of that work in our context, namely, the classical atonement theory, more technically known as the theory of substitutionary sacrificial atonement. We will critique this understanding of Christ's work, reject it as inconsistent with a loving God and untrue to Jesus Christ, and offer an alternative understanding, a kind of demonstration soteriology (theory of the saving work of Christ) known as theology of the cross. We will then examine the implications of theology of the cross for our understanding of the dynamics of salvation. The second broad category is the understanding of Christian ethics. We will consider the prevailing understanding of Christian ethics as a system of rigid laws, critique that understanding, reject it as inconsistent with the true nature of grace, and offer an ethical understanding grounded not in law but in love.

It is important to keep one thing in mind. In discussing topics such as the nature of Christ's saving work (which, of course, assumes that there is something saving about Christ's work) or the nature of the cross, we are not talking about objective reality. As we have seen, we cannot know objective reality or even if there is such a thing. We are talking about subjective experience, as we always are when we talk about faith. We are talking about the meaning of myth. In the material that follows, we reject the classical theory of atonement. In doing so we are saying not that this theory is objectively wrong but that we find this interpretation of the saving work of Christ unconvincing. We find it to be a barrier to the acceptance of the Christian faith by numerous people in our current context. We will not stop to repeat this point as we go along. In the material that follows, we will be operating in a state of post-critical naiveté. Please remember always that even when we don't stop to make the point explicit we are dealing in Part Three of the present work with the meaning of myth and symbol, not with something that we claim to be objective fact.

8

Beyond the Classical Theory of Atonement

ON ASH WEDNESDAY, 2004, a movie hit American theaters that caused quite a stir. It was Mel Gibson's *The Passion of the Christ*, a graphic, bloody cinematic portrayal of the end of Jesus' earthly life. The movie received massive pre-release publicity. Conservative evangelical churches promoted it aggressively as a magnificent tool for reaching people church professionals always condescendingly call "the un-churched." The movie's own promotional materials predominantly used one slogan to sum up the movie's message. Those materials said, in bold, even lurid letters, "Dying was His reason for living." Gibson's gruesome movie was both grounded in and reinforced the public awareness of a theory about the meaning of Jesus Christ. It is a meaning that focuses exclusively on his suffering and death. It is the understanding that a wholly innocent Jesus took upon himself all the sin of humanity, then suffered horribly and died to pay the price for human sin. It is a theory that has Biblical roots. In its most popular form today, however, it dates back only to the early twelfth century and the publication of Anselm of Canterbury's book *Cur Deus Homo?*, *Why Did God Become Human?* (or *Why God-Man?*—either translation fits the text). This theory of salvation is so widespread among us that for great numbers of people both inside and outside of the churches it has become nearly identical with Christianity itself. One particular theology, which never truly was or could be the entirety of the Christian faith, has very nearly swallowed the entire religion whole. Although it has wide appeal in Evangelical and Fundamentalist circles, I am convinced that it has become one of the primary obstacles to Christian faith in the world today.

From the very beginning Christians have had a powerful sense that Jesus, in his birth, life, teachings, death, and resurrection, has saving significance. We have sensed that there is something about him that restores our relationship with God in a way that brings what we have always called salvation. From the very beginning Christians have struggled to find language to express that sense, that perception, that experience of the saving power of Jesus Christ. The New Testament writings themselves express different understandings of Jesus' saving work. Those writings express the different experiences of different early Christians as those early believers struggled to find the words to communicate what they knew to be true. Although most Christians today probably believe that the classical atonement theory is *the* Biblical understanding of the saving work of Jesus, this is not the case, as an examination of some of the key New Testament texts will show.

The earliest Christian texts that we have are the authentic letters of Paul. In those letters, Paul expresses the saving work of Jesus Christ in the language of reconciliation and solidarity. One very important text for an understanding of Christ's work as bringing not atonement but reconciliation between God and creation is 2 Corinthians 5:16–19, which reads

> From now on, therefore, we regard no one from a human point of view; even though we once knew Christ from a human point of view, we know him no longer in that way. So if anyone is in Christ, there is a new creation: everything old has passed away; see, everything has become new! All this is from God, who reconciled us to himself through Christ, and has given us the ministry of reconciliation; that is, in Christ God was reconciling the world to himself, not counting their trespasses against them and entrusting the message of reconciliation to us.

Paul does not say *how* God reconciled Godself to us in Christ. Apparently he felt no need to explain. The important point for our purposes is that Paul does not say that the reconciliation was effected through a substitutionary atoning sacrifice on Jesus' part.[1] He says that the reconciliation that Christ effected between God and the world was God's doing in Jesus. In Christ Jesus, we are reconciled with God because that was God's will and purpose in Jesus Christ. There is no reference to Christ's death or suffering here, although the cross is central to Paul's theology (and to mine) in a different way, as we will see below. In this very early Christian statement, Paul simply expresses his experience that in Christ he is reconciled to God, indeed, the whole world is reconciled to God.

---

1. I recognize of course that many people may infer substitutionary sacrificial atonement in Paul's statements here and in the Romans passage discussed below. I believe, however, that reading these passages that way projects onto Paul's words a later understanding that he in fact did not have.

Beyond the Classical Theory of Atonement

The central text that expresses the saving work of Jesus Christ in terms of God's solidarity with the world is Romans 8:38–39. Written later in Paul's life, it reads, "For I am convinced that neither death, nor life, nor angels, nor rulers, nor things present, nor things to come, nor powers, nor height, nor depth, nor anything else in all creation, will be able to separate us from the love of God in Christ Jesus our Lord."[2] In and through Jesus Christ, God stands with us in life and in death, come what may, no matter what. That was Paul's experience that he expressed so powerfully in this magnificent passage. It is a very early Christian understanding of the meaning of Jesus Christ's work, of what it means for us to call Jesus Savior.

There is at least one other New Testament understanding of the saving work of Christ that we must mention before we turn to the classical atonement theory. It is called the ransom theory of atonement. One key text is Mark 10:45, which reads, "For the Son of Man came not to be served but to serve, and to give his life a ransom for many."[3] Many contemporary Christians may read this statement as meaning the same thing as classical atonement theory, but it does not. As we will see, in that theory Jesus pays a debt humanity owes to God. In ransom theory, a price is paid, but not to God. The ransom theory assumes that humanity is held in bondage to sin by Satan. Satan has in effect kidnapped us from God and is holding us hostage. In order for Satan to set us free from sin, Satan must be paid a ransom. A price must be paid to the devil. Jesus Christ is that price. He bears the price of sin although he was without sin and thereby pays off the devil by suffering all the devil can inflict by way of human suffering and death. The ransom theory, in which the price is paid to Satan not to God, is one of the prominent theologies of salvation in the New Testament.

Although, as noted above, the classical statement of substitutionary sacrificial atonement theology did not appear until the early twelfth century, it does, in fact, have roots in the New Testament. One place where it appears in at least embryonic form is the Letter to the Hebrews. That letter presents Jesus Christ as the great high priest who is both the one who offers

---

2. This is my favorite passage in the entire Bible, which is why it appears above the Introduction at the beginning of this book. It sums up my own experience of God in Jesus Christ better than any other passage. For me, in a very real sense, these words of Paul's are the Gospel, and everything else is gloss.

3. This saying attributed to Jesus is repeated at Matthew at Matt 20:28. See also 1 Tim 2:6.

sacrifice to God like the priests of the Jerusalem Temple and the one who is himself the sacrifice for human sin, the ultimate scapegoat, the blameless one offered up as a sacrifice to God to procure God's forgiveness of human sin. Hebrews says, "Although he was a Son, he learned obedience through what he suffered; and having been made perfect, he became the source of eternal salvation for all who obey him, having been designated by God a high priest according to the order of Melchizedek."[4] And . . .

> For it was fitting that we should have such a high priest, holy, blameless, undefiled, separated from sinners, and exalted above heaven. Unlike the other high priests, he has no need to offer sacrifices day after day, first for his own sins, and then for those of the people; this he did once for all when he offered himself. For the law appoints as high priests those who are subject to weakness, but the word of the oath, which came later than the law, appoints a Son who has been made perfect forever.[5]

Hebrews says that Christ offered a single sacrifice for sins for all time.[6] For the anonymous author of Hebrews, Jesus was the ultimate sacrifice for human sin.

It is clear what this author has done. He too experienced salvation in and through Jesus Christ. He searched for language in which he could express that experience and convince others of its truth. He found that language in the sacrificial system of first century Judaism. Until the Romans destroyed the Temple in 70 CE, first century Judaism centered on animal sacrifice, which was performed in the Temple. Animal sacrifice could have meanings other than atonement for sin,[7] but a conception of animal sacrifice as a means of forgiveness was part of Judaism in New Testament times. The author of the Letter to the Hebrews has used that conception to express his understanding of the meaning of Jesus' death.

It may seem odd that a Jewish writer would substitute a human being for a sacrificial animal in a theory of atonement, but there is precedent for it in the Hebrew Scriptures. Second Isaiah (Isaiah chapters forty through fifty-five) contains three passages known as the Suffering Servant songs. One of those, Isaiah 53:4–12, contains language that could be used to sup-

4. Heb 5:8–10.
5. Heb 7:26–28.
6. Heb 10:12.
7. See Marcus J. Borg and John Dominic Crossan, *The Last Week, A Day-by-Day Account of Jesus' Final Week in Jerusalem* (San Francisco: HarperSanFrancisco, 2006) 36–38.

Beyond the Classical Theory of Atonement

port the view of Jesus as a substitutionary atoning sacrifice for human sin. That passage begins

> Surely he has borne our infirmities and carried our diseases; yet we accounted him stricken, struck down by God, and afflicted. But he was wounded for our transgressions, crushed for our iniquities; upon him was the punishment that made us whole, and by his bruises we are healed.[8]

This third Suffering Servant song also says, "It was the will of the LORD to crush him with pain,"[9] and "The righteous one, my servant, shall make many righteous, and he shall bear their iniquities."[10] It is easy to see how early Christians could find in these words of Second Isaiah an answer to their question of the meaning of Jesus' unjust suffering and death. As an historical matter, they are certainly the source of the early Christian understanding of Jesus as an atoning sacrifice for human sin.

The classical atonement theory, the understanding that Jesus took our place and in his body paid the price for human sin though he himself was sinless, thus has roots in the Bible, in both the New Testament and the Hebrew Scriptures. Yet as we have just seen, it is only one of the New Testament understandings of the saving work of Jesus Christ. The fact that it has nearly completely displaced all other understandings comes not from the fact that certain Bible verses can be cited to support it but from the prominence it received after the publication in the year 1107 of the book we mentioned above, *Cur Deus Homo?* by St. Anselm of Canterbury.[11] *Cur Deus Homo?* is a thoroughly medieval book. It is a fine example of the Scholasticism of the High Middle Ages that also produced the towering figure in the history of Christian theology St. Thomas Aquinas. True to the Scholastic tradition, it is thoroughly rationalistic. Anselm claims to establish his thesis on the basis of reason alone. Yet as brilliant as it is, it is firmly rooted in the culture and the ethic of its time.

Anselm states the problem he addresses in the book this way:

---

8. Isa 53:4–6.
9. Isa 53:10a.
10. Isa 53:11c.
11. 1107 sounds like a long time ago to most of us, but please consider. The year 1107 is closer in time to us than it is to Jesus. Thus, the common understanding of the classical atonement theory that comes from Anselm can be said to be a relatively recent development in the history of Christianity.

> For what reason and on the basis of what necessity did God become a man and by His death restore life to the world (as we believe and confess), seeing that He could have accomplished this restoration by means of some other person (whether angelic or human) or else by merely willing it?[12]

It is a legitimate question and a very important one for every Christian. Why did God become human in Jesus of Nazareth? For that God did just that is the central Christian confession.

Anselm begins his answer by saying that every person owes a debt to God. The debt arises from the fact that we do not make our will subject to the will of God. Anselm says "A person who does not render God this honor [of making his or her will subject to God's will], takes from God what is His and dishonors God, and this is to commit sin." Sin, then, is acting according to one's own will and not according to God's will. The problem with sin is that it "dishonors" God. We must do something to atone for our sin, and merely returning what we have taken, that is, merely repenting and subjecting our wills to God's will in the future, is not enough. Rather,

> on account of the insult committed, [the sinner] must give back more than he took away. . . . [F]or one who violates the honor of some person, it does not suffice to render honor, if he does not make restitution of something pleasing to the person dishonored, in proportion to the injury of dishonor that has been inflicted. . . . Thus, therefore, everyone who sins must pay to God the honor he has taken away, and this is satisfaction, which every sinner must make to God.

Anselm's conception of the redemptive work of Christ is then thoroughly grounded in a medieval sense of the honor that a subordinate person owes to a superior one. Sin is sin for Anselm because it dishonors God.

Anselm then considers whether it is "fitting for God to remit sin out of mercy alone, without any payment of the debt." He answers that it is not: "To remit sin in such a way is the same as not to punish it. And since to deal justly with sin, without satisfaction, is the same as to punish it, then,

---

12. All quotes from *Cur Deus Homo?* are from an abridged version of the book found on the Internet at http://shoeleg.yak.net/49. The analysis here is informed by a lecture that the Rev. Dr. Michael Rashko, professor of systematic theology and church history at the Seattle University School of Theology and Ministry, gave in the late 1990s in a church history class.

if it is not punished, something inordinate is allowed to pass." Moreover, "if an unpunished sin is remitted . . . one who sins and one who does not sin will be in the same position before God. And that would be unseemly for God." There is much more to Anselm's analysis of the necessity of punishment for sin, but the point is made. It would be "unseemly" for God to forgive sin without demanding a restoration of God's honor through punishment of the sin. Therefore, God does not simply forgive sin out of mercy or because God wills to do so, but God demands a punishment. God demands that a restitution be made, that a price be paid.

The next step in the analysis that we must consider is Anselm's argument that humans cannot make satisfaction for their own sin. If we attempt to make satisfaction for our sin by doing what God expects of us, through "repentance, a contrite and humbled heart, fasting, and all sorts of bodily work, mercy in giving and forgiving, and obedience," as Anselm puts it, all we are doing is giving God what is God's due in the first place. Humans have nothing to offer God that is not already God's and therefore cannot make satisfaction for their own sin.

Another reason why humans cannot make satisfaction for their own sin is the gravity of that sin. We sin so gravely whenever we knowingly do anything, however small, that is contrary to the will of God that nothing we can give in return can adequately pay the debt to God that our sin creates. God demands satisfaction in proportion to the extent of the sin, Anselm says, and human sin is so great that humans have nothing to offer that is truly proportionate to the extent of human sin.

Since humans then cannot save themselves, they must be saved through Christ. The work of salvation "can only be accomplished if there is someone who pays to God, for man's sin, something greater than every existing thing besides God." The only person who could do that is someone who himself "surpasses everything that is less than God" and who is himself "greater than everything that is not God." Since only God surpasses everything that is not God, "only God can make this satisfaction." Yet the satisfaction for human sin must also be made by a human, since it is human sin for which satisfaction is being made. Therefore, "if only God can make this satisfaction and only a man ought to make it: it is necessary that a God-man make it." The one who makes atonement for human sin must at the same time be fully divine and fully human. The only way that could happen would be for God to assume a human nature. Anselm, of course, argues that this had to be done through a virgin birth, but the main point is that God became "God-man" in Christ. Christ died, although for Anselm only his human nature died. Christ the God-man voluntarily laid down his human life and therefore made the payment that no mere human could make for human sin.[13]

Anselm's analysis is thus thoroughly medieval. It is rigidly rationalistic in the Scholastic tradition. It is grounded in the feudal system of honor and allegiance that subordinates owe to superiors. It also reflects a medieval conception of human sin. In this view all human sin, no matter how trivial from a human point of view, is such an affront to God's honor that a price has to be paid beyond mere repentance and a commitment to lead a holy life. The basic idea is that it is unjust and "unseemly" for God simply to forgive human sin, which is so evil that even the littlest sin is an infinite affront to God's honor, without demanding a price. The life of Jesus the God-man was that price, for no other price, no mere human price, could possibly be high enough to restore God's honor. Anselm may not use the phrase, but he would completely agree with the marketing slogan for "The Passion of the Christ." Dying was Christ's reason for living. He became one of us and died because that was the only way God could forgive human sin without committing an injustice, that is, without getting from humanity what was God's due, what human sin had taken from God, and then some.

This understanding of the work of Jesus Christ has indeed virtually swallowed Christianity whole. Relatively few Christians in our context today would find anything in it to which to object. Yet I am convinced that the classical atonement theory is a major obstacle to Christian faith today for those who are not Christians and for a great many people who cling to Christianity despite their reservations about it. I also believe it to be theologically unsound and Biblically unnecessary. To the objections to the classical atonement theory we must now turn.

The classical atonement theory that we have just reviewed is, I am convinced, something from which Christianity needs to be liberated. It is something with which a great many Christians struggle, or perhaps it is just something that a great many Christians ignore, not accepting it but not having any alternative understanding of the significance of Christ's

13. The story of Christ's Passion and death in the Gospel of John fits this theology very well. As we have seen already, in John, Jesus is in charge of the events of his suffering and death and enters them voluntarily, without reservation. The theology of the other canonical Gospels fits Anselm's theory far less well.

redeeming work to put in its place. In popular consciousness it is, as we have said several times before, virtually synonymous with Christianity itself. Clearing away the classical atonement theory and replacing it with a healthier, more life-giving and life-enhancing understanding are necessary steps in overcoming obstacles to faith among us today. The first step in that process is to demonstrate that, so far from being the central message of the faith, the classical atonement theory is in fact bad theology on a number of different levels.

We notice first that Anselm's notion that it would be "unseemly" for God simply to forgive human sin without a price being paid is not Biblically required. We noted that New Testament authors such as the author of the Letter to the Hebrews found a Scriptural basis for a theology of sacrifice in, among other places, Isaiah 53. There are, however, several other passages in the Hebrew Bible where God forgives human sin simply because God wills to do so. At Jeremiah 31:34 we read: "For I [Yahweh] will forgive their iniquity and remember their sin no more." There is no mention of sacrifice here. At Numbers 14:19–20 Yahweh answers Moses' prayer that he forgive the iniquity of the people simply by declaring: "I do forgive, just as you have asked." Psalm 65:3 reads: "When deeds of iniquity overwhelm us, you forgive our transgressions." Anselm thought it "unseemly" for God simply to forgive sin, but Hebrew Scripture doesn't.

Next we examine Anselm's own logic in his classic formulation of the theory. There are at least two problems inherent in that logic itself. Recall that for Anselm the problem with sin is that it is an affront to God's honor. Anselm makes a direct analogy between the affront to the honor of a person created when another person withholds something from her to which she is legally entitled. Anselm's conception of honor is thoroughly medieval, and we can reject his analogy on those grounds; but there is a more profound problem with this approach. Anselm assumes without question that human concepts such as honor apply to God. If a feudal lord's honor is offended when a vassal withholds the service or the tax which is the lord's due under the standards of the time, then it follows without question for Anselm that the Lord's honor is offended when the Lord's vassals, we humans, withhold from the Lord that which is the Lord's due, namely, our allegiance and obedience.

This unquestioning application of human conceptions to God is simply inadmissible. God may in some sense be personal, or our relationship to God may be analogous to certain human relationships; but God is not human. God transcends our petty human conceptions and our petty human relationships absolutely. If there is any meaning to us in the statement that God has honor, and I don't think that there is, it is inconceivable that that divine honor in any way depends on anything we humans do or fail to do. The problem with sin is not and cannot be that it offends God's honor. That notion makes God entirely too human. Perhaps more importantly, it makes God entirely too petty. The theology of the cross that we develop in the next chapter holds that God suffers when humanity suffers. That too is at least analogous to a human emotion or experience. It is, however, not the result of humans inflicting any direct pain on God, as Anselm thought human sin directly offended the honor of God. It is a result of God's free decision to stand in solidarity with us humans in all phases of our lives. It is a result of God's nature as love. It does not reduce God to a petty human the way Anselm's analysis does.

There is at least one more logical flaw in Anselm's argument that is worth addressing. Anselm posited that we humans have nothing that we can pay to God as the price of our sin that isn't already God's due and that therefore humans cannot in any event atone for their own sin. He says, in effect, that all we can do is stop sinning, and not sinning is our duty to God whether we have ever sinned in the first place or not. Therefore, not sinning in the future cannot be the something more that is God's due as recompense for the affront to God's honor that is sin. There is, however, one thing that humans can do that goes far beyond merely not sinning. Humans can die. Humans of course do die, all of us. The Christian tradition held from the beginning, with Paul, that "the wages of sin is death."[14] If, as the tradition holds and as Anselm probably believed, death came into the world as a result of human sin (specifically the sin of Adam passed on to all subsequent people), then it would be reasonable to hold that each human's death is the something extra that each human owes to God for sin.[15] Anselm's logic seems to support the idea that each human's death is the atonement for that person's sin, a conclusion that would of course make Christ, as Anselm understood him, entirely unnecessary. Anselm claimed to establish the necessity of God becoming human in Jesus Christ

---

14. Rom 6:23.

15. I do not actually believe that death is the result of sin. I think it is the result of our being creatures and not gods. The point, however, is not whether I believe that death is a consequence of sin but whether Anselm did, and I assume that he did, along with the Christian tradition at large.

Beyond the Classical Theory of Atonement

on the basis of reason alone. His attempt to do that, like all attempts to establish religious propositions on the basis of reason alone, failed.

Yet even if Anselm's presentation of the classical theory of atonement were logically flawless, we would still have to reject substitutionary sacrificial atonement as a flawed theology. It is a flawed theology for at least three additional reasons. They are in short, first, that the classical atonement theory assumes that the work of Christ is primarily about obtaining forgiveness of sin, and this assumption in turn is based upon the assumption that sin is the universal human dilemma, that sin is primarily that from which we need saving. Second, the idea that Jesus is above all else a sacrifice is inconsistent with Jesus' own self-understanding as it is presented in the Gospels and in particular is inconsistent with Jesus' rejection of the Temple system and its sacrificial worship. Finally, substitutionary sacrificial atonement presents an unacceptable image of God. It is inconsistent with a God of grace, mercy, and love.

We established early in this work that the legitimate function of any religion is to connect people to God and God to people. Implied in that statement of the purpose of religion is the notion that something separates people from God. In other words, our understanding of the purpose of religion implies that we humans suffer under some kind of existential dilemma. There is something that produces in us an existential angst, an anxiety about our existence. To some extent in New Testament times, and certainly in the Middle Ages that gave us, among so many others, Anselm of Canterbury, an awareness of human sin and a desperate desire to be forgiven was the prevailing existential dilemma in western Christianity. His anxiety of sin and forgiveness was one of the ways in which Martin Luther, for example, was a thoroughly medieval man. It was his near panic at the sinfulness that he perceived in himself that eventually drove him to Paul's theology of justification by grace through faith that became the bedrock of the Protestant Reformation. Medieval Europe was fixated on human sin and its well-deserved punishment. The lurid portrayals of hell in medieval art and in literature are ample evidence of the people's preoccupation with sin and forgiveness. The classical atonement theory at least has the virtue of addressing that existential anxiety in a powerful and, for countless people through the ages, convincing way.

Yet sin is not the only existential dilemma we humans face. Indeed, as Paul Tillich and Douglas John Hall have pointed out, sin is not necessarily the primary agent of angst for most people in our contemporary context. In our context, where most of us live relatively comfortable and relatively long lives, the idea of an immediate, eternal torment because of our sin has lost its grip on us. Certainly in the more or less liberal mainline Protestant churches (or should I say the Protestant churches that we used to call mainline?) most of the people do not carry much guilt about sin. In the more liberal of those churches, as in at least some United Church of Christ congregations that I know of, the people will not even let the pastor include a confession piece in the worship service because they don't perceive that they have anything to confess. Certainly many of us who live and work in the more liberal Christian traditions recognize that position as unrealistic and theologically unsound. We know the truth in Paul's statement that all sin and fall short of the glory of God[16] and 1 John's statement that if we say we have no sin we deceive ourselves and the truth is not in us.[17] Nonetheless, it is true that sin is not the issue for the people of these traditions that it was for Anselm of Canterbury or for Martin Luther. Even those of us who include a confession piece in our liturgies sometimes feel the need to apologize for doing so, which really is why we do a "call to confession" that explains to the people why we're doing confession at all. An awareness of sin simply is not what keeps most people in our context awake at night.

Tillich believed that the primary existential dilemma for most modern people was not sin but meaninglessness, and I believe that he was right. When people fall into despair today they are much more likely to despair of finding any meaning in their lives than they are to despair of finding forgiveness of their sin. The modern secular existentialist has given up on finding any meaning in human existence. A great many people in our context today who know nothing of philosophical existentialism nonetheless experience, if only perhaps at the subconscious level of their psyches, that their lives have no meaning. They may be "successful." They may be financially wealthy and hold positions of power and prestige in society. The very high rates of divorce, alcoholism, drug addiction, and suicide among those "successful" people among us tell us, however, that all is not well with their souls. Sometimes these people come to church, and when we ask them why they say, "because I want to give something back to my community." That oft-repeated refrain means, I believe, that people are looking for meaning, and they know they cannot find it in their

16. Rom 3:32.
17. 1 John 1:8.

self-centered, "successful" lives. Their statement, it seems, must have some such deeper meaning, for if all they were truly looking for were in fact a chance to give back to the community, joining the local Kiwanis or Rotary Club would be a more direct way to do it than is joining most churches. Likewise, I am convinced that the very high addiction and suicide rates among our young people, our teenagers, result from the fact that our culture convinces them that their lives have no meaning. Our commercial culture bombards them every day with the message: your purpose in life is to be a consumer so that large corporations can make lots of money, and you are the only one you need to care about. Whether they can articulate it or not, young people sense the lie in those messages, but our culture gives them nothing to put in their place. Meaninglessness is a much more significant existential dilemma among us than is sin.

The classical atonement theory, however, has nothing to say about any existential dilemma except sin. It presents a mechanism through which God supposedly has forgiven human sin. Despite the theological problems with that mechanism, classical atonement theory does at least give one explanation of how it is that God forgives sin. It has nothing to say, however, about the existential dilemma of meaninglessness or any other possible human existential dilemma. It does nothing, for example, to address the human fear of non-being, the fear, so closely related to a sense of meaninglessness, that when it's all over it's all over, that only nothingness awaits us at the end of our human journey. Classical atonement theory addresses sin and only sin. Perhaps that is why conservative Christian churches, for whom that theory has devoured the entire faith, keep preaching that what people need more than anything else is forgiveness of sin. If all you have is a hammer, every problem looks like a nail. If all you have is an answer for sin, then every human problem looks like sin. For those of us who recognize that our fundamental anxiety is primarily about something other than sin, the classical atonement theory is largely irrelevant. Christianity that consists mostly of that theory is irrelevant. It simply does not give us what we need. In other words, it does not connect us with God. It is therefore, for us, bad religion.

Yet even if the classical atonement theory were not largely irrelevant to so many people in our context today, it would still be bad Christian theology. The reason it would still be bad Christianity is that it is untrue to Jesus Christ, the one in and through whom Christians claim to know God, the one whose disciples Christians claim to be. Jesus, you see, rejected the entire notion of sacrifice as the appropriate human response to God. A brief look at two familiar episodes from the Gospel of Mark will illustrate the point.

The first episode is the famous story of the "widow's mite."[18] Jesus is sitting in the Jerusalem Temple during the last week of his life. He sees wealthy people putting their contributions into the treasury of the Temple. Then he sees someone Mark calls "a poor widow" come to put money in as well. She deposits two copper coins, which Mark tells us are worth a penny. Jesus says nothing to her. Instead he seizes upon the incident as a teaching moment for the Disciples. He says to them, "Truly I tell you, this poor widow has put in more than all those who are contributing to the treasury. For all of them have contributed out of their abundance; but she out her poverty has put in everything she had, all she had to live on."[19]

It is perhaps not immediately apparent that this story constitutes a rejection by Jesus of sacrificial worship, yet that is precisely what it is. When we read the story of the widow's mite with the passage that comes immediately before it and the passage that comes immediately after it we see that it is part of a carefully constructed condemnation of the Jerusalem Temple. The passage just before the widow's mite has Jesus teaching in the Temple.[20] He condemns the scribes, who were Temple officials of the time. He condemns their hypocrisy in the way they parade their piety before the public while at the same time they "devour widows' houses." He concludes that they will receive "the greater condemnation."[21] The reference to "widows' houses" in this passage clearly ties it to the story of the widow's mite that immediately follows.

The passage immediately after the story of the widow's mite is Jesus' prediction of the destruction of the Temple.[22] He tells a disciple who marvels at the grandeur of the Temple buildings that "Not one stone will be left here upon another; all will be thrown down."[23] The Temple is the "house" of the scribes. Because they devour widows' houses, their own house will be devoured. The story of the widow's mite in the middle of this struc-

---

18. Mark 12:41–44.
19. Mark 12:43–44.
20. Mark 12:38–40.
21. Mark 12:40.
22. Mark 13:1–2.
23. Mark 13:2.

ture illustrates how the Temple authorities "devour widow's houses." The widow's contribution wasn't voluntary. She was doing what she could to pay the Temple tax required of all Jews. She gave the last little bit that she had because those Temple authorities had told her all her life that she would be a sinner if she did not. She paid in the last she had to live on because she wanted to be right with God when she died. Her act is not one of unreasonable generosity; it is a sign of her oppression by the religious authorities of her time. Because of the way the Temple authorities oppress people like the poor widow, the entire structure of their power will be overthrown. In this story Jesus is rejecting the Jerusalem Temple with its system of sacrifice outright. He is saying that the way to be right with God is not to engage in the rituals of the Temple, it is to do justice for people like the poor widow.

In the story of the widow's mite, Jesus condemns the Temple, but it is still possible that all he is condemning is the corruption of the Temple authorities, not the sacrificial system of the Temple itself. Another familiar Gospel story, I believe, puts to rest that possible interpretation.[24] It is the story usually, and very erroneously, called "the cleansing of the Temple." It is one of the few Gospel stories that appear in all four Gospels. We will focus on the earliest of the versions, the one in Mark.[25]

On the day after his triumphal entry into Jerusalem,[26] Jesus goes to the Temple, the seat of the religious powers of the day and the place of sacrificial worship. As soon as he entered he

> began to drive out those who were selling and those who were buying in the temple, he overturned the tables of the money changers and the seats of those who sold doves; and he would not allow anyone to carry anything through the temple. He was teaching and saying: "Is it not written, 'my house shall be called a house of prayer for all the nations'? But you have made it a den of robbers."[27]

The first important thing to understand is that the people who were selling doves and the money changers weren't doing anything wrong in

---

24. I recognize that Borg and Crossan disagree with this analysis. See their book *The Last Week*, 31–53. On page forty-nine, for example, they write, "There is nothing wrong with prayer and sacrifice [i.e., the proper functions of the Temple]—they are commanded in the Torah." I respectfully disagree, for the reasons stated in the discussion that follows.

25. Mark 11:15–19. The other versions are found at Matt 21:12–13; Luke 19:45–46; John 2:13–16.

26. Mark 11:1–11.

27. Mark 11:15–17.

terms of the sacrificial system of the Temple. Borg and Crossan, of course, recognize this fact. They acknowledge that

> the money changers and animal sellers were perfectly legitimate and absolutely necessary for the temple's normal functioning.... Money changers were needed so that Jewish pilgrims could pay the temple tax in the only approved coinage. Buying animals or birds on site was the only way pilgrims could be sure the creatures were ritually adequate for sacrifice.[28]

Yet Jesus, in a prophetic act that echoes the prophetic acts of Jeremiah and the other great Hebrew prophets, disrupted and prevented their legitimate actions, overturning their tables and seats and driving them out of the Temple. If these people and their activities were legitimate in terms of the sacrificial system of Temple worship, why did Jesus do it? What was his problem with them and their activities?

He clearly did not do it go "cleanse" the Temple. The moneychangers and the sellers of sacrificial animals were not people of whom the Temple needed cleansing. They weren't defiling it; they were enabling its operation in the way it was intended to operate. We must, therefore, understand his action not as a purification of something of which he approved but as a symbolic overthrowing of something of which he disapproved. Because the people he drove out were essential to the functioning of the Jewish system of sacrificial worship, Jesus' action is a symbolic rejection of that system. This action throws new light on his prediction of the destruction of the Temple that we considered above and that follows the story of his driving out the money changers and the sellers of animals by more than a chapter in the Gospel of Mark. That prediction is part of Jesus' rejection of the entire Temple system of worship. For him, God does not desire sacrifice. God desires justice. Indeed, at Matthew 9:9, Jesus quotes the prophet Hosea when he says to the Pharisees, "Go and learn what this means, 'I desire mercy, not sacrifice.'"[29] Sacrifice does not get people right with God. Lives of justice do. The life of faith isn't about sacrifice. It is about loving God, neighbor, and self and about doing justice.

It is, therefore, ironic at best that the Christian tradition has turned Jesus into the ultimate sacrifice. The classical atonement theory, with roots in the Bible and fully developed by Anselm, makes Jesus something

---

28. Borg and Crossan, *The Last Week*, 48.
29. Quoting Hos 6:6.

Beyond the Classical Theory of Atonement

that is contrary to everything he taught about God and our life with God. Jesus stands in the great Jewish prophetic tradition that rejected sacrifice. He stands in the tradition of Amos, who said, "Even though you offer me your burnt offerings and grain offerings, I will not accept them; and the offerings of well-being of your fatted animals I will not look upon ... but let justice roll down like waters, and righteousness like an ever-flowing stream."[30] He stands in the tradition of Micah, who said, "Shall I come before [the Lord] with burnt offerings, with calves a year old? Will the Lord be pleased with thousands of rams, with ten thousands of rivers of oil? ... He has told you, O mortal, what is good; and what does the Lord require of you, but to do justice, and to love kindness, and to walk humbly with your God?"[31] Jesus doesn't want sacrifice. He wants faith, peace, and justice. He would be appalled that the Christian tradition has turned him into the ultimate scapegoat, that we have made him something that he himself rejected. It is not too strong to say that the Christian tradition's making Jesus into a sacrifice for sin is a betrayal of Jesus.

It is a betrayal of Jesus, but reaching that conclusion does not exhaust the theological problems with the classical atonement theory. There is one more big one that we must address, namely what that theory says about God. I once heard of a Biblicist preacher who, preaching about substitutionary sacrificial atonement, held a baby in his arms. He stretched out the precious, innocent infant's arm and held open his hand. He said something like, "Who among you would love another so much that you would drive a nail through this hand? We wouldn't, but God did. God drove nails through the body of His Son to save you." He thought he was preaching salvation, but what was he really saying? He was saying not that God is more loving than we are (which is certainly true) but that God is more brutal, crueler, and more sadistic than we are. Perhaps the single greatest sin of the classical atonement theory is that it makes a monster of God. It makes God a bloodthirsty ogre so concerned with God's own honor that God will commit an unspeakable atrocity, the brutal slaughter of an innocent man, as a precondition for the forgiveness of human sin. The classical atonement theory is in truth nothing but a theory of cosmic child abuse, as feminist theologians have taught us in recent years.

---

30. Amos 5:22,24.
31. Mic 6:6–8.

Proponents of the classical atonement theory sometimes insist that the requirement of a sacrifice before God can forgive sin is necessary to preserve divine justice. God is, they quite rightly say, a God of both mercy and justice. If God simply forgave sin without requiring a penalty, the argument goes, God would preserve the divine sense of mercy but not the divine sense of justice. The error in this argument is that it misunderstands divine justice. We will consider the nature of God's demand for justice that we see in Jesus in more detail in the final chapter. The point here is that God's demand for justice is not a demand for justice *for God*. God is not concerned with a limited human concept like justice for Godself. God's demand for justice is a demand for justice for us, for God's people. It is most particularly a demand for justice for "the least of these."[32] The notion that the bloody sacrifice of God's own son is necessary to preserve God's justice is another example of how the classical atonement theory improperly projects limited human concepts onto God, where they do not apply.

The classical atonement theory will simply not survive critical scrutiny. It is not Biblically required. Its classic formulation by Anselm of Canterbury is based upon an impermissible anthropomorphizing of God in terms of medieval codes of honor and is logically flawed. It betrays Jesus, and it makes a monster of God. Yet this untenable theory is the public face of Christianity in our context today. It is a major obstacle to the Christian faith among us. We have shown its error, but the question remains: with what are we going to replace it? After all, we too have experienced the saving power of Jesus, and not just his great moral teaching. We have experienced salvation in him. He connects us to God and God to us. We believe that he is indeed the Savior. How are we to understand that experience, to express it in a meaningful way to our contemporaries? The answer I am convinced lies in what Jürgen Moltmann has called a "not much loved" minority voice in the history of Christianity known as the theology of the cross. It is to a discussion of that alternative understanding of the saving work of Jesus that we now turn.

---

32. Matthew 25:40.

Questions for Reflection and Discussion

1. Were you ever taught that Jesus "died or us," or "died for our sin?"
    > If so, were you taught that Jesus died to "pay the price for sin?"
    > Were you taught that Jesus had to suffer and die before God would forgive human sin?
    > Were you taught that that is what the Bible says?
    > If so, what parts of the Bible contain that message?
2. Do you believe that justice requires that a price be paid before God can forgive human sin?
    > If so, what does "justice" mean in this context?
    > Is it justice for humanity?
    > Is it justice for God?
    > Which of these does God care about?
3. What picture of God does the classical theory of atonement paint for you?
    > Do you agree with the contention in chapter 8 that this theory amounts of a theory of cosmic child abuse?
    > Why?
    > Or why not?

9

The Meaning of the Cross: The Demonstration of God's Solidarity

CLASSICAL ATONEMENT THEORY DOESN'T work and is a barrier to the Christian faith in our context today. Yet Christians from the very beginning have experienced saving significance in Jesus Christ—and not just in his life but in his death. Jesus' death is one of the defining characteristics of Christianity. Of all the world's major religions, only Christianity follows a crucified savior. In other words, only Christianity follows a savior whom the world's powers executed as a common political criminal. Jesus' execution at the hands of the Romans should have been the end of his movement.[1] First century Judea had numerous would-be Messiahs who developed followings among the people just as Jesus had. The Romans executed them, and they were never heard of again. Surely the Romans expected the same thing would happen with Jesus, but it didn't. His followers continued to speak of him and to preach the good news about the Kingdom of God that they had learned from him. Certainly their experi-

---

1. The matter is beyond the scope of this work, but it is important to point out that it was the Romans, not the Jews, who executed Jesus. For more on this subject see John Dominic Crossan, *Who Killed Jesus: Exposing the Roots of Anti-Semitism in the Gospel Story of the Death of Jesus* (San Francisco: HarperSanFrancisco, 1995). There is no doubt about that fact as an historical matter. The Jewish authorities of Jesus' time did not have the authority to crucify people. That was a Roman method of execution, one used primarily for people the Romans perceived to be political threats. The effort of the Gospels, especially Matthew and John, to make the Jews responsible for Jesus' death has had tragic consequences throughout the history of Christianity. It has served as the Biblical basis for institutionalized anti-Judaism that led to deaths of millions of Jewish people over the centuries, culminating in the Holocaust. If there is one verse that we should drum out of the Bible it is Matthew 27:25: "Then the people as a whole answered [Pilate, who had washed his hands of Jesus' blood], 'His blood be on us and on our children.'" This verse has had perhaps the most pernicious effect of any verse in the Bible. I refuse to read this line when reading the Passion story from Matthew in worship.

The Meaning of the Cross: The Demonstration of God's Solidarity

ence of his continuing presence with them that we call the Resurrection was part of the reason his movement did not die with him. Here we need to note that his followers' experience of his death also helps account for the survival of his movement. Thus Paul, the author of the earliest Christian writings that have survived, proclaims Christ's Resurrection. He says, "If Christ has not been raised, then our proclamation has been in vain and your faith has been in vain."[2] More central to Paul's proclamation, however, is the Crucifixion. He says, "For Jews demand signs and Greeks desire wisdom, but we proclaim Christ crucified, a stumbling block to Jews and foolishness to Gentiles, but to those who are the called, both Jews and Greeks, Christ the power of God and the wisdom of God."[3] Clearly, any apologist for Christianity must explain the meaning of the cross of Christ in a way that makes sense in his context so that the cross, so easy to see as a sign of abject failure, does not again become foolishness and a stumbling block in the way of faith. Theology of the cross, as it is stated in the New Testament primarily by Paul, as Martin Luther picked it up at the time of the Reformation, and as Jürgen Moltmann and Douglas John Hall have developed it in our day, is that way.

To understand theology of the cross, it is necessary first to understand a different approach to the question of soteriology, that is, the question of the nature of Jesus' saving work, than the sacrificial approach of Anselm. This different approach too received its classic formulation in the twelfth century, this time by a somewhat younger contemporary of Anselm's named Peter Abelard. It is called demonstration soteriology. Anselm taught, as we have seen, that the saving work of Jesus consisted of his substitutionary atoning sacrifice for human sin. Abelard, unfortunately more famous for his affair with a woman named Heloise than for his theology, taught that Jesus' atoning work consisted not of his being a sacrifice for human sin but of his demonstrating on the cross God's love for humankind. That demonstration has saving significance for people because in observing Jesus on the cross they see the ultimate demonstration of God's love. For Anselm the human existential problem was sin. For Abelard it was more a lack of knowledge of God's love. The cross addresses that existential problem by demonstrating to those with eyes to see that God loves them. In Abelard's writings it is never entirely clear how the

2. 1 Cor 15:14.
3. 1 Cor 1:22–24.

cross demonstrates God's love, but Abelard insists that it does. Theology of the cross is a demonstration soteriology somewhat in the tradition of Abelard, but it supplies what is missing in Abelard's work, the explanation of how the cross demonstrates God's love for humanity.

Theology of the cross is grounded in two closely related foundational Christian doctrines—Trinitarianism and Incarnation.[4] A basic understanding of these two doctrines is a prerequisite to understanding theology of the cross. Since at least the fourth century CE, Christianity has espoused a Trinitarian view of God. Although the New Testament has no fully developed doctrine of the Trinity, that understanding of the nature of God has at least tenuous Biblical roots. The clearest statement of the classic Trinitarian formula of God as Father, Son, and Holy Spirit is found at the end of the Gospel of Matthew, in the passage known as the Great Commission. The penultimate verse of Matthew's Gospel reads, "Go, therefore, and make disciples of all nations, baptizing them in the name of the Father and of the Son and of the Holy Spirit, and teaching them to obey everything that I have commanded you."[5] The Christian

---

4. Some might argue that Trinitarianism and Incarnation are themselves barriers to faith in our context, that they are anachronisms that made sense in the Hellenistic world of the fourth century CE but not in ours. It certainly would be easier simply to reject them, as Unitarianism does. Nonetheless, for the reasons stated here, I prefer to keep them. They are central to the orthodox Christian tradition and to theology of the cross. Douglas John Hall, the preeminent contemporary proponent of theology of the cross, in his trilogy cited in the Introduction to this work, presents a penetrating critique of the Hellenistic philosophical language in which the Nicene Creed and the Formula of Chalcedon express them. Hall re-imagines these doctrines, rejecting what he calls the substantialistic ontology of their classic formulations and replacing it with a relational ontology that he asserts is truer to the Biblical understanding of reality. Hall's reformulation of the doctrines of the Trinity and the Incarnation is fascinating and challenging. It offers a way of understanding them that may be more accessible for many people in our context. It is an understanding that is perfectly consistent with the theology of the cross presented here.

5. Matt 28:20. This verse, which is the only verse in the Bible in which the classic Trinitarian appears in full form, raises numerous thorny theological issues. It has been used to justify Christian imperialism virtually from the time it was written, and certainly since Christianity became the official religion of the Roman Empire in the fourth century CE. The question of Christian imperialism is beyond the scope of this work, but it should be clear from what has been said about the legitimate function of religion and about the nature of religious truth that Christian imperialism is ruled out in this understanding of the faith. Just as any religion is true to the extent that it connects people with the spiritual, so any religion can bring salvation, the nature of which we will consider later in this work. There is also the problem of the exclusively male language of the traditional Trinitarian formulation. There is no good solution to this problem. In worship I prefer to use Creator,

The Meaning of the Cross: The Demonstration of God's Solidarity

understanding of God differs from the radical, and to the Christian mind quite static, monism of Islam. God for Christians is the Trinity, one God in three Persons, the Father, Son, and Holy Spirit. "Person" here is not to be understood in the colloquial sense. The Persons of the Trinity are not people. They are God as Three in One. They are not Three *or* One, they are Three *and* One. They are at the same time separable and inseparable. Much ink has been spilled and forests of trees have given their lives for the paper used in trying to explain the Trinity. In the end, however, the Trinity defies explanation. It is a paradox. It is a mystery. Its character as paradox and mystery makes it not less true but more true. The mystical, paradoxical nature of the Trinity preserves the transcendence of God, because the Trinity transcends human comprehension or description. For purposes of theology of the cross, it is particularly important to remember that the Father and the Son are both one and not one, the same and different at the same time.

The Christian doctrine of Incarnation also has a Biblical anchor, the Prologue to the Gospel of John that reads in relevant part, "In the beginning was the Word, and the Word was with God, and the Word was God. . . . And the Word became flesh and lived among us, and we have seen his glory, the glory as of a father's only son, full of grace and truth."[6] For Christians, Jesus is the Son of God Incarnate. He is the Second Person of the Trinity (Who John calls "the Word" but Who the Christian tradition calls the Son) become a human being in Jesus of Nazareth. Like the Trinity, the Incarnation is a mystery and a paradox. Jesus Christ is two natures in one person, true God from true God, to use the ancient language of Christian confession, and fully human at the same time. He is both God and a human being, with neither nature in any way diminishing the other. To the human mind, it isn't possible. To the Christian believer, it isn't possible either; it's just true. As with the Trinity, the mystic, paradoxical nature of the Incarnation preserves the mystery of how the impossible

---

Christ, and Holy Spirit, although "Creator" is less personal and has a different connotation than Father. Here, however, because my understanding of theology of the cross is so closely bound to traditional Christian Trinitarianism, I will use the traditional language. In no way do I mean to suggest that God or any of the persons of the Trinity are male. My decision to stick with the classic language is merely a reflection of my despair at finding anything that works better in the context of this analysis.

6. John 1:1, 14.

could happen, how God could come to us as one of us.[7] For Christians Jesus is Emmanuel, one of his Biblical names that means "God with us."[8] It is a name not much used except at Christmas, where it is read as part of Matthew's nativity story. The idea that it expresses, however, is central to theology of the cross. In Jesus Christ God was and is with us, as one of us and as the Son of God.

The mythic Christian confession that Jesus Christ is Emmanuel, God with us, informs our understanding of the significance of Jesus Christ throughout his life, from his birth through his ministry, his death, and his resurrection. We will focus on the issues of his teaching as the teaching of God later in this work. Theology of the cross focuses on the meaning of the Christian understanding that in Christ's Crucifixion we see not only a human being unjustly and brutally executed but God the Son Incarnate in that human being unjustly and brutally executed. On the cross of Jesus Christians see both an innocent man and God Godself.[9]

Because we confess that Jesus Christ is God the Son Incarnate, for us God enters into everything that Jesus is, everything that Jesus said, everything that Jesus did, everything that happened to him. In him God was born as a human being. Not as some divine entity that just looked like a human being. Truly as a human being.[10] In him God lived a truly human

---

7. Hall applies his relational ontology to the Incarnation as well as to the Trinity. In this analysis, Jesus is God Incarnate in that he represents God to humanity and humanity to God. This representational understanding also works perfectly with the theology of the cross I develop here, which should not be surprising in light of the extent to which that theology is indebted to Hall throughout.

8. Matt 1:23.

9. The Christian tradition has always stressed Jesus' innocence of the charges the Jewish authorities and the Romans brought against him. Certainly from the perspective of divine justice, Jesus was innocent. As God Incarnate he could not be anything but innocent. Yet overemphasizing his innocence can blunt the revolutionary nature of his message. We will consider that message further in chapter 11. For now suffice it to say that from the perspective of the Romans at least, he really was guilty. His message of the Kingdom of God was, and is, radically anti-Imperial, whether the empire in question be the Roman Empire of the ancient world or the neo-colonial empire of American economic and military hegemony in the world today.

10. The idea that Jesus wasn't truly human but that he was God walking around just appearing to be human is the belief that the early church branded as heresy under the name Docetism. The Gospel of John is open to the charge of Docetism. At times in John Jesus can be truly human, as when he cries at the death of his friend Lazarus (John 11:35). At other times he can seem hardly human at all, as in John's Passion narrative that we have already mentioned earlier in this work. The Gospel of Mark is the key Gospel for

The Meaning of the Cross: The Demonstration of God's Solidarity

life. He had parents. He began human life as an infant and grew to adulthood. He worked, and he learned. He preached and he taught. He loved, and he had conflicts with others. He was loved, and he was despised. He was defended, and he was betrayed. He felt joy, and he suffered. He lived, and he died. In Jesus, God experienced all of these parts of human life and many more besides in God's own person.

In Jesus, God experienced human life and, more importantly, in Jesus confessed to be God Incarnate we *see* God experiencing human life. In Jesus as the Son of God Incarnate, God *demonstrated* to us that God shares our lives, all of our lives. The pre-Christian Jewish tradition in which Jesus stood knew that God was always with us. The Psalmist wrote, "Where can I go from your spirit? Or where can I flee from your presence?"[11] He knew that the answer was "nowhere." God is always present with us. Yet in Jesus Christ something more happens. God's presence with humanity becomes manifest, it becomes embodied, it becomes Incarnate. People had heard of God's constant presence with them; in Jesus Christ they saw it with their own eyes.[12] We see it with the eyes of faith.[13] We see God entering into human life. We see God sharing human life—*all* of human life.

The question we set out to answer here, however, is the question of the meaning less of Jesus' life than of his death. Our understanding of Jesus as God the Son Incarnate in whom God experienced all the aspects of human life leads us to an answer to that question. The meaning of Jesus' brutal, unjust death is that in that death we see God experiencing the worst that human life offers. We see God experiencing the worst that human sin can inflict upon other humans. We see God entering into human suffering and experiencing human suffering directly, immediately, in God's own person. We see God taking the effect of sin into God's own body. We see

---

theology of the cross, for in Mark there is no question that Jesus is human and that he truly suffered and died. Much contemporary mainline Protestant theology attempts to regain a sense of Jesus' true humanity against a tradition that has overstressed his divinity. Douglas John Hall's work is a good example of the trend.

11. Ps 139:7.

12. Just as Job confessed after God spoke to him out of the whirlwind (Job 42:5).

13. It is perhaps necessary to state here once again that we are talking about mythic not historical truth. We are not talking about history *wie es eigentlich gewesen*, how it actually was. We are talking about the mythic truth that Christianity sees in the history, a truth that transcends the mere facts of history and that history as an academic discipline can neither prove nor disprove.

Emmanuel, God with us, entering with us into human suffering. We see God with us suffering with us.

And we see God with us dying with us. On the cross of Jesus, God the Son dies a human death. Throughout the history of Christianity theologians have tried to avoid that conclusion by making distinctions between Jesus' divine and human natures. They say he died in his human nature but not in his divine nature. Theology of the cross properly understood rejects that distinction. If, as we confess, Jesus was while truly human also truly God, then God died on the cross of Jesus. On the cross of Jesus, God entered into and experienced even human death. We should not shy away from this perhaps shocking conclusion. In Jesus Christ as Emmanuel, God with us, God resolved to come to us as one of us and to experience the entire scope of human life. God resolved to demonstrate to us God's unshakable presence with us throughout that entire scope of human life. Human life includes human death. God did not stop short of experiencing that ultimate human reality. God did not stop short of demonstrating God's presence with us in that ultimate human experience.

There is one more human experience that God shared on the cross of Christ, and it is perhaps the most paradoxical of all. We humans often feel that God has abandoned us. We feel God-forsaken. The human experience of the absence of God is at least as pervasive as the human experience of the presence of God. Twentieth century philosophical existentialism profoundly expressed that sense that God was absent from the world and from our lives. Samuel Becket's play *Waiting for Godot* is a profound literary expression of that experience.[14] Even the great twentieth century German theologian Dietrich Bonhoeffer built his theology on the idea that humanity had come of age and that God had therefore withdrawn from the world and left us to learn to live without God, to develop a life of faith in the absence of God.[15] On a more personal level, we have all had

---

14. Beckett himself denied that his play was about the absence of God, but, even though he wrote the play in French, the similarity of the name of the character who never appears to the English language's chief symbol for the spiritual cannot be coincidence. Moreover, even if Becket did not intend the play to have that meaning, modern hermeneutical theory recognizes that works of literature can have a "surplus of meaning." It is legitimate for us to see the play as an allegory on the absence of God even if its author did not.

15. Bonhoeffer is better known for his death at the hands of the Nazis interpreted as martyrdom than for his theology. This is unfortunate, as his theology is profound and challenging. It surely would have become much better known and more influential had he survived World War II.

The Meaning of the Cross: The Demonstration of God's Solidarity

times of despair, pain, or grief when God has certainly felt much more absent than present in our lives. The greatest paradox of the cross of Jesus is that in the person of Jesus on the cross, God felt abandoned by God.

Different Gospels attribute different words to Jesus as he dies on the cross. John has him uttering the very God-like "It is finished."[16] God on earth has finished the divine mission and can now go home to heaven. Mark surely understood the meaning of the cross more profoundly. Mark's Jesus, in true agony, nailed to one of the most inhumane torture and execution devises the sinful mind of humanity has ever concocted, cries out in despair the opening lines of Psalm 22, "My God, my God, why have you forsaken me?"[17] Some theologians have tried to blunt the impact of this cry by pointing out that Psalm 22 eventually becomes a Psalm of trust in God, but surely that effort reflects nothing more than an unwillingness to accept the awful truth of the cross. On the cross of Jesus, God entered into the human experience of abandonment by God. God personally experienced abandonment by God. In a paradox that is perhaps beyond true comprehension but that captures the powerful spiritual truth of Jesus' death, we say that, on the cross of Jesus, God demonstrated God's presence with us even in the experience of being abandoned by God. The cross of Jesus transforms Godforsakenness into God's presence in the absence of God.

In Jesus, God demonstrates to us God's presence with us in every aspect of human life, yet there is another word that captures the significance of Jesus' life and death even more profoundly than presence. That word is solidarity. Solidarity indicates a more intimate connection than presence. Solidarity is a standing with and standing for, not merely standing by. Presence can be indifferent, or even hostile. That's not how God is present with us. God's presence is supportive. God's presence is sympathetic in the technical sense of the word. God feels what we feel. God experiences what we experience. God laughs when we laugh and rejoices when we rejoice. God cries when we cry and mourns when we mourn. There is even a sense, mysterious though it may be, that God dies when we die. That is the meaning of the cross of Jesus, where we see God's solidarity displayed for the eyes of faith to see.

---

16. John 19:30.
17. Mark 15:34.

God stands in solidarity with us, and God's solidarity demonstrated fully to us in the life and death of Jesus Christ means that nothing can separate us from God or God from us. We have already cited Paul's profound statement of God's solidarity and even used it at the head of this work to set the tone for everything that follows, but it bears repeating over and over again: "For I am convinced that neither death, nor life, nor angels, nor rulers, nor things present, nor things to come, nor powers, nor height, nor depth, nor anything else in all creation, will be able to separate us from the love of God in Christ Jesus our Lord."[18] The cross of Jesus shows us in the most vivid way possible that God is with us, standing in solidarity with us, no matter what.

God's solidarity with us is the meaning of the cross, but our attributing meaning to the cross, even if it is a different meaning than that which the classical atonement theory ascribes to it, raises the question of whether Jesus had to suffer and die as that classical theory contends. Certainly the Gospels assert that his suffering and death were a necessity.[19] The Gospel of Mark, from which Matthew and Luke took the passages, contains three so-called "Passion predictions." The first is Mark 8:31 which reads, "Then he [Jesus, of course] began to teach them [the Disciples] that the Son of Man [Jesus' common term of self-reference] must under go great suffering, and be rejected by the elders, the chief priests, and the scribes, and be killed, and after three days rise again." The other Passion predictions are substantially similar and are found at Mark 9:31 and Mark 10:32–34.

Our understanding of the cross as a demonstration of God's solidarity with humanity even in suffering and death leads us to the same conclusion, but with a very different connotation. Mark's Jesus was right that he had to undergo suffering and death, but not because that in itself was his purpose for living, as it is for the classical atonement theory. His purpose was precisely to enter into, to share, and thus to sanctify all aspects of human life. Stopping short of suffering and death would have left the mission unfinished, since suffering and death are unavoidable parts

---

18. Rom 8:38–39.

19. At least, the synoptic Gospels (Matthew, Mark, and Luke) assert that his suffering and death were a necessity, as we will see shortly. The Gospel of John sees only his death as a necessity, since in John the Crucified Jesus doesn't really suffer. The term "synoptic Gospels" means that these three Gospels can be "seen together" because of their many similarities. It is a useful term for distinguishing them from the Gospel of John, which as any careful reader will notice is very different from the other three.

The Meaning of the Cross: The Demonstration of God's Solidarity

of the human experience. The radical extent of God's solidarity with us humans would not have been fully demonstrated if the demonstration in Jesus Christ had not included suffering and death. God did not send Jesus to suffer and die, but God did not send Jesus *not* to suffer and die either. God's purpose in Jesus was to demonstrate the divine solidarity with us. Therefore it was both foreseeable and necessary that Jesus would suffer and die.

This understanding of the necessity of Jesus' death avoids one of the big pitfalls of the classical atonement theory. That understanding makes Jesus' death essentially irrelevant to us. In that understanding, Jesus' death demonstrates nothing about *our* lives. It is just something that happened to *him*. It has nothing to do with how we live and how we die, because, after all, dying was *his* purpose for living, not ours. This fallacy removes most of the meaning from the cross. Rather than recognize that suffering and death are unavoidable parts of human life, it allows the perpetuation of the fallacy that faith prevents bad things from happening to us. That very bad things happened to Jesus has a cosmic significance for the classical atonement theory in buying our forgiveness, but for that theory it does not follow that God is with us in the bad things. For theology of the cross, the revelation precisely that God *is* with us in the bad things is the primary meaning of Jesus' death.

There is a closely related issue we also need to consider. Throughout the history of Christianity, and indeed in the other great monotheistic faiths, there is a widespread belief that God controls everything that happens in life. There is a widespread belief that whatever happens, good or bad, happens because God wills it to happen. There is a corollary of this belief that is very prominent in the history of Christianity, namely, that if we believe hard enough and pray hard enough, bad things won't happen to us or our loved ones. This idea is found throughout the Bible, perhaps especially in the Psalms. A good example is Psalm 91, which includes these lines:

> Because you have made the LORD your refuge, the Most High your dwelling place, no evil shall befall you, no scourge come near your tent. For he will command his angels concerning you to guard you in all your ways. On their hands they will bear you up, so that you will not dash your foot against a stone.[20]

20. Ps 91:9–12. These verses appear in the popular Christian song "Eagle's Wings." It's a beautiful, moving song, but we must not take it literally.

This Psalm also has God say, "Those who love me, I will deliver; I will protect those who know my name. When they call to me, I will answer them. . . ."[21] Verses like these have commonly been taken to mean that bad things don't happen to those who have enough faith and who pray hard enough. This is an understanding of God's grace that theology of the cross rejects. It is an understanding that is inconsistent with a theology that asserts that in Jesus Christ even God the Son suffered and died. Theology of the cross rejects the notion that bad things won't happen to God's faithful ones because, after all, bad things happened even to Jesus. They happened to Jesus because he was living a fully human life. We see in him precisely that God does not prevent bad things from happening to God's faithful ones but rather that God is present with them in those bad things, that God stands in solidarity with them in those bad things, in suffering and in death.

We need to say a bit more about this point because the belief that faith and prayer keep bad things from happening to us and cause good things to happen for us is so wide-spread among us. People in my congregation have told me that they even know people who claim that when they pray for God to find them a parking place on a crowded street they always find one. That may be a silly application of this belief, but it is often far more pernicious. What pastor has not been faced with the anguished question from a faithful soul who has just lost a loved one to death: "Why did God do this to us?" Or to my loved one. Or worse, to me. So many Christians believe that their faith will protect them and their loved ones, and it just isn't true. Let me make it more personal once more.

I have previously described in this work a powerful spiritual experience that I had a few days after my wife of thirty years died of breast cancer. Her name was Francie. She was only fifty-five years old. She was a wonderful, vivacious, intelligent, caring woman, a wonderful mother to our two adult children, a wonderful wife to me, and a professional sign language interpreter who devoted her professional life to helping the deaf make their way in an uncomprehending and uncaring world. She died far too young, at the height of her professional life and at a time when she, our children, and I should have had many more years together by the standards of our modern society. Tragically, countless Christian pastors have told countless Christians in similar situations that if they had prayed

---

21. Ps 91:14–15a.

The Meaning of the Cross: The Demonstration of God's Solidarity

harder, if their faith had been stronger, their loved one would not have died. In a sermon I preached shortly before Francie's death I called this notion a Satanic lie. I am convinced that it has destroyed more faith than perhaps any other Christian contention.

Throughout Francie's illness and death, I never once asked "Why is God doing this to her?" I certainly did not ask "Why is God doing this to me?" I knew then and I know now that God wasn't doing it. Francie wasn't a particularly religious person (although in her way she was far more spiritual than I am), but she knew it too. One day during her final hospitalization, during a particularly rough time when the medical people were trying to do something to make her more comfortable, doing it wrong, and making her even more uncomfortable, she had a vision. She saw God's outstretched hand. She saw herself and me held in that divine hand, and she knew that we were safe there. After she died, we put on her grave marker the words "Safe in God's Hands." She was, and she is.[22]

The human existential truth is that bad things happen to everyone. Good people aren't excluded. Wonderful women at the apex of their lives die of breast cancer. Children contract leukemia and die before they ever have the chance to grow up. Children starve to death or die of preventable diseases simply because of the place of their birth. No amount of faith, no amount of prayer, does or can prevent these tragedies. God does not prevent these tragedies, but neither does God cause them. They are inevitable consequences of the undeniable fact that we are creatures not gods. Ultimately the notion that if our faith is strong enough nothing bad will happen to us will fail each and every one of us, for we are all mortal. We will all die. The question is not how to prevent bad things from happening; the question is how to hold on to the presence of God in the bad things, as Rabbi Kushner has so wonderfully explained.[23] For us Christians, the answer to that question is—the cross of Jesus.

The Christian tradition has attributed too much control over events in our lives to God. Because that attribution of divine control is

---

22. William Sloan Coffin, so often brilliant in expressing profound theological truths in short, pithy sayings, has expressed this one by saying: "God provides minimum protection, but maximum support...." In *Letters to a Young Doubter*, (Louisville: Westminster John Knox Press, 2005) 71.

23. Harold S. Kushner, *When Bad Things Happen to Good People*, (New York: Avon Books, 1983). For a discussion of this issue from the perspective of theology of the cross see Douglas John Hall, *God and Human Suffering, An Exercise in the Theology of the Cross* (Minneapolis Augsburg Publishing House, 1986).

ultimately inconsistent with human experience, there was bound to be a reaction against it sooner or later. One such reaction came during the Enlightenment in the form of Deism, which, as we have seen, had God creating the world then withdrawing completely so that God was not even present in creation. That understanding too was bound to fail because it too contradicts human experience by denying not only God's control but God's presence.

Theology of the cross represents a kind of synthesis of these two extreme beliefs. It walks a middle way between ascribing to God too much control and removing God from creation altogether. Neither of those approaches truly captures the human experience of the spiritual. Theology of the cross captures human experience far better than do either a theology of God as micromanager of the world or a Deistic removal of God from it. It does not deny the reality of evil, of suffering, or of death. Rather, it enables us to walk into evil, suffering, and death with courage and hope because we know that everywhere we go, God goes with us. God will not prevent evil, suffering, or death; but God stands in solidarity with us as we encounter them, giving us strength and bringing us peace in whatever happens.

This understanding of theology of the cross provides at least something of an answer to the age old question of theodicy, the justification of God in the face of evil. Archibald MacLeish's character J. B., in the great play of the same name, expresses the dilemma of theodicy beautifully when he says, "If God is God He is not good, if God is good He is not God."[24] Throughout human history people have struggled to understand why if God is good, kind, and merciful there is so much suffering and evil in the world. Resolving that issue requires us to rethink our understanding of God, and theology of the cross does precisely that. Theology of the cross answers J. B.'s *cri de coeur* by saying that God is God, but that does not mean that God is responsible for everything that happens in creation. Rather, God is present in everything that happens in creation. God too suffers the misery and evil in creation. God stands with us in it and works always to bring new life out of it. Theology of the cross does not expect God to end suffering and evil, something that human experience abundantly proves that God does not do. Rather, it knows that God goes with us into suffering and evil and gives us the strength, courage, and peace

---

24. See www.religioustolerance.org/reac_ter3.htm.

The Meaning of the Cross: The Demonstration of God's Solidarity

to face it, endure, and work with God to end it. A theology that expects God to end evil cannot explain evil. Theology of the cross explains evil as the result of the fact that we are creatures not gods and as the result of humanity's belief that we are in fact separate from God. Theology of the cross seeks to overcome evil by overcoming that misperception.

There is a possible objection to our understanding that the significance of Jesus Christ is not his atoning sacrifice but his demonstration of God's solidarity with us in all aspects of human life that we must still address. It is the objection that theologians call the scandal of particularity. We say that in Jesus on the cross God experienced human suffering and death because Jesus experienced human suffering and death, and Jesus was God the Son Incarnate. Yet there is a vast ocean of human experience that Jesus did not experience. He was a particular human being, and like every particular human being he lived in a particular place and a particular time. He grew up in a particular human culture and a particular religious tradition. He had a particular gender and sexual orientation.[25] The Gospels present him as unmarried and celibate, so as far as we know he did not experience sexual relations or married life.[26] He died relatively young, so he did not experience the infirmity and failing mental capacities of old age. Perhaps most importantly, he was a man. He did not experience what it means to live life as a woman, not even as a woman of his place and time. Some might argue that Jesus does not, therefore, truly demonstrate God's solidarity with all humans in all places and times.

We must reject this objection. Incarnation necessarily implies particularity. If God truly became Incarnate in Jesus of Nazareth particularity is unavoidable because Jesus of Nazareth was a particular person, just as we all are. The truly important point is that in Jesus God the Son became human. Jesus did not live my life. He did not live your life, whether you be male or female. Nonetheless, he lived a human life. He died a human

---

25. We do not know what Jesus' sexual orientation was. Some contemporary theologians speculate that Jesus was gay. They point to the fact that he apparently was unmarried and that the Gospel of John has a mysterious figure called "the disciple whom Jesus loved." I consider such arguments to be rank speculation. The fact is that we do not know what Jesus' sexual orientation was. Statistically it is more likely to have been heterosexual than homosexual, but we just don't know. I consider it best to leave off the speculation and live with what we do know from the Gospels and with what we do not know.

26. Some contemporary theologians argue that Jesus was in fact married, probably to Mary Magdalene. My remarks about the speculation regarding Jesus' sexual orientation in the preceding footnote apply to this issue as well.

death. That is what matters. That he did not live my life does not diminish my experience of knowing the solidarity of God with me in my life through him because, as different as we are, Jesus was a human being like me. He was a human being with immense empathy for all people, as his embracing of the outcasts (including especially women) demonstrates. In Jesus God came to us as *one* of us and demonstrated God's solidarity with *all* of us. The particularity of the Incarnation does not diminish that fact but enhances it because Incarnation is impossible without particularity.[27]

God's solidarity with us demonstrated in the life and death of Jesus is, when we truly understand it, the best news there ever was or ever could be. It means that even in our times of greatest pain and greatest grief God is there with us, holding us in God's everlasting arms of grace, keeping us existentially safe from all harm. Though we die, God is there with us, dying with us, and keeping us close in death and beyond death. Even more importantly, though our loved ones die God is there with them, keeping them close in death and beyond death. God is there with us, grieving with us and holding us until we can, with time and with God's grace, move beyond our grief to the newness of life that God always offers us. God is there offering us the fruits of the Spirit, offering us peace, courage, and patience as we go through what as humans we must go through. No matter what happens to us in life, and even in death, the spiritual power of the universe that we call God never forsakes us, never abandons us, never condemns us. Even when we feel most abandoned by God, when we feel truly Godforsaken, we know that God is there in that abandonment, in our experience of being forsaken. We know it because we see it demonstrated in Jesus' cry of dereliction from the cross. God is with us *always*, absolutely no matter what. That is the meaning of the cross. That is theology of the cross.

27. At least one feminist theologian is famous for saying that a male savior cannot be a savior for women. For the reasons I have stated here, I respectfully disagree. I freely acknowledge that my disagreement comes from my *Sitz im Leben*, my place in life, as male. I cannot change that fact, nor do I apologize for it. Like every human, like Jesus, I am a particular person not a generalized one. I recognize that positions like the one rejecting a male savior for women come from a place of deep anger over the Christian tradition's sinful and profoundly distressing history (and to a considerable extent present reality) of patriarchy, androcentrism, and misogyny. Elizabeth A. Johnson, the great contemporary Catholic feminist theologian, taught me in a class at Seattle University that I cannot be a feminist theologian because I am not a woman. When I asked her what I *could* do she said, "Stand in solidarity with the feminist theologians. Be an ally." That is what I have tried to do ever since.

The Meaning of the Cross: The Demonstration of God's Solidarity

Questions for Reflection and Discussion

1. Who is Jesus for you?

    Is he a human being, albeit it perhaps a great or even unique one?

    Is he a great teacher?

    Is he a prophet?

    Is he the Son of God?

    Is he God Incarnate?

    If so, what does that statement mean to you?

2. Do you need to be saved?

    If so, from what do you need to be saved?

    Sin?

    The fear of death (the fear of nothingness)?

    Meaninglessness?

    Something else?

    What do you need in order to be saved from that from which you need to be saved?

3. Christianity is unique among the world's great religions in that it follows a crucified Savior, and the faith has always ascribed profound meaning to Jesus' suffering and death and considered them to have been necessary.

    Was it necessary for Jesus to suffer and die?

    Why, or why not?

    Do Jesus' suffering and death have more meaning than the suffering and death of other people?

    If not, why not?

    If so, what is that meaning for you?.

10

The Dynamics of Salvation

1. THE POPULAR MEANING OF SALVATION: GOING TO HEAVEN WHEN WE DIE

FROM THE VERY BEGINNING Christians have experienced salvation in Jesus Christ. The experience of the earliest Christians that Jesus as they had known him during his lifetime among them had brought them salvation in a way they had never known before is a big part of the explanation for the continuation and spread of the Jesus movement after the execution of its founding figure. From their day to ours Christians have sought and found salvation in and through him. In popular Christianity in our context salvation becomes the function, and sometimes the only function, of the faith. Christians ask, "Are you saved?" Or, "When were you saved?" They mean by these questions have you taken Jesus Christ as your personal savior, or at what specific date and time did you do it. The prominence of these questions in contemporary American Christian circles, problematic as they may be, simply continues the two thousand-year-old Christian experience that in Jesus Christ there is salvation. Any attempt at liberating Christianity, at overcoming the obstacles to faith in our time, must address the question of the meaning of salvation.

Salvation has come to have a very narrow, limited meaning in contemporary popular American Christianity. It has come to mean little more than getting to go to heaven when you die. Being saved has come to mean avoiding hell and gaining heaven. It gets reduced to the bumper sticker I saw once, consisting of a border of flames around the words, "Where will you spend eternity?" The assumption of this five word summation of Christianity is clear. The default answer is "hell." The same idea is expressed in a mailing members of my congregation received in November,

The Dynamics of Salvation

2006, from a local Baptist church in Monroe, Washington. In that mailing, the church's pastor claims that the question "Where do I go when I die?" is one that "everybody secretly thinks about but almost never discusses out loud." He claims that the most important event of his life was "the day I made sure I was going to heaven." That day occurred when this pastor was all of five years old when "I heard that Jesus loved me, and I put my trust in Him alone to take me to heaven." The mailing included a little pamphlet that restates the classical theory of atonement as "three truths you must understand," namely, that your problem is sin, Christ died for our sins, and in doing so Christ paid the price for our sin.[1] The assumption is clear. Unless you do something about it, you will spend eternity in a place of unspeakable torment. The thing you have to do about it, the thing you have to do to avoid that fate (which to this way of thinking you otherwise so richly deserve) is to accept Jesus Christ as your personal Lord and Savior.[2] This reductionist view of Christianity is very wide-spread among us and strongly colors the popular view of our faith.[3]

Salvation as getting to go to heaven when we die is, I believe, a significant barrier to faith in our context. It rests upon certain assumptions.

---

1. The literalist, classical atonement Christianity of this mailing and the liberated Christianity of this book are so different that one is tempted to say that they are in fact different religions. I know progressive Christians who consider progressive Christianity in fact to be a different religion from traditional American Christianity. The problem with concluding that liberated and liberating Christianity is a different religion than literalist, classical atonement Christianity is that despite all their differences, both types of belief are spiritual systems centered on the person of Jesus as the Christ. We may understand him differently, but he is the focus of our faith for both groups. Therefore I, and most progressive Christians I know, are not willing to give up the sacred name Christian. We have nothing else to call ourselves even if we wanted a different name, which I for one do not.

2. This pastor's letter said that "Christ is the only way" to get to heaven. Yet notice what he says actually assured him of heaven. It isn't Christ. It was his decision at the age of five to trust Jesus to get him to heaven. In this view, salvation comes not from Christ but from the believer's decision. In other words, faith becomes a work that is necessary for salvation. This view quite simply denies that grace is grace.

3. I recognize that for many conservative Christians the experience of Christian conversion, which they call the experience of Christian salvation, involves more than the conviction that now they will get to go to heaven when they die. Many of these folks speak powerfully and truthfully about how God changed their lives, freeing them from destructive habits and even addictions and leading them toward wholeness of life after they were saved. Nonetheless, the new life that they find in the faith is not for them salvation. It is something that Jesus can give them precisely *after* they are saved, by which they mean after they get their ticket to heaven punched by having the right kind of conversion experience and taking Jesus as their personal Lord and Savior.

The first is, of course, that there is an afterlife. Salvation as going to heaven when we die assumes that there is some immutable, immortal part of us that survives our physical death and continues to exist in a form that is recognizably us in some other world or some other dimension of reality. This is not the place to examine the validity of that assumption. The point is that it is an assumption that a great many people in our context, rightly or wrongly, do not make. Our secular culture generally assumes that death is the end of all aspects of our being. This assumption is of course consistent with and grounded in the materialist worldview. If the physical is all there is, and if our physical bodies die as we know they do, then there is nothing that survives our deaths. Since no aspect of our being survives our deaths, there is no afterlife. Christianity that is primarily about the fate of some aspect of our being that we call a soul that survives our physical death does not and can not speak to people with that understanding of reality. It has nothing to say to them because it makes a fundamental assumption that they do not share.

The second assumption that the understanding of salvation as getting to go to heaven when we die makes is that the fate of that eternal soul is something that we need to be concerned about. It assumes that our souls are at risk of damnation, that God will punish us with eternal torment if we do not attain the salvation that Christianity (and to this way of thinking only Christianity) offers. Most people who accept the reality of the immortal soul also accept the truth of this second assumption. The second assumption, however, does not necessarily follow from the first. It is possible to believe that we have an eternal soul but also to believe that its eternal fate is something that God has already taken care of, that it isn't anything that we need to worry about or that we can do anything to control. I take up this issue in the section below on the universality of grace, and I will not spend more time on it here. Suffice it to say for now that there is at least a minority voice in the Christian tradition that believes that through Christ all souls are already saved in the sense of salvation we are discussing here. The assumption that the fate of our soul is something we need to be concerned about is a barrier to faith in our context in part because, as we just noted, so many people in that context don't believe in a soul that survives death at all. In addition, it is a barrier to faith for more thoughtful people who realize that it paints a very unpleasant picture of God as one who will punish human failings in this life with eternal torment, hardly an image of a loving, compassionate, and graceful God. The understanding of salvation as getting to go to heaven when we die is a barrier to faith among us that we must work to overcome if we are to liberate Christianity in our context.

2. LIBERATING SALVATION

Liberated Christianity, the understanding of Christianity that we are developing here, leads to a different understanding of salvation. To understand the transformed meaning of salvation that flows from our understanding of the purpose of religion as connecting us with God and from our understanding of the cross as the symbol of God's unshakable solidarity with us in whatever happens in life, and in death, we need to take a closer look at the concept "salvation" to discover what it might actually mean.

Christianity's conviction, from the beginning, that what theologians call the Christ event—the birth, life, teaching, suffering, death, and resurrection of Jesus of Nazareth—has saving significance rests upon a particular assumption about the nature of human existence. It assumes that we need salvation, that is, that there is something from which we need to be saved. We looked at this notion briefly above, where we noted that classical atonement theology at least has the advantage of being one solution to the existential dilemma of sin even though it has nothing to say about any other existential dilemma from which we might suffer. We need now to take a closer look at Christianity's assumption that there is something from which we need saving.

Thoughtful humans throughout history have sensed that there is something wrong with human life. We have sensed that life as we know it is not life as it should be. People have understood this nearly universal, inchoate sense that human existence is somehow disordered in many different ways. The most common expression of that idea in Christianity has been that humans are sinners who need to be saved from their sin. This understanding of the disordered nature of human existence focuses on the undeniable fact that all humans (or, for Christians, all humans except one) do things that people generally consider to be wrong. We do things that our religious traditions teach us violate the will of God, usually seen as being expressed in sets of rules or laws understood to have a divine origin. Whether we accept those codes of rules and laws as divine or not, we cannot deny that human life is universally characterized by violence, dishonesty, greed, exploitation of others, and other behaviors that human cultures and the world's great religions universally consider to be morally wrong. We know they are wrong, but we do them anyway. That is indeed a fundamental disorder in human life from which we need saving.

Yet sin understood in this way is not the only way in which cultures have understood the human existential dilemma. As we noted in Chapter Nine, it is probably not the most common way in which people in our context understand that dilemma. We noted that meaninglessness is a more prevalent understanding of what is wrong with life among us than is sin. We won't repeat that discussion here, but please keep it in mind. We will include a discussion of the existential dilemma of meaninglessness in our consideration of how our understanding of liberated Christianity addresses the human existential dilemma.

Another way of understanding the human existential dilemma is through the concept of nothingness. This understanding is closely related to meaninglessness. We fear that our ultimate fate is nothingness. We live in constant fear of falling out of existence into nothingness. This is the fear of death combined with the fear that nothing lies beyond our death. Paul Tillich saw human life as suspended between being and nothingness, constantly threatened with falling into nothingness, of losing its tenuous grasp on being. Because God was for him pure being, or the ground of being, God was what gave us existential being (which is different from pure being in that it isn't pure) and kept us from falling into nothingness.

Although perhaps most of us never get beyond that inchoate sense that there is something wrong with life to a more articulate expression of the problem, there are then several different ways of understanding the human existential dilemma. These different ways of understanding the matter focus on different aspects of the problem, but we need to ask if there is anything that they all have in common. Is there any common thread running through them that might give us a clue as to how liberated Christianity might address them? I think there is. I think that the common thread among the different understandings of the human existential dilemma is that they all express the understanding, or at least the fear, that we live separated from God. We sense that we live separated from ultimate reality, from the ground of our being, from our source and our goal. We may believe that we are separated from such ultimate reality because we do not believe that there is such an ultimate reality. Or we may believe that although it exists (or, as Tillich would prefer, although it is real) we

The Dynamics of Salvation

are not adequately connected with it.[4] In either case, the problem is that we live separated from it.

It may be fairly clear that the existential dilemmas of meaninglessness and nothingness are grounded in a sense of separation from ultimate reality, from God. We will have more to say about them and about how liberated Christianity addresses them shortly. It may, however, be less clear that the existential dilemma of sin is grounded in the same sense of separation. The reason that this connection may not be clear is that the concept of sin has lost most of its original meaning. Sin has come to mean not an existential condition but rather particular acts that violate God's laws. We speak less of sin than we do of sins, by which we mean actions, not a state of being. Yet sin properly understood is less a particular act than it is living in separation from God. Perhaps better, it is living in violation of God's will for us that leads to us living in separation from God, or at least believing that we do.

That, I think, is the mythic meaning of the story of Adam and Eve in the Garden of Eden that Christianity has long pointed to as the beginning of sin.[5] In that well-known story the first people, the man Adam and the woman Eve, disobey God's injunction that they should not eat the fruit of the tree of the knowledge of good and evil that grows in the garden. As a punishment, God drives them out of the garden. God was immediately present in the Garden. God walked in the garden and spoke directly with God's two people. The driving from the garden is a mythic expression of the human awareness that we no longer live in such immediate connection with God.[6] We live east of Eden, to some extent at least separated from God. In the stories of the Hebrew Bible that follow the expulsion from the Garden of Eden, God is not totally absent to be

---

4. Paul Tillich teaches that God does not exist. God is real, but it is inaccurate to say that God exists. In Tillich's system, existence is a category of created being not a category of pure being. God is pure being not created being. Therefore, the category "existence" does not apply to God. This understanding has led to some very baffled responses when people who know that I am a Christian pastor have asked me if I believe in the existence of God and I answer no.

5. Gen 2:4—3:24.

6. I, of course, do not mean "no longer" literally. This story is a great myth. It is not history. Things happen in a temporal sequence in the story. They have to. That's how stories work. The story's mythic significance, however, is not temporal. We aren't really talking here about what once was but is no more. We are talking about a timeless existential reality. We just have to use categories of created existence like time to tell the story.

sure, but God's presence is always less direct and immediate than it was in the Garden of Eden.[7] Sin, the consequence of the original disobedience in the garden, is then living in at least relative separation from God.[8] The fundamental human existential dilemma then is that we live, or believe that we live, in separation from God. Separation from God is that from which we need to be saved.

Given that fundamental truth about all of the conceptions of the human existential dilemma, it is easy to see how the understanding of Christianity that I am developing here addresses that dilemma. The meaning of salvation in our liberated Christianity becomes clear. In particular, we see how theology of the cross that we developed in the previous chapter addresses and resolves the basic human dilemma of separation from God. The meaning of the cross is, as we have seen, precisely that we are *not* separated from God. In the cross of Christ, we see demonstrated to the fullest extent God's solidarity with us in all aspects of human life, including even unjust suffering and death. God could not demonstrate more clearly that our perception that we live separated from God is an illusion of our own making. From God's side of the relationship, it just isn't true. Jesus Christ, especially Jesus Christ nailed to the cross, is Emmanuel, God with us. The truth is that God is with us, not apart from us, not separated from us. The basic human existential dilemma turns out to be a mirage.

We need, however, to look more closely at how theology of the cross addresses each of the understandings of the human existential dilemma that we have enumerated here. Let us first address the understanding of the human existential dilemma as the fear of nothingness. Theology of the cross saves us from the fear of nothingness because it shows us that God, who is the opposite of nothingness, who is ultimate reality, who is being itself again to use one of Tillich's terms, never deserts us. We need not fear nothingness because ultimate being stands in complete solidarity with us in life and in death. God, being itself, holds us in existence and keeps us from falling into nothingness. We may not understand what God's soli-

---

7. One exception to this general rule appears at Exodus 33:11, which states that "the Lord used to speak to Moses face to face, as one speaks to a friend." Despite this exception the general rule stands.

8. Note that as the Hebrew Bible tells the story of humanity's relationship to God and God's relationship especially to the Hebrew people the Law does not appear until after the expulsion from the Garden of Eden. The Law itself is then an expression of the perceived existential truth that we live in separation from God. It is an attempt to deal with that perceived reality.

The Dynamics of Salvation

darity looks like after death. Death remains ultimately a mystery because no living human has yet truly experienced death, and, as we have seen, all human knowledge and all human truth are ultimately based upon experience.[9] Nonetheless, we can leave the nature of human existence after death up to God because we know that whatever form that existence takes, even if it does not involve the survival of some consciousness recognizable as our pre-death selves, it does not entail nothingness. It does not entail radical separation from God. We know that because Jesus Christ, God with us, God Incarnate, demonstrated it to us upon the cross.[10]

Liberated Christianity, with its theology of the cross, also resolves the human existential dilemma understood as meaninglessness or purposelessness. A sense of meaninglessness arises from a belief that there is nothing for us to live for other than ourselves. It is the awareness, perhaps even at the level of the unconscious, that our lives don't matter to anyone, that they don't mean anything to anyone other than ourselves. Meaninglessness arises from selfishness. It arises from an excessive focus on the self and on personal gratification, from lives that are directed only inward, on ourselves. Certainly selfishness and greed are values that characterize our current context. We are bombarded hundreds of times every day, usually in the form of advertising but also in the messages of our politicians (who always tell us what they will do for *us*, not for others and especially not for the poor and the marginalized), that our purpose in life is to look out for ourselves alone. Our culture tells us that greed is good because our material greed produces profits for the economic concerns

---

9. There are of course the reports of people having what we call "near death experiences." The point is precisely that these are *near* death experiences. They are not death experiences. The people who have had them cannot tell us what death truly is because they were not themselves ultimately dead.

10. Contemporary Christianity, indeed Christianity since it became the established religion of the Roman Empire in the fourth century CE, has so emphasized getting to heaven as the goal of the religious life that for many people in our context the afterlife is what all religion is principally about. Yet a concern with an afterlife is a relatively late development in the Judeo-Christian tradition. For most of its history Judaism had no significant conception of an afterlife. There is no reference in the Hebrew Bible to an afterlife characterized by judgment, reward, and punishment until the Book of Daniel, the last of the books of the Jewish and Protestant Bibles to be written, dating from approximately the third century BCE. In the rest of the Jewish Bible each person's fate after death was Sheol, a kind of shadowy netherworld of pseudoexistence. The Jewish faith developed without a conception of an eternal soul destined for heaven or hell depending on how a person lived during this life on earth. It is clear, then, that religion does not have to be about an afterlife. Indeed, religion at its best is not.

and the moneyed classes in whose interest our society actually functions. Acting as our culture expects us to, we strive for financial and material success. We try to "get ahead," which means to rise to positions of ever greater personal power and material wealth.

Our culture tells us that the greatest value beyond our own physical wellbeing is to care for our immediate family. We consider it a great moral achievement to care for and protect those closest to us, our immediate relations, especially our children. I certainly do not want to suggest that caring for our children is not a legitimate moral value. It is. The point is that our culture has so narrowed the scope of our concern for others that caring only for that very small group with whom we are most closely related has become a great virtue rather than a moral minimum. Caring for our immediate family is actually no great moral achievement. Our scripture knows this truth. In the Gospel of Matthew, Jesus says: "For if you love those who love you, what reward do you have? Do not even the tax collectors do the same?"[11] The culture of our context has become so individualistic, so narrowly focused in the moral concerns it expects of us, that the existential dilemma of meaninglessness is the inevitable result.

Human experience teaches us that selfishness, while it may be touted as a value by our secular culture, is a recipe for spiritual stagnation or even death. Modern psychology knows this truth well. Contemporary theories of psychological or psychospiritual development do not culminate with a state of self interest. Their highest stage of development is the stage in which a person is able to transcend her own narrow self interest and, from her position as a centered self in the world, live for others, caring more about others than about her own narrow self. The realization of our full human potential lies beyond selfishness in reaching out to others.

This too is a truth the Gospels know well. In the Gospel of John, Jesus says, "No one has greater love than this, to lay down one's life for one's friends."[12] In Matthew, Jesus calls us to do even more than that. He says, "Love your enemies, and pray for those who persecute you."[13] Jesus' Great Commandment is that we love the Lord our God with our entire being and that we love our neighbor as our self.[14] To Jesus, "neighbor"

---

11. Matt 5:46.
12. John 15:13.
13. Matt 5:44.
14. Matt 22:37–39.

The Dynamics of Salvation

meant much more than those who live next door. When asked in Luke who is our neighbor, he tells the Parable of the Good Samaritan.[15] One point of the parable—there are other important ones that are beyond the scope of the present discussion—is that the concept "neighbor" applies even to those whom we detest, as the Jews of Jesus' day detested the Samaritans. Jesus rejects any narrow or biologically conditioned limitation on the scope of our concern for others. He affirms the ancient commandment to honor one's father and mother.[16] He also says, however, "Whoever comes to me and does not hate father and mother, wife and children, brothers and sisters, yes, and even life itself, cannot be my disciple."[17] And, "For whoever does the will of my Father in heaven is my brother and sister and mother."[18] Certainly Jesus did not call us actually to hate our immediate family members. He did, however, call us beyond any narrow moral concern for them to a broad, even limitless concern for all of God's people. It is our culture's rejection of the wisdom that says we are not called to be selfish that has produced the existential dilemma of meaninglessness among us.

Liberated Christianity offers salvation from that existential dilemma. It offers it in the teachings of Jesus that we just quoted. It offers it, however, in an even more fundamental way as well. Excessive focus on the self separates a person from God. At least it produces an anxiety, perhaps subconscious, that we are in fact separated from God. Although there is never any separation from God as God views the relationship between God and people, there can seem to be separation from God as we view the relationship. That seeming separation produces a sense of meaninglessness because the human spirit is never truly satisfied with a narrow focus on the self. The cross of Jesus saves us from meaninglessness because it saves us from separation. It demonstrates that any sense we have of separation from God is entirely of our own making.

Because we live in solidarity with God, our lives have meaning. They have meaning first of all because they matter to God. They matter so much to God that, as John says, God gave God's only begotten son that we might we might have eternal life.[19] In our understanding here, this

---

15. Luke 10:29–37.
16. Mark 10:19; Luke 18:20.
17. Luke 14:26.
18. Matt 12:50. See also Mark 3:35.
19. John 3:16.

means that we might be saved from our perceived separation from God. Our lives have meaning as well because we know that *all* human lives are as precious to God as our own is. We therefore know that we can work in solidarity with God doing God's will in the world when we work to make the lives of others better. Our lives can have the meaning of bringing others to know that they too are not truly separated from God and God's solidarity. Our lives can have the meaning of enhancing the lives of those of God's people who suffer from poverty, disease, despair, oppression, exploitation, or the ravages of war. Our lives can have the meaning of working to realize the Kingdom of God on earth, that kingdom of peace and nonviolence, of justice, compassion, and mercy for all people. God's solidarity with us opens up a world of meaning for our lives and saves us from the existential dilemma of meaninglessness.

There is another issue that has long been central to Christianity that we need to take up. It is the question of whether or not we need to do anything to gain salvation. Do we earn salvation by how we live or by what we believe? Or is salvation God's free gift of grace, given unconditionally and regardless of any action, belief, or merit on our part? In the Christian tradition, this is usually called the issue of "justification." It was, of course, one of the central issues of the Protestant Reformation, with the Protestants arguing for justification by grace through faith and the Catholics arguing for justification through works. This issue fits into our analysis here in the discussion of salvation, and I will use salvation rather than justification without more analysis of whether or not they technically mean the same thing.

The answer to the question of whether we have to do anything to earn salvation in our system of liberated Christianity requires us to make a fundamental distinction. I have already suggested it. We need to ask whether anything is required of us from God's side of the God-human relationship and whether anything is required from us from our side of that relationship. It turns out that the answer differs depending upon which side of the relationship we are looking at. Let us look first at God's side. As we have maintained throughout, Jesus Christ, especially Jesus Christ on the cross, is the demonstration of God's solidarity with humans in all aspects of human life. It follows that Jesus did not create that solidarity. It has always existed. The Christ event is a demonstration of God's presence with us and God's solidarity with us that has always been there. Christ

The Dynamics of Salvation

was not needed to create God's solidarity with humanity; he was needed to demonstrate it to us in its fullness.[20]

Since as we have just seen salvation means for us God's presence and solidarity with us, and since God's presence and solidarity have always been humanity's ultimate reality, there is nothing we can or must do to earn that divine solidarity. It has always been there. It *is* always there. It was there before we were old enough to do anything but cry when we were hungry or uncomfortable. It has been there throughout our lives. It is there when we deny it. It is there when we ignore it. It is there when we go astray and behave in ways that are painful to God, when we harm ourselves or others. It is there when we are not capable of perceiving it, as in the dementia that so often characterizes old age. It is there because God has determined that it will be there. God's presence and solidarity with us is God's decision, demonstrated on the cross of Christ. It has nothing to do with any decision of ours. We can't earn it. We don't have to. God has decided how God will relate to us, and we can do nothing to change how that relationship looks from God's side.

The matter is very different when we look at the divine-human relationship from the human side. Whether God is present with us and in solidarity with us isn't up to us, but whether or not we are aware of God's presence and solidarity is. God doesn't force Godself upon us. We are saved, but it is quite possible for us not to know that we are saved. Indeed, most of us don't. The real issue before us humans is not whether we are saved. It is whether or not we will acknowledge our salvation and work to live into it, to incorporate it in the way we live, to reap its benefits for our lives and for the world. The questions that arise when we choose the latter course and seek to live into our salvation are how do we do that and what does it look like when we do.

---

20. This claim, which some Christians will find shocking because they have been told for so long that Christ brought a salvation that didn't exist before him, raises the question of what it means to say that Christ died for us. In our understanding of the faith, does it mean anything to say, as Christians have always said, that Christ died to save sinners? Indeed, it raises the question of whether these claims have any meaning at all. They do, but their meaning is very different from the traditional Christian understanding. Christ's death did not create salvation. It did, however, demonstrate our salvation to the fullest, as we have already said. We must now understand the claim that Christ died for us to mean that he died to demonstrate God's solidarity with us. We must understand the Christian claim that Christ died to save us to mean that he died to demonstrate to us our salvation, not to create it.

The first step in appropriating our salvation for our lives is to open our eyes to the fact that we are indeed saved and that there is nothing we need to do to achieve salvation. We must give up our attachment to the idea that somehow we must earn salvation. Christianity has taught for so long that we must do something to earn salvation that giving up that notion is not an easy thing for most of us.[21] We fear that free salvation removes all motivation for living moral lives. We resent the notion that people whom we consider evil are as saved as we are, at least as far as God is concerned, a conclusion that necessarily follows from the understanding of salvation I have developed here.[22] Our response to that objection to free salvation must simply be: Get over it! Free salvation is God's way. We must realize that truth if we are to appropriate our salvation in our lives.

Various spiritual disciplines are also helpful in appropriating our salvation into our lives. Contemplation of the cross of Christ is one very helpful one. When we contemplate the cross not as a sign of substitutionary sacrifice necessary to appease an angry God but as the symbol of our salvation in the form of God's immutable solidarity with us in our lives and in our deaths we find our connection with God and God's connection with us. When we contemplate the cross as the symbol of our salvation, we move beyond ourselves into the realm of the spiritual. The power of the Spirit pours into our lives. That power lifts us up and brings the fruits of the spirit—peace, strength, courage, hope, love, and joy. We are lifted beyond ourselves into the presence of God, and that presence becomes real for us. As we contemplate the cross of Christ, as we meditate on its meaning or simply stand in its presence, we understand our salvation with our minds. More importantly we take it into our hearts, into our souls, into the depth of our being. That salvation, which was always there, becomes real for us, and we grow in faith and in the assurance of God's unfailing grace and love.

The other traditional Christian spiritual disciplines are also helpful. Prayer is, of course, the foundational spiritual discipline in Christianity

---

21. Even Protestant Christianity, which teaches that we are justified by God's grace through faith, has given the message that we have to do something to earn salvation, namely, we have to believe the right things, we have to accept Jesus Christ as our personal Lord and Savior. In most of Protestant Christianity, belief becomes a work necessary for salvation.

22. We will consider these issues further in the section below on the universality of grace.

The Dynamics of Salvation

and the other great religions.[23] Prayer can be a powerful aid in bringing the reality of our salvation to our consciousness. Prayer isn't necessarily asking God for something. It isn't necessarily saying anything to God at all. Language is helpful in prayer only if it increases our awareness of God's presence in our lives. Silent prayer may be more effective in doing that for some people. Others find their connection with God comes alive in body prayer or through a prayerful discipline such as walking the labyrinth. Sacred music is a particularly powerful form of prayer for many of us, whether we perform it or simply listen to it. All of these are legitimate and appropriate spiritual disciplines if they help make our salvation real for us, if they help us to appropriate it into our lives.

No discussion of Christian spiritual disciplines that help us appropriate our salvation in our lives would be complete without a mention of Christian worship and of the sacraments that are a part of worship.[24] Gathering for worship has been the central activity of the Christian community virtually from the very beginning. The earliest Christian communities were house churches. People gathered at the home of a fellow believer for prayer and for a meal, the agape meal that evolved into the symbolic meal of the Eucharist. For most Christians today and throughout Christian history, being part of the church has meant above all else attending communal worship on Sunday morning. It is possible to maintain Christian faith in isolation. People have done it and do it today. Nonetheless, faith, that decision and commitment to live our spiritual lives within the Christian tradition, flourishes in community. It flourishes particularly in communal

---

23. Many of us have questions and reservations about prayer. Most of these reservations come from our understanding of prayer as asking God to do something for us or for others. Intercessory prayer is indeed problematic in the liberated Christianity we have outlined here. We understand God as presence, not as cause. We do not believe that God intervenes in the world; rather we believe that God is present in solidarity with us in the world. It is a legitimate question to ask if intercessory prayer is appropriate in this theological system. Clearly if the reason we do it is to try to influence events and outcomes it is not. That is not how God works. The purpose of any prayer is to make the presence of God in our lives real to us, to bring it to our consciousness, and to strengthen our awareness of our connection with God. In this system intercessory prayer is appropriate to the extent, and only to the extent, that is fulfills that function.

24. A brief comment on the nature of the church in liberated Christianity is appropriate here. If the function of religion is to connect us to God and God to us, the function of the church as the institutional expression of a religion is to facilitate that connection, that is, to facilitate our awareness of God's solidarity with us. Any church is legitimate to the extent that it does that and illegitimate to the extent that it connects us to something less than God, usually to itself.

worship. Sharing our faith with fellow Christians reinforces our own faith and helps us to grow in the knowledge of God's love. Exercising our faith together with others strengthens it and brings it more alive in our lives. Regular attendance at worship that feeds our souls is an important spiritual discipline that helps us appropriate our salvation.

The sacraments are a central part of Christian worship.[25] All Christian traditions practice baptism. Although baptism is sometimes misunderstood as a sacrament for the forgiveness of sin, especially so-called "original sin,"[26] its proper function is as the sacrament by which one becomes a member of the Christian community. Baptism, which is a symbol of God's presence and solidarity with the person being baptized, is properly done as part of communal Christian worship. It can help us appropriate our salvation in our lives precisely because it is a visible symbol of salvation. It reminds us of our own baptism, whether we actually remember it or not, when we were the recipients of that great symbol of salvation. Baptism is done only once, but we may celebrate the Eucharist as often as we like. It, too, is a communal act of worship that should be done privately only in exceptional circumstances, as when a pastor or other authorized person brings the elements from a communal worship service to a member of the community who is unable to attend. In the Eucharist we physically take symbols of Christ into our bodies. The Eucharist is a powerful symbolic enactment of God's solidarity with us. In it, we symbolically act out our salvation. Frequent participation in the Eucharist is a particularly powerful aid in making our salvation real in our lives.

I must here mention one other helpful spiritual discipline, one that has been particularly important in my own life. It is the discipline of the study of theology. The study of theology is perhaps not often thought

---

25. Because I practice my faith in a Protestant tradition, I will consider here only two sacraments, baptism and the Eucharist. I, of course, acknowledge that the Catholic tradition celebrates seven sacraments. I have no quarrel with that practice, since within the Catholic Church all seven act as true sacraments, connecting people with God and strengthening their faith.

26. Original sin has great significance in the western Christian traditions of Catholicism and Protestantism. It derives from the teachings of St. Augustine of Hippo (354–430) and has colored most of Western Christianity from his time on. It is far less prominent in eastern Christianity, and it is unknown in Judaism, despite the fact that it rests upon an interpretation of the Jewish story of Adam and Eve in the Garden of Eden. Although I recognize that separation from God, as we perceive it, is a problem for all people, I do not consider the concept of original sin particularly helpful and will not discuss it further here.

The Dynamics of Salvation

of as a spiritual discipline. Yet anything can be a spiritual discipline that strengthens our connection with God, that is, that makes that connection more real and more alive for us. The study of theology has done that for me. My journey to ordained ministry began in mid-life with a new-found passion for Christian theology. Perhaps because you are reading this book theology has been a spiritual discipline for you too, or perhaps it will become one. In certain Christian circles of my acquaintance so much emphasis is placed on faith as a matter of the heart that the undertakings of the mind are minimized or even dismissed as a legitimate pathway to faith and to God. My experience tells me otherwise. The life of faith can begin with intellectual curiosity. It can't stop there of course, but my hope and my prayer are that some of you may find the theology presented in this book to be a helpful part of your own journey of faith, your own discovery of your connection with God.

Appropriating our salvation into our lives is, however, not for the fainthearted. Dramatic things happen to us when we do it. God is a divine presence and stands in solidarity with us, but that presence and that solidarity are not static. God isn't just there. God saves us, but God also calls us. God calls us to transformation. In Christ Jesus, God has shown us what the ideal human life looks like. In Christ Jesus, God taught us God's ways, the ways of peace, justice, and radical inclusivity that we will consider at some length later in this work. In God's presence with us, we hear the divine call to transformation after the model of Jesus. God calls us to be God's prophets of peace and justice. God calls us to transformed values, values of spirituality not materiality, of peace not war, of justice not oppression, of inclusion not exclusion. God calls us to transform not only ourselves but to do nothing less than to transform the world. When we truly live into our salvation we do indeed become instruments of God's peace, as St. Francis so famously prayed. We become instruments of worldly transformation. When we truly know, not with our minds only but with our whole being, that God has saved us, we respond with lives transformed into true disciples of Christ.

Salvation then is not getting to go to heaven when we die. Salvation is the presence of God in our lives and our awareness of that presence. Salvation is the awareness that, no matter how much we may perceive one, there is actually no separation between us and God. Salvation is the knowledge of God's solidarity with us in life and in death. That knowledge can overcome whatever existential dilemma we experience, be it sin, or nothingness, or meaninglessness.[27] We appropriate our salvation through spiritual disciplines like prayer and meditation, and especially through contemplation of the meaning of the cross. We appropriate our salvation through communal Christian worship, particularly through participation in the holy sacrament of the Eucharist. Our knowledge of our salvation changes us; it transforms us. It can transform the world. It makes the sometimes hidden reality of the presence and solidarity of God apparent and effective in our lives and in God's world.

3. THE UNIVERSALITY OF SALVATION

Our analysis thus far of the dynamics of salvation drives in the direction of what is for many a startling conclusion. We have already suggested it. Our understanding of liberated Christianity leads to the conclusion that salvation is universal. Everyone is saved. Everyone! No exceptions! The solidarity of God with humanity that Jesus Christ demonstrated in his life and in his death is solidarity with *everyone*. It has to be. Especially on the cross, Jesus Christ as God Incarnate, as Emmanuel, God with us, is demonstrating the divine relationship with humanity. That demonstration remains what it is, the ultimate demonstration of God's solidarity with God's human children, without any participation in the demonstration from our side. The demonstration on the cross is an act of God, not an act by any human being other than the God/man Jesus. We can appropriate the divine solidarity that the cross demonstrates into our lives or not, as we saw in the previous section. Our failure to do so, however, does not change the character of the demonstration for those who perceive and experience its meaning precisely as a demonstration of God's solidarity. When we confess that God's relationship with humanity is one of presence and solidarity, we necessarily confess that God's presence and solidarity are with everyone.

---

27. You may detect echoes of Gnosticism in this analysis. I do not shy away from the similarities. Gnosticism teaches that the human existential dilemma is a lack of knowledge. Typically for the Gnostics the knowledge that we lack is the knowledge that our true nature is spiritual and not physical. I reject that analysis because I believe that God created us precisely as inspirited bodies and that our creation as physical beings is good, as Genesis 1 teaches. I agree with the Gnostics, however, that the fundamental human existential dilemma is a lack of knowledge. It is a lack of knowledge of the reality that in truth we are not separated from God, as I have attempted to explain in this chapter.

The Dynamics of Salvation

One way to understand this issue is for us to introduce the concept of grace, which we have not focused on to this point, at least not explicitly.[28] Grace has always been a central Christian concept. In the Bible, grace has the primary meaning of God's favor.[29] At least one secular dictionary defines the word in its theological sense as meaning "the unmerited love and favor of God toward man [sic]."[30] Grace was, of course, a key concept for the Apostle Paul, from whose writings the Christian understanding of the term chiefly comes. This is not the place for a detailed examination of Paul's theology of justification by grace. Suffice it to say that, for Paul, the chief characteristic of God's grace is that it is free and unmerited. Thus he says, "But the free gift is not like the trespass. For if many died through the one man's [Adam's] trespass, much more surely have the grace of God and the free gift in the grace of the one man, Jesus Christ, abounded for many."[31] And, "But if it is by grace, it is no longer on the basis of works, otherwise grace would no longer be grace,"[32] that is, it would no longer be free but would be earned as a reward for good works. Grace for Paul is God's free and unmerited gift of justification through Jesus Christ.

We can say then with confidence that grace, if it is truly grace, must be for everyone. If it is not, if it is for some but not others, then it must depend upon some action or characteristic of those to whom it is given that distinguishes them from those from whom it is withheld.[33] If that

---

28. For an interesting if in the end not entirely satisfactory discussion of the concept of grace leading to an understanding of universal salvation, see Philip Gulley and James Mulholland, *If Grace is True, Why God Will Save Every Person* (San Francisco: HarperSanFrancisco, 2003).

29. *The HarperCollins Bible Dictionary*, s.v. 'Grace" (by Calvin J. Roetzel) (San Francisco: HarperSanFrancisco, 1996).

30. *Webster's New World Dictionary of the American Language*, s.v. "Grace," (Cleveland and New York: The World Publishing Company, , 1966).

31. Rom 5:15.

32. Rom 11:6.

33. There is one way to avoid this conclusion, namely, through the doctrine of double predestination. Double predestination holds that God has from the beginning of time predestined some people to be saved and some people to be damned. The doctrine is particularly associated with Calvinist Christianity. Although my own United Church of Christ is primarily (if not quite exclusively) a Calvinist tradition, I know no one who believes in double predestination any longer. I certainly do not. I believe that it makes God capricious and arbitrary and that it destroys the concept of human freedom. It is inconsistent with the theological system I develop in this work. I reject it, and I will not discuss it further here.

were true, grace would not be grace. It would not be God's free gift. It would be a reward, not a gift. As the authors of *If Grace is True* cited above recognize, if grace is true, and if it is truly grace, then it is for everyone. The same is true of salvation, which is an expression of and depends upon God's grace. If God is gracious, if God gives the free and unmerited gift of justification (or, to use the language we have used here, salvation seen from God's side of the relationship), then God gives it to everyone.

The universality of grace and of salvation is a very difficult concept for most Christians to grasp. In my experience it meets with stiff resistance even from Christians who are relatively knowledgeable and progressive in other areas of their thinking about the faith. I believe that this resistance has two basic root causes. One is the age-old Christian teaching, which finds plenty of support in the New Testament, that salvation is in fact not for everyone but is only for those who believe in Jesus Christ. The other is a moral reservation about a conclusion that seems to say, and that indeed does say, that God does not send evil people—Adolf Hitler is the example most commonly advanced—to hell. I have been asked several times, "do you mean to say that Hitler was saved?" My affirmative answer is usually met with confusion or a bemused and condescending dismissal of me and my heretical theology. Many people believe that universal salvation removes all motivation for people to behave in a moral way. Let us examine each of these objections in turn.

The New Testament verses that support the idea, or that over the centuries have been used to support the idea, that only Christians are saved, are legion. We cannot possibly examine all of them here, nor do we need to. We will cite only some of the more important ones. There is, of course, the Letter of James that Martin Luther wanted to drum out of the canon precisely because it makes grace conditional. That letter famously says that faith without works is dead.[34] Even Paul can seem to make grace conditional on occasion. He refers at times to those whom God has "chosen," with the implication at least that God's grace is for them alone. Thus Romans 11:5, right before Romans 11:6 quoted above, says, "So too at the present time there is a remnant, chosen by grace." He tells the Christians of Thessalonica that God has "chosen" them.[35] There is no way to dismiss these statements of Paul's that seem to limit the scope of God's grace. All

---

34. Jas 2:26.
35. 1 Thess 1:4.

The Dynamics of Salvation

we can say is that he was inconsistent on the point, and we believe that his universalizing statements are truer to his central concept of grace than are his narrowing ones.

A prime source for the notion that bad behavior will land your soul in hell is the Gospel of Matthew. Matthew has Jesus say that at the end time "The Son of Man will send his angels, and they will collect out of his kingdom all causes of sin and all evildoers, and they will throw them into the furnace of fire, where there will be weeping and gnashing of teeth."[36] Matthew's Jesus also says that the kingdom of heaven is like a net that catches the bad fish with the good. At the end of the age "the angels will come out and separate the evil from the righteous and throw them into the furnace of fire, where there will be weeping and gnashing of teeth."[37] In the great final judgment scene of Matthew 25 that functions as a constitution for all Christian social justice work, Matthew's Jesus says of those who did not care for him in the persons of "the least of these" that they "will go away into eternal punishment, but the righteous into eternal life."[38] I suppose for a convinced Biblicist the presence of these passages in Matthew ends the discussion. It does not end it for us. The other Gospels have no such emphasis on eternal punishment. I take Matthew's love affair with the furnace of fire, or the outer darkness, where there will be weeping and gnashing of teeth to be his metaphorical way of expressing God's displeasure with sinful behavior. We need not conclude, however, that God's displeasure translates into eternal punishment.

Perhaps even more foundational for the notion that only some, and only Christians, are saved are the exclusionary passages in the Gospel of John. Two of them have had special significance in the history of Christianity. The first is John 3:16–18.[39] We all know the famous John 3:16, the New Testament citation that zealous believers who are also sports fans love to hold up in football stadiums. It reads, "For God so

36. Matt 13:41–41.
37. Matt 13:47–50.
38. Matt 25:46.
39. The words of John 3:16–18 are usually understood to be words John attributes to Jesus, yet this is not necessarily so. The NRSV contains a translators' note at the end of verse 15 that reads, "Some interpreters hold that the quote concludes with John 3:15." If this is true, the famous words of John 3:16–18 are not even attributed to Jesus but are clearly John's. The Jesus Seminar does not believe these words to be Jesus' in any event, and I agree, but we need not go into that thorny issue. For our purposes at the moment what matters is that they are in the Gospel of John, not whether or not Jesus actually said them.

loved the world that he gave his only Son, so that everyone who believes in him may not perish but may have eternal life." This verse is itself exclusionary. It starts out with what could be a statement of universal grace: "For God so loved the world that he gave his only Son. . . ." That much we can agree with, assuming, of course, the theology of the cross that we have developed here to express the meaning of God's gift of Jesus. Verse sixteen, however, already adds a qualifier: "so that *everyone who believes in him* may not perish. . . ." John immediately limits the effect of God's gift of God's Son to those who believe in the gift. Verse seventeen could also be read as describing universal grace. It reads, "Indeed, God did not send the Son into the world to condemn the world, but in order that the world might be saved through him." Perhaps because he sensed that this line might suggest a universal salvation that he could not accept, John immediately adds verse eighteen. It is one of the most exclusionary verses in the entire Gospel, indeed in the entire New Testament. It reads, "Those who believe in him are not condemned; but those who do not believe are condemned already, because they have not believed in the name of the only Son of God." Then there is the almost equally famous John 14:6: "Jesus said to him, 'I am the way, and the truth, and the life. No one comes to the Father except through me.'"[40] That verse has most often been read to mean the same thing as John 3:18. No one can come to God, that is, no one can be saved, who does not believe in Jesus. Clearly for John salvation is conditional. It depends upon believing in Jesus. The Gospel of John is the primary source for the nearly universal Christian practice of turning faith, understood as belief in the objective truth of certain facts about Jesus, into a work that is necessary for salvation.

Must we conclude that this interpretation of the faith is the correct one, or the only correct one, because the Gospel of John so clearly says that it is? It should be clear by now that my answer to that question is a resounding no. My rejection of this interpretation is grounded in the understanding of what the Bible actually is that we examined earlier in this work. To recap: The Bible is a human document that reflects the ex-

---

40. I once heard the story of a Hindu wise man who was asked by a Christian what his response was to this verse. The Hindu wise man said that he agreed with it completely. The Christian was puzzled. The Hindu explained: It says Jesus is the way, the truth, and the life. To determine if that is true we must ask: What is the way that Jesus is? It is the way of peace, mercy, compassion, and justice. That is indeed the way. It is indeed the only way to God. This Hindu wise man understood this verse far better than have most Christians.

The Dynamics of Salvation

periences and understandings of the people who wrote it. The Gospel of John, like everything else in the Bible, is a particular author's understanding and interpretation of the faith. The mere fact that any proposition appears, or can be made to seem to appear, in the Bible never ends any discussion of the truth of that proposition. We have here John's experience and understanding. As with everything else in the Bible, we must hold that experience and understanding up to our own experience and understanding. If ours do not agree with John's, and mine don't on this point, then we must dig deeper to try to understand why John said what he did and to discern if a change in our own thinking is required in light of what we learn about John.

The exclusionary passages in John are explained, I am convinced, by the historical circumstances in which that Gospel was written. Scholars generally agree that the Gospel of John was written late in the first century CE or perhaps even during the first decade of the second century CE. It was written for a community of Jewish Christians and/or Gentile Christians who had affiliated themselves with Jewish synagogues without actually converting to Judaism. After 70 CE, when the Romans destroyed the Temple in Jerusalem and Judaism began its transformation from the sacrificial system of Temple worship into the rabbinic Judaism that we know and cherish today, tensions between Jews and the so-called Gentile God-fearers who accepted Jesus as the Messiah on the one hand and Jews who did not on the other increased over time. Christianity, which originally had been a small sect within Judaism, and its Jewish parent faith parted ways. Christianity came to be seen, especially by the Jews but also by the Roman authorities, as a separate religion. As the Jewish communities throughout the Roman Empire struggled to define and maintain their own identity after the destruction of Jerusalem and the Temple, they began to expel the Christians from the synagogues. Many of the Christians who were now excluded from their former spiritual homes became quite angry at the Jews with whom they had previously been so closely affiliated. That anger, which is understandable from a human point of view but which we can hardly call truly Christian, found expression in the anti-Judaism of the Gospel of John and in that Gospel's insistence that Jesus was the only way to God.

The anti-Judaism and the Christian exclusivism of John are an expression not of divine truth but of the anger of a small, largely powerless, and vulnerable community[41] against a parent religion that had disinherited them.[42] John's claims that Jesus is the only way to God are his way of saying to the Jews, "You're wrong. You can throw us out; but we have the truth, and you don't." This ancient anger against our faith's parent religion is hardly something we must share. Indeed, given the horrendous history of Christian anti-Judaism, it is something of which we must repent and that we must discard as anachronistic and untrue to the better values of our faith. The New Testament passages that make grace and salvation conditional are not divine truth for us. They do not require or support a rejection of the universal nature of grace and of salvation.[43]

Before we take up the second objection to the universality of salvation, we need to pause here to say some more about another significant barrier to the Christian faith in our context that we addressed in Chapter Four. It is the issue of Christian exclusivism. The analysis we have just given of the exclusivist passages of John relating to putting conditions on grace has something to say about that issue as well. As we have already noted, throughout its history Christianity has taught that it has the only truth and that only it can bring salvation. Our faith has historically been far more exclusionary than have the other two great Abrahamic faiths, Judaism and Islam. To most people in our context, Christian exclusivism simply makes no sense. It isn't logical that God would create only one way to salvation, a way that just happens to be our way, then provide that that one way is the religion of only some of God's people. Moreover, in the cos-

---

41. Becoming disassociated from Judaism made Christianity more vulnerable in large part because as long as it was seen as a Jewish sect it enjoyed the Jews' immunity from certain obligations within the Roman Empire, in particular the obligation to worship the Emperor. When Christianity became a separate religion it lost that immunity.

42. The same analysis explains the virulent anti-Judaism of the Gospel of Matthew. Like John, Matthew was written in and for a predominantly Jewish, or formerly Jewish, community. The Gospel of Mark, which was written earlier than either Matthew or John, and the Gospel of Luke, which was written for a Gentile audience not a Jewish one, are much less anti-Judaic than are Matthew and John.

43. For many Christians the conviction will remain that there *must* be a punishment after death for truly evil people, like Adolf Hitler, Josef Stalin and so many other human monsters over the centuries. I suggested above that I am essentially an agnostic on questions of an afterlife. If there is one in which some aspect of our being that is recognizably us survives, I do not believe that it includes a hell of eternal torment. Some have suggested that the punishment of the Adolf Hitlers of the world consists of their own remorse, their self-recrimination once they realize in the presence of God how evil their deeds actually were. I suppose this is as good a resolution as any for those who believe in an afterlife of the consciousness and must hold on to a belief in some kind of punishment.

The Dynamics of Salvation

mopolitan world of today too many of us know people of other faiths, or of no particular faith, whom we know to be decent, moral, spiritual people who simply follow spiritual paths, religious or secular, different from ours. The claim that so many Christians make that only their faith is true and that God rejects people of all other faiths, or of no faith, just doesn't make sense any more (if it ever did, which I doubt). Christian exclusivism is a major barrier to Christianity among us.

This exclusivist contention is, of course, radically inconsistent with the understanding of the nature of religious truth we have developed in this work. We have seen that any religion is true to the extent that it connects people with the spiritual and that with which it connects people is truly the spiritual. Since it cannot be denied that all of the world's great religions truly connect people with the spiritual, it cannot be denied that all of those religions are true to the extent that they do so. None of them does it perfectly. Certainly Christianity does not. All religions have within them the risk of connecting people with something that is not truly the spiritual. Christianity regularly commits that error by, among other things, connecting people more with a book or with an ecclesiastical institution than with the truly spiritual. Other religions have their own similar failings. Nonetheless, they all do connect people with the spiritual as well. They wouldn't have survived to become great world religions if they did not. Liberated Christianity as we are developing it here absolutely rules out religious exclusivism. The preceding analysis shows that Christian exclusivism is not the divine mandate that it can sometimes appear to Christians to be.

We return now to the second major objection that is raised to the universality of salvation. That objection, that if all are saved there is no motivation for people to behave morally, is perhaps more difficult to deal with than was the first objection we dealt with above. The church has used the threat of eternal damnation as a control mechanism over the people for so long that the notion that the only reason people ever behave in a moral way is out of fear is deeply ingrained within us. We fear that if the threat is removed people will conclude that anything goes and that greed, violence, and other sinful behavior will be totally unchecked. If grace is truly unconditional, why shouldn't we sin, seeing as how sin can seem to be so much more fun than being moral?[44]

---

44. One of my favorite expressions of this idea is a line from the Billy Joel song "Only the Good Die Young" that goes, "I'd rather laugh with the sinners than cry with

St. Paul faced the same objection to his message of grace nearly two thousand years ago. Since, as Paul taught, the grace we received through Jesus Christ had abolished the law, some drew the unwarranted conclusion that Christians were free to sin because they stood in God's grace. Paul responded:

> What then are we to say? Should we continue in sin in order that grace may abound? By no means! How can we who died to sin go on living in it? Do you not know that all of us who have been baptized into Christ Jesus were baptized into his death? Therefore we have been buried with him by baptism into death, so that, just as Christ was raised from the dead by the glory of the Father, so we too might walk in newness of life.[45]

Paul gives us the answer to this objection, albeit in his typically somewhat obscure language. He says that we cannot "go on living" in sin once we have "died to it," using the symbolism of baptism as a rebirth into a new life in Christ. Paul is saying, I think, that once we truly know the grace of God in Christ Jesus we will "walk in newness of life"; that is, we will no longer walk in the ways of sin but in the ways of God's righteousness. Sinful behavior, that is, selfish or violent behavior that is harmful to ourselves or to others, behavior that does not constitute loving God, self, and neighbor, is not an option for those who truly know God's grace. Of course, none of us lives God's law of love perfectly. Only Jesus did that. The point is that in a system of universal grace and salvation, the motivation for moral behavior is not fear of punishment. It is the desire to respond to love with love, to respond to grace with grace.

That desire after all, is what makes what we call moral behavior truly moral. Behavior that is ultimately grounded in self-interest, that is ultimately selfish (which behavior that is grounded in a fear of eternal punishment finally is) is not truly moral behavior. It remains in the end concern more about oneself than about God or God's people. Great good may come from such behavior. Indeed, much of the good Christian people have done over the millennia has come out of this fearful self interest. In

---

the saints. The sinners are much more fun." Perhaps another barrier to faith that we need to overcome is the notion that religion is always and necessarily a serious, joyless affair. So many of our churches are what the great contemporary Christian musician Ken Medema calls "the Frigidaire Presbyterian Church." (Substitute your own denomination for Presbyterian.) We really do need to get over it.

45. Rom 6:1–4.

The Dynamics of Salvation

the final analysis, however, that behavior, while pleasing to God on one level, is not truly moral behavior. The religion of fear does not produce truly moral people. It produces fearful, self-interested people.

The religion of fear may be a useful tool of social control, but we must ask ourselves whether social control is a legitimate function of religion. It certainly has been a historically prominent function of religion. Once Christianity became the established religion of the Roman Empire in the fourth century CE, social control in the interest of the ruling classes became one of its most important functions. We, however, live in an era of Christian disestablishment.[46] Social control is not our function. There is no reason for us any longer to maintain a religion of fear. We are free to develop a true religion of grace.

We conclude then that universal grace does not remove all motivation for moral behavior. It simply changes the nature of the motivation. It removes fear from the equation and frees us to be truly moral children of God, living out of love rather than out of selfish concern for our own eternal fate. Some may call this approach idealistic and unrealistic. If it is, so be it. Jesus Christ was nothing if not an idealist. He certainly had a thoroughly realistic understanding of the sinful nature of the world. He did not, however, therefore retreat into a religion of manipulation and control through fear. Rather, he demonstrated to the full God's free, unmerited grace for all people. He demonstrated to the full God's unfailing presence and solidarity with all people. That grace is universal. If it is truly grace, it cannot be otherwise.

---

46. There has been much wailing and gnashing of teeth in so-called mainline Protestantism over its loss of status, a loss that truly amounts to de facto disestablishment. We need to get over it. We need to see the loss of our strong connections to the powers in our country not as true loss but as an opportunity for greater faithfulness to the Gospel of Jesus Christ. Douglas John Hall's trilogy cited in the Introduction to this work contains a penetrating analysis of the loss of our status as what he calls "the stained glass version of the dominant culture." See also Hall's little book, *The End of Christendom and the Future of Christianity* (1997; repr. Eugene, Oregon: Wipf and Stock Publishers, 2002).

Questions for Reflection and Discussion

1. What was your first understanding of salvation?

    Did it mean getting to go to heaven when you die?

    Did it mean anything else?

2. Recall your answers to the questions at the end of chapter nine on your need for salvation. Those questions apply to chapter ten as well.

    Does God save you?

    How?

    How do you know?

3. Have you experienced God's grace active in your life?

    Describe that experience (or those experiences)

    Has that experience (or those experiences) made a difference in your life?
    How?

    Did you do anything to earn that experience of God's grace?
    If so, what?
    If not, what does that tell you about the nature of God's grace?

4. Chapter ten asserts that God's salvation is universal, that is, that all are saved, at least as far as God is concerned.

    Have you been taught otherwise?

    Do you now agree or disagree with Chapter Ten's assertion of universal salvation?
    Why, or why not?

11

Christian Social Ethics:
The Teachings of Jesus for Our Time

THE GENERAL PUBLIC PERCEPTION of what it means to be a Christian in our context is a major obstacle to faith. We have already examined many of the connotations of the term "Christian" among us. So far in this regard, we have focused on the Biblicist understanding of Christianity as an obstacle to faith. There are, however, other connotations that the term "Christian" has among us that make Christianity unattractive and even repellant to a great many people. These connotations have to do with the positions the most vocal and visible American Christians take on social and ethical issues. If one listened only to the James Dobsons, Jerry Falwells, and Pat Robertsons of American Christianity one would conclude that Christianity is rabidly homophobic, supports a Victorian, patriarchal view of the family as ordained by God and denies the equality of women, equates God's will with American imperialism, and has little or no concern for the poor and the marginalized of the world beyond a certain level of charitable work that may provide some temporary relief for some people but that does nothing about the social systems that produce poverty and marginalization in the first place. Christian "values" get reduced to opposition to gay marriage and abortion. One would conclude that Christians are uniformly opposed to separation of church and state and wish to impose a Christian theocracy upon our American democracy. One could even get the idea that the values of Christianity and the values of the Republican Party are virtually identical, that one cannot be both a Christian and a political and social progressive.

Sometimes the most visible Christian leaders descend into self-parody, as when Jerry Falwell grandiloquently announced that the children's television character Tinky Winky is gay.[1] Sometimes they call for actions that are demonstrably un-Christian, as when Pat Robertson called on the United States government to assassinate President Chavez of Venezuela. Sometimes they commit moral outrages in the name of Christ, as when Fred Phelps and his followers (I refuse to call him "the Reverend Fred Phelps" as the news media always do) picket the funerals of American service personnel killed in Iraq, claiming that their deaths are God's punishment for this country's alleged toleration of homosexuality. Our largest Protestant denomination, the Southern Baptist Convention, disgraces all of Christianity by saying that women should not serve as pastors; and the largest Christian denomination in the world, the Roman Catholic Church, reinforces the view of Christianity as misogynistic by declaring that anyone who even discusses the ordination of women distances herself from the communion of the Church. The parade of outrages could go on almost forever.

Sometimes it seems as if Christianity is intent on self-destruction, yet the view of what it means to be a Christian that these outrages create is a tragic mischaracterization of true Christian values. Christianity has done such a good job at perverting its own core values and has so compromised with the values of the world that overcoming this public perception of Christian values is a monumental task. It won't be easy. It is, however, an absolute necessity if we are to liberate Christianity from the misperceptions that prevail both within and outside the churches and overcome a major obstacle to the faith in our context. As long as the distorted, I dare to say even demonic,[2] view of Christian values that prevails among us today remains unchallenged, the obstacles to the Christian faith in our context will remain insurmountable for most people.

Significant efforts are under way to change that horrendous misperception of Christian values. I will mention a few of them very briefly. Chief among them is Jim Wallis's organization and journal Sojourners. Wallis is a self-avowed Evangelical Christian who understands that Christian values include a lot more than opposition to gay rights and

---

1. Not long after Falwell gave us all a good laugh with that absurd bit of pomposity my late wife and I attended a concert by the Seattle Men's Chorus, one of the many excellent gay choruses in our country. At one point in the concert a young man came skipping across the stage wearing a Tinky Winky backpack. The place erupted in laughter. It was a delightful spoof of Falwell's bigoted nonsense.

2. I use the term "demonic" in its technical sense of not being its true self, of not being what God created it to be.

abortion. He is very moderate on those issues, but on issues of peace and economic justice he speaks God's truth with a clarity and a passion that make him a true prophet among us. His book *God's Politics: Why the Right is Wrong and the Left Doesn't Get It*[3] is a must read for anyone who seeks to understand how Christianity truly informs believers' views on values issues today.[4] The Rev. Fred Plummer's organization, The Center for Progressive Christianity, has developed and promotes an enlightened view of Christianity and Christian values. Its "8 Points" of progressive Christianity are a good starting point for anyone seeking to understand the alternative of progressive Christianity.[5] Walter Wink, to whose work we will return in what follows, has done pioneering work on Jesus' teaching of assertive, creative non-violence as the true Christian response to evil. Efforts have begun to reform the public's understanding of Christian values. The success of that reformation is essential to the liberation of Christianity today.

The values of liberated Christianity are already implied in the preceding paragraphs. Yet the matter is so important that we must devote substantially more attention to it. How does our understanding of liberated and liberating Christianity inform our conception of Christian values? Is there anything in our understanding of the nature of religious truth, of the Bible as a collection of human mythic stories, and of our concept of God's solidarity with us as demonstrated in the life, teachings, death, and resurrection of Christ that drives in the direction of a particular understanding of ethics and values? I believe that there is, and to an analysis of that issue we now turn.

One point should be clear from the very beginning. The mere fact that a values position is or can be made to seem to be supported by some passage in the Bible is in no way determinative on any issue of values. We have already established that the authority of the Bible does not arise

3. Jim Wallis, *God's Politics, Why the Right Gets It Wrong and the Left Doesn't Get It* (San Francisco: HarperSanFrancisco, 2005).

4. Wallis makes the important point, among many others, that the conclusion that in the 2000 Presidential election "values voters" voted overwhelmingly for George W. Bush is mistaken because the polls that reached that conclusion separated issues of peace and economic justice from the category "values."

5. The 8 Points are available at www.tcpc.org. I once asked Rev. Plummer why the 8 Points do not expressly include a commitment to Jesus' way of nonviolence. He was unable to give a satisfactory answer. The Center needs, in my opinion, to expand their 8 Points to nine to include that commitment.

from divine origins. It has no divine origins, at least not in any objective, absolute sense. Biblical statements on values issues are frequently expressions of the cultural values and norms of the time and place which produced the statements. As with everything else in the Bible, we must hold these statements up to the mirror of our own experience of God and our own understanding of Christian values to see if they express divine truth *for us* or not. We will refer to the Bible frequently in what follows but not as a proof text for any value position.

As Christians, our starting point for a discussion of virtually any issue and certainly of any issue of values or morals must be Jesus. Christians properly look to him for guidance in every aspect of their lives. He is the one in and through whom we see the ultimate demonstration of the nature of God and of God's will for the world. In his Resurrection we see God's sign and seal that he is indeed the one who shows us God's ways. We confess that he is God the Son Incarnate; that is, in him we experience the true presence of God among us. On the cross he demonstrated God's unshakable solidarity with us in everything that happens to us, as we have already discussed. In his life and in his teachings, he demonstrates to us the will of God for how we are to live our lives. Precisely because we are Christians, his moral teachings must be our guide as we make our own decisions in life.

The importance for us of Jesus' teachings raises something of a problem. The only sources we have on the teachings of Jesus are the Gospels.[6] There are several issues about the Gospels and their presentation of Jesus' teachings that we must address at the outset if we are to use these sources appropriately. We must keep in mind that each of them presents a different view of Jesus. We have already noted that all of the Biblical books are human constructs that reflect the cultural understanding and beliefs and the literary conventions of their time. The Gospels are, then, not biography or history as we understand them. They are theological tracts that tell stories to make theological points, and they don't all make the same theological points.

---

6. There are, of course, many more Gospels than the four that made the cut and became part of the Christian Bible. Nonetheless, in this chapter when I say Gospels I mean the four canonical Gospels of Matthew, Mark, Luke, and John. These are the four that have become foundational for Christian life and Christian beliefs. They are the four that most matter to us.

Christian Social Ethics: The Teachings of Jesus for Our Time

Perhaps more important is the thorny issue of the historicity of the sayings that the Gospels attribute to Jesus. Much scholarly sweat has been shed trying to determine which of those sayings Jesus may actually have said and which are later expressions of the experiences and beliefs of the early Christian community that produced the Gospel in which they appear. Certainly it is important to realize that the mere fact that some words in the Gospels appear in red (in most popular editions) indicating that they are the words of Jesus does not establish that Jesus actually said those words as an historical matter. In recent years, the Jesus Seminar in particular has done a great deal of work trying to differentiate the historically authentic sayings of Jesus from the inauthentic ones. The results of that labor are found primarily in their book *The Five Gospels*.[7] Their conclusions are interesting and perhaps instructive despite the fact that their claims to have found objective criteria for distinguishing between authentic and inauthentic Jesus sayings are unconvincing.[8] They certainly appear to be correct when they say that none of the sayings attributed to Jesus in the Gospel of John are authentic sayings of Jesus. The differences between John's Jesus and the Jesus of the synoptic Gospels are so great that the historical Jesus cannot have been both. In the synoptic Gospels, Jesus preaches the Kingdom of God.[9] In John he preaches belief in himself, something that seems highly improbable as an historical matter. I understand the sayings about himself that John attributes to Jesus, especially the great "I am" sayings, not as something Jesus said but as the faith confession of the Johanine community. Nonetheless, the fact remains that the Gospels are the only source we have for Jesus' teachings. We will,

---

7. Robert W. Funk, *The Five Gospels: What Did Jesus Really Say? The Search for the Authentic Words of Jesus* (San Francisco: HarperSanFrancisco, 1997). The book deals with five Gospels not four because the Jesus Seminar included the non-canonical Gospel of Thomas in its study of the sayings attributed to Jesus.

8. The problem is not that their criteria and their decisions are subjective. All human life is subjective. The problem is that they claim an objectivity that they do not and cannot have.

9. The Gospel of Matthew mostly uses the phrase "the Kingdom of Heaven" rather than the Kingdom of God. Scholars explain this different usage as Matthew's compliance with the Jewish prohibition against speaking the name of God. Matthew clearly means the same thing by it as Mark and Luke mean by the Kingdom of God. Nonetheless, Matthew's usage has had unfortunate consequences. It has given support to the misguided notion that the Kingdom about which Jesus spoke is located in heaven. It isn't. It is located here on earth, as we explain in what follows. I will use the term Kingdom of God in referring to all three Gospels except when quoting Matthew.

therefore, use them as we believe we must use all Biblical material, trying to understand them in their original context and holding them up to our own experience of God. This method of course dwells in subjectivity, but we have insisted throughout this work that subjectivity is unavoidable for us humans. All we can do is state our reasons for finding some of Jesus' teachings to be divine truth for us and finding others not to be, then letting each reader decide for herself if her experience of God leads to the same conclusion.

Before we look at some of the more important of those teachings, we need to get one issue out of the way. As mentioned in a footnote above, the Christian tradition has, at least since the establishment of the faith as the official religion of the Roman Empire in the fourth century CE, tended to direct believers' attention out of this life and onto an afterlife by transferring the Kingdom of God, about which Jesus speaks so much in the synoptic Gospels, out of this world and into heaven. Putting the Kingdom of God in heaven and not in this world badly distorts the meaning of the faith. As we noted above, Matthew's use of the term Kingdom of Heaven instead of Kingdom of God has facilitated that distortion of the term's meaning. There is one other passage, this one from John, which has been even more misleading and even more misused in this regard. In the eighteenth chapter of John, Jesus has been arrested and has been taken from the high priest to Pilate, the Roman governor, for trial and execution. In an exchange with Pilate about the charge against Jesus that he claims to be "the king of the Jews," Jesus speaks a line that has come into English usage as "My kingdom is not of this world."[10] This translation, which comes from the King James Version, has been used to convince generations of Christians that Jesus' life and teachings are not about this world, that they are only about how one gets to heaven and what things are like "up there."

There is a serious problem with this translation and the understanding of the location of God's kingdom and the nature of the Christian life that it supports. In John's account, Jesus does not say "my kingdom is not of this world." In the Greek original, he says "my kingdom is not *ek tou kosmou*."[11] *Tou kosmou* means "this world." There's no problem there.

---

10. John 18:36 KJV.

11. There is an inherent problem in close linguistic analyses of sayings of Jesus like the one we are doing here. We will see another of them farther on when we take up Walter Wink's exegesis of the Jesus saying from Matthew "do not resist an evildoer" (Matt

The problem is with the preposition "*ek*." "*Ek*" does not mean "of," at least not in the sense so often given to it of belonging to. It means "from" or "out of." It indicates a place out of which something comes or its point of origin. We see it as a root in English words like "ecstatic," which literally means standing outside of oneself, and "ecclesiastic," which comes from the Greek *ekklesia*, the word for church that literally means those called out from the world to be a people apart. The meaning of the statement John attributes to Jesus is that his kingdom does not originate in or have its basis in this world. The statement is about the kingdom's source not its location. The New Revised Standard Version translation recognizes this fact when it changes the translation of this phrase to "my kingdom is not *from* this world" (Emphasis added). The King James Version's use of the preposition "of" to translate "*ek*" has led to a great misunderstanding of what John's Jesus actually says.[12]

We turn then to what Jesus actually teaches about Christian values in the public arena. When we examine what he says about values we notice first of all that he says nothing about the issues that have come so to define Christian values in the public consciousness in our context. We notice first of all that he says absolutely nothing about homosexuality or homosexual acts. There isn't a single mention of them in any of the Gospels. We will take up the issue of the true Christian position on homosexuality below.

5:39). The problem is that we have the words attributed to Jesus in Greek, but Jesus did not speak Greek. He spoke Aramaic. We focus so much on the meaning of the Greek because it is all we have. This is perhaps one more reason for being more concerned with the sources we have than with speculation about what Jesus may actually have said as an historical matter. When the Jesus Seminar says that a particular saying is an authentic saying of Jesus the most they can really say is that it is a Greek translation of what they think is an authentic saying of Jesus.

12. I find it interesting that this translation, which supports the notion that God's people are supposed to be concerned with heaven more than with affairs on earth, comes from a translation sponsored by an earthly king. Certainly the interpretation that flows from the translation inures to the benefit of earthly powers, be they kings or some other type of earthly ruler.

The matter is beyond the scope of this work, but the Gospel of John is almost universally misunderstood to be about heaven and not about of this world. This misunderstanding comes primarily from John's frequent use of the phrase "eternal life." We take that to mean never-ending life with God in heaven. It doesn't. The Gospel of John itself gives us the term's meaning. In that Gospel Jesus says, "And this is eternal life, that they [Jesus' disciples] may know you, the only true God, and Jesus Christ whom you have sent" (John 17:3). Eternal life then is something we obtain in this life by knowing God and Christ. It isn't about heaven at all.

Suffice it to say for now that the great emphasis contemporary Christianity puts on condemning homosexuality is puzzling in light of Jesus' total silence on the issue. The Gospels also contain no statement of Jesus about abortion or when human life begins. Arguments from silence are dangerous, but those Christians and their leaders who work so hard at making Christian values be about those two issues must at least acknowledge that they are making a great deal about matters that Jesus didn't even mention.

Those same Christians and their leaders also strive to make Christian values be primarily about family. We have already looked at this issue in our discussion above of the human existential dilemma of meaninglessness. We need not repeat that discussion here. Suffice it to say that the reduction of Christian values to so-called "family values" that is so prevalent among us is odd at best given Jesus' apparent rejection of the nuclear family as the primary unit of our concern.

Jesus doesn't talk about homosexuality, and he doesn't talk about abortion. He rejects the family as the core unit of values. In other words, he doesn't talk about the issues that have come to characterize Christian values in the public consciousness, and he affirmatively rejects the focus on the family of most Evangelical Christianity. What values then does he talk about? We can organize his teachings under three headings, namely, nonviolence, economic justice, and radical inclusivity, expressed in large part through a rejection of individual purity as the goal of the religious life. We will take up each of these in turn. We will then take a closer look at the issue of homosexuality, the issue that most characterizes the differences between popular Christianity in our context and the liberated and liberating Christianity we are developing here.

1. JESUS' "THIRD WAY" OF CREATIVE NONVIOLENCE

There is simply no doubt that Jesus taught nonviolence and rejected all resort to violence as a tactic for resisting evil. The earliest Christians understood this fact very well. They were all pacifists. They refused to serve in the Roman or any other army. They did not resort to violence to defend themselves against persecution, even when it cost them their lives, as it sometimes did. Until the establishment of Christianity as the official religion of the Roman Empire in the fourth century CE, Christianity was thoroughly pacifist. In other words, it was, at least on this issue, true to the teachings of the one it called (and we call) Lord and Savior.

The Gospel passages that present Jesus' teaching of nonviolence are well known. One of them is found in the Gospel accounts of Jesus' arrest. In Matthew, we read that when Jesus was arrested, "one of those with Jesus put his hand on his sword, drew it, and struck the slave of the high priest, cutting off his ear." Jesus rejected this attempt to prevent his arrest by violence. In Matthew's account, he says, "Put your sword back into its place; for all who take the sword will perish by the sword."[13] In Luke's version of the same story, Jesus responds to the act of violence by saying, "No more of this!" Then to drive the point home, he reaches out and heals the man who had been wounded.[14] This story also appears in John, where it is none other than Peter who cuts off the man's ear. John's Jesus also rejects this act of violence aimed at saving him from arrest and execution.[15]

Jesus' most famous teachings on nonviolence are part of the Sermon on the Mount in the Gospel of Matthew. The crucial passage reads

> You have heard that it was said, 'An eye for an eye and a tooth for a tooth.' But I say to you, Do not resist an evildoer. But if anyone strikes you on the right cheek, turn the other also; and if anyone wants to sue you and take your coat, give your cloak as well; and if anyone forces you to go one mile, go also the second mile.[16]

This passage is often cited together with another one that follows right afterward. That one reads, "You have heard that it was said, 'You shall love your neighbor and hate your enemy.' But I say to you, Love your enemies and pray for those who persecute you."[17] Phrases like "turn the other cheek," "go the extra mile," and "love your enemies" have passed into our

---

13. Matt 26:51–52.

14. Luke 22:50–51.

15. John 18:10–11. It should be pointed out that the story has a different meaning in John. John's Jesus rejects the act of violence not because it is violent but because he doesn't want anyone to interfere with his carefully orchestrated and controlled arrest and crucifixion, which are necessary for him to complete his divine mission. He says, "Put your sword back into its sheath. Am I not to drink the cup that the Father has given me?" We should not, however, conclude from John's theological twist on the story that John's Jesus did not reject violence on moral grounds.

16. Matt 5:38–41.

17. Matt 5:43–44. Jesus, or more likely Matthew, actually got this one a bit wrong. Nowhere in Hebrew Scripture does it actually say "hate your enemies." We must concede, however, that the way enemies are treated in much of the Hebrew Bible and the way God is said to have destroyed Israel's enemies on many occasions could easily lead to the belief that hatred of enemies was appropriate.

common vocabulary as metaphors for pacifism or at least for a compliant, non-combative attitude in life.

This understanding of these passages is correct to the extent that it recognizes that Jesus rejected hatred and violence as appropriate responses to anything or anyone we encounter. Jesus rejected violence, but we run the risk of a serious misunderstanding of his teaching if we stop our analysis at that point. These verses have a shadow side that has had tragic consequences throughout Christian history. They have far too often been used to counsel people in positions of subordination and exploitation, especially women, simply to accept their fate, not to resist, and indeed to love those who oppress them by doing nothing to extricate themselves from their intolerable situation. A shameful aspect of Christian history is the way Christian pastors, perhaps truly believing that they were speaking the will of God, have sent women back into abusive relationships with the advice to turn the other cheek and love their abusers. If this were in fact what these passages from Matthew actually meant, we would perhaps have to reject them as inconsistent with our experience of a loving and caring God who desires wholeness of life for all people, especially for the marginalized and the oppressed. As it turns out, they actually mean something quite different.

Walter Wink has powerfully demonstrated that passivity is in fact not what Jesus is counseling in these passages. The analysis that follows is his.[18] Wink teaches that Jesus' way is neither the way of violence nor the way of sheepish passivity. Jesus' way is a "Third Way," the way of creative, assertive, nonviolent resistance to evil. Wink bases his analysis primarily on Matthew 5:38–41 quoted above. He first gives an extensive linguistic analysis of the Greek word translated as "resist" in the phrase "do not resist an evildoer." He concludes that it is a word from Greek military usage that

---

18. Wink has published extensively on the issue of Christian nonviolence. Most important is his trilogy on "the powers." All published by Fortress Press, Minneapolis, they are: *Naming the Powers: The Language of Power in the New* Testament (1984), *Unmasking the Powers: The Invisible Forces That Determine Human Existence* (1986), and *Engaging the Powers: Discernment and Resistance in a World of Domination* (1992). Wink has summarized and popularized this work, especially the third book of the trilogy, in his book *The Powers That Be: Theology for a New Millennium* (New York: Galilee Doubleday, 1998). That book is an indispensable guide to any Christian who wants truly to understand how radical Jesus' teaching of nonviolence is and how it calls us to creative acts of nonviolence in opposition to evil. I cannot recommend it too highly. The following analysis is Wink's, although of course any error in presenting his interpretation is solely mine.

means to resist with armed force. Jesus' statement "do not resist an evildoer" means something like do not go out in armed ranks to fight an evil doer. It is not a blanket injunction against resistance. It is an injunction against armed, violent resistance.

Wink believes that what follows in this passage are three illustrative examples not of passivity but of assertive nonviolent resistance. We fail to see this meaning in them because we do not live in their first century Jewish context. The first example, in Matthew, reads, "But if anyone strikes you on the right cheek, turn the other also." We often overlook the fact that Matthew has Jesus say, "if anyone strikes you on the *right* cheek." We hear it simply as if anyone strikes you on the cheek, or if anyone strikes you at all. Yet Wink argues that Matthew says "right cheek" for a reason.[19] In first century Jewish culture the left hand was considered unclean. No one used it as the dominant hand.[20] Because the image of a person striking another person on the cheek necessarily assumes that the striker is using his right hand, the reference to the victim being struck on the right cheek necessarily means that the blow is with the back of the striker's hand. Try it, and you'll see; however, of course don't actually hit anyone to prove the point. Wink says that a backhanded blow to the cheek was the way a person in a superior position would strike a person in an inferior one. Equals fought with fists such that a blow with the right hand would land on the other person's left cheek. This illustration of Jesus' point assumes that the person struck on the right cheek is in an inferior position to the person hitting him. This understanding gives turning the other cheek a whole new meaning. The other cheek is now the left cheek. Presenting the left cheek to a right-handed assailant forces the assailant either to break off the attack or to treat the victim as an equal by striking him directly with the fist. Turning the left cheek elevates the victim to the level of the assailant and gives the assailant an impossible choice between defeat and recognizing the equality of the one he considered inferior. Turning the

19. Wink's analysis does not work with the parallel passage in Luke. There Jesus says "if anyone strikes you on the cheek, offer the other also" (Luke 6:29a).

20. This prejudice against the left hand lasted well into the twentieth century. Perhaps if you are naturally left-handed you have experienced well-meaning teachers who forced you to learn to write with your right hand. Our word "sinister" comes from a root that means left. The parallels between this prejudice against the naturally occurring state of being left-handed and the naturally occurring state of being homosexual are remarkable. Both are minority characteristics natural to some people against which the dominant culture has had a strong prejudice.

other cheek is, as Wink explains it, a creative, assertive, nonviolent response to an assault by a superior upon an inferior. It is a third way. It is not violent, neither is it passive acquiescence in evil.

The same is true of the other two examples Matthew's Jesus gives of how to respond to certain types of evil. Wink explains that the reference to someone suing to take one's coat assumes a court of law in which a creditor was suing to collect a debt. In that world most people would have owned only two garments, an outer covering here called a coat and an undergarment here called a cloak. If when a successful creditor took the debtor's outer garment to satisfy a debt the debtor gave the cloak as well, the debtor would have been left standing in the courtroom naked. In the Jewish culture of the time, nakedness was not shameful for the person who was naked; it was shameful for the person who saw the other person's nakedness. Giving the cloak as well is not an act of generosity. It is an act of shaming an oppressor for taking one of the very few things a poor person of that day owned. It, too, is an example of creative, assertive nonviolent resistance to oppression.

Wink says that the reference to going the second mile assumes a situation that prevailed in first century Judea. A Roman soldier was authorized to require a Jewish civilian to carry the soldier's gear one mile.[21] He would be breaking the rules and exposing himself to punishment if he required such an impressed civilian to carry the gear more than one mile. By going a second mile, the victim of the soldier's oppression put the soldier in an impossible position. He would have to plead with the person to stop carrying his gear. He would have to force the person to stop carrying his gear. The victim would have turned a minor episode of exploitation by the Roman soldier into a miserable situation for the soldier.

Wink's fascinating exegesis of this passage makes it clear that while Jesus is counseling nonviolence, he is not in fact counseling passivity. Although the actions mentioned sound meek and passive to us, in their original context they were not. Rather, the three situations Jesus mentions are examples of creative, assertive, nonviolent resistance to evil. Jesus here is not teaching us simply to fold in the face of evil. He is teaching us that violence is not God's way. Creativity, assertiveness, and even humor are God's way, as the example of giving the cloak as well demonstrates. We are

---

21. Or one *stadium*. The actual unit of measure doesn't matter.

to love our enemies, as Jesus also says.[22] That does not mean, however, that we must passively accept evil. It certainly does not mean that oppressed people have no moral right to oppose their oppression. They do, and Jesus does not teach otherwise.[23]

Nonviolence is clearly Jesus' way. It is therefore the way of the Christian. Yet Christians have been extremely creative in coming up with justifications for avoiding this central teaching of the one we call Lord and Savior. The dominant Christian position on the use of violence since the fourth century CE has not been nonviolence; it has been the so-called "just war theory." Christian just war theory arose after the establishment of Christianity as the official religion of the Roman Empire. Up until that time Christians eschewed all violence and refused to serve in the Roman army. Once the Empire became Christian, many faithful Christians perceived a dilemma. Jesus taught nonviolence, but the now Christian Roman Empire was under violent attack by non-Christian barbarians. Surely Jesus did not mean that they could not fight to defend a *Christian* empire. So the leading theologians of the time, most notably St. Augustine of Hippo, developed a theory of the just war to justify Christians who were fighting the enemies of Christian Rome.

Classic Christian just war theory holds that a war is just, and the use of violence is therefore justified, if five criteria are all met. Three of the criteria deal with the cause of the war, and two deal with how the war is fought once it has begun. For a war to be just it must be 1) defensive, 2) declared by a legitimate state authority, 3) a last resort, 4) use the minimum amount of force necessary to achieve the defensive objective, and 5) avoid inflicting casualties on noncombatants. St. Augustine taught that if these conditions were met, Christians could engage in warfare.

---

22. The Church of the Brethren, one of the historic peace churches, puts out a bumper sticker that reads, "When Jesus said love your enemies, I think he probably meant don't kill them." Indeed.

23. The most common objection to nonviolence in my experience is that it "doesn't work." People assume that violence is a more effective response and deterrent to violence. This assumption simply is not correct. For a detailed examination of the effectiveness of nonviolent movements against oppression see the work of Walter Wink. I will mention briefly only the fact that violence primarily begets more violence, as the intractable Israeli-Palestinian conflict, in which both sides seem committed to the use of violence, abundantly proves. Creative nonviolence drove the British from India, led to the passage of the 1964 Civil Rights and the 1965 Voting Rights Acts in our own country, and ended apartheid in South Africa. It works. For more on the effectiveness of nonviolence see Walter Wink's little book *Jesus and Nonviolence, A Third Way* (Minneapolis: Fortress Press, 2003).

Christians of good conscience have accepted the just war theory for centuries as a matter of necessity, but we must make two observations about that acceptance. The first is that anyone who accepts the just war theory must acknowledge that it is a compromise of Jesus' teachings.[24] In my experience people who advocate the just war theory rarely do. They contend rather that it is legitimate Christian teaching. It is not. It is a compromise between Christ's teachings and the demands of the world. If we accept the just war theory at all (and I do not), we must at least acknowledge that undeniable fact.

The second observation is that the just war theory opened the door to the acceptance of war by Christians in a way and to an extent that surely would have appalled even St. Augustine himself. Virtually no war that has ever been fought has truly satisfied the criteria of just war theory. Even the American involvement in World War II, which most of us accept as "the good war," or at least the necessary and just war, fails to meet these criteria. We were attacked, massively and openly by Japan at Pearl Harbor and to a lesser extent by the German U-boat campaign against American shipping in the North Atlantic. Some armed, defensive response might have been justifiable under just war theory. We have to ask, however, did our insistence on "unconditional surrender" meet the criterion of using the minimal amount of force necessary to achieve the defensive end of the war? Perhaps an argument can be made that it did, but on its face it does not appear to have done so. Beyond that, the criteria of not inflicting casualties on noncombatants was simply thrown out by all parties to the war. The indiscriminant bombing of enemy cities, whether with conventional weapons or nuclear ones, clearly violates that necessary criterion for a just war.

My point is not to belittle the service of the brave American men and woman who fought that war, my father included. The decisions about unconditional surrender and carpet bombing of enemy cities were not theirs. My point is only that we cannot call the fighting of that war just under the classic Christian just war theory. Much less can we call the Vietnam War or the American invasion of Iraq in 2003 and its aftermath just under

---

24. Dietrich Bonhoeffer was a committed pacifist who nonetheless made the decision to join a conspiracy to assassinate Hitler because he saw no other way to end World War II and the evil of the Nazi regime. Bonhoeffer, however, never contended that his decision was truly Christian. He acknowledged that it violated Jesus' teachings, saying only that he did what he thought he had to do and that he asked God's forgiveness for having done so.

that theory. The American invasion of Iraq does not even meet the first criterion of being defensive. The introduction of the just war theory into Christianity led to the virtual abandonment of Jesus' teaching of nonviolence. In our own country today, certain Christian groups, including most prominently the Southern Baptist Convention, endorse manifestly unjust wars like the one in Iraq and virtually equate Christianity with American geopolitical interests. The liberation of Christianity requires that we return to Jesus' original teachings and advocate creative, assertive, but always nonviolent responses to evil. It is the only truly Christian way.

Beyond just war theory, Christians have been creative in their use of certain Scripture passages as a rationalization for avoiding Jesus' clear teaching of nonviolence. One of the passages most often cited to prove that Jesus didn't really mean it when he taught nonviolence is Matthew 10:34, which reads, "Do not think that I have come to bring peace to the earth; I have not come to bring peace, but a sword." Christians who reject nonviolence and wish to resort to the world's way of war cite this verse as justification for any resort to violence that they happen to find expedient. Read in its context, however, this verse clearly does not establish that Jesus condoned violence:

> Do not think that I have come to bring peace to the earth; I have not come to bring peace, but a sword.
> For I have come to set a man against
> his father,
> and a daughter against her mother,
> and a daughter-in-law against her
> mother-in-law;
> and one's foes will be members of
> one's own household.[25]

The verse is part of the second of five large collections of the sayings of Jesus in the Gospel of Matthew. Matthew presents these sayings as instructions to the Disciples as they leave on a mission trip. In the passage we are considering, Jesus is telling the Disciples what they can expect the result of the Gospel they bring to be. The author of the Gospel of Matthew, of course, wrote these lines several decades after Jesus' death. In their historical setting they are describing not what Jesus' intent was but rather the situation in the families of the members of Matthew's community. The

---

25. Matt 10:34–36.

Gospel of Jesus Christ did in fact divide families. It still does. The term "sword" here is a metaphor for that divisive effect of the Gospel, as the immediate reference to family divisions with the connecting word "for" clearly shows. That setting family members against each other was not Jesus' intent seems obvious. Scriptural support for that contention can be found in several passages in which Jesus restates the Mosaic commandment to honor our parents.[26] It was not Jesus' intent, but the Gospel did cut through families like a sword in New Testament times. That is what Matthew is talking about here. It is a gross misreading of this passage to use it as a Christian justification for the use of violence.[27]

There is also a passage in Luke's Passion story that could be used to suggest that Jesus supported the resort to violence at least on occasion. Upon closer examination, however, it turns out that this passage does not mean what proponents of the use of violence construe it to mean. This passage reads

> He [Jesus] said to them, "When I sent you out without a purse, bag, or sandals, did you lack anything?" They said, "No, not a thing." He said to them, "But now, the one who has a purse must take it, and likewise a bag. And the one who has no sword must sell his cloak and buy one. For I tell you, this scripture must be fulfilled in me, 'And he was counted among the lawless'; and indeed what is written about me is being fulfilled." They said, "Lord, look, here are two swords." He replied, "It is enough."[28]

Two aspects of this passage make it clear that Jesus is not here authorizing his disciples to use violence. The first aspect that makes this point is the line that begins, "For I tell you. . . ." Luke has Jesus refer to a passage from Isaiah 53:12, part of one of the "suffering servant songs" of Isaiah that Christians have long thought of as predicting the coming of Jesus. That verse says that the servant "was numbered with the transgressors. . . ." Jesus tells his followers to carry a sword so that this scripture will be fulfilled in him. The point apparently is that merely carrying a sword would make Jesus and his band "lawless" (as in Luke) or "transgressors" (as in

---

26. See Matt 15:4 and 19:19; Mark 7:10 and 10:19, and Luke 18:20.

27. It is significant that this Jesus saying from Q reads differently in Luke. At Luke 12:51 Jesus says, "Do you think that I have come to bring peace to the earth? No, I tell you, but rather division." Luke's version of the saying makes it clear that the word "sword" in Matthew's version is a metaphor and is not to be taken literally.

28. Luke 22:35–38.

Isaiah). The second aspect that indicates the nonliteral nature of this passage is Jesus' response when the disciples produce only two swords. He had said that everyone who had no sword must acquire one. Yet when the twelve disciples produce two swords, Jesus says, "It is enough." Two swords are not enough for twelve people if we are to take literally the direction that everyone must acquire a sword. The swords that Jesus approves can serve only a symbolic function. Clearly these verses are here only as a typical New Testament prophecy fulfillment passage and in no way constitute an authorization for Christians to use violence.

Another Gospel story that Christians who choose not to live by their Master's teaching of nonviolence often use as a rationalization for their decision is the story of Jesus overturning the tables of the money changers in the Temple. We considered this story at some length in Chapter Nine as evidence of Jesus' rejection of sacrifice as the proper worship of God. We must now consider these stories further to see whether they in fact justify Christians in resorting to violence. It is clear that they do not. Mark's version of the story is the oldest. It says that Jesus "began to drive out those who were selling and those who were buying in the temple, and he overturned the tables of the money changers and the seats of those who sold doves; and he would not allow anyone to carry anything through the temple."[29] The first thing to notice is that there is no reference in this story to Jesus inflicting physical harm on anyone. He interfered with their business. He "drove" them out, but the text does not say that he used violence to do it. He dramatically upended their tables and their chairs. He disrupted their commerce. He did not harm any of them. The only thing remotely resembling a weapon used in any of the versions of this story appears in John's account. There we read that Jesus made a "whip of cords." He used it, however, only against the livestock that was being sold in the temple, not against the people. John states, "Making a whip of cords, he drove all of them out of the temple, both the sheep and the cattle."[30] He made a whip so he could control the animals, not so he could harm the people.

Jesus here is not engaging in an act of violence against people. He is committing an act of assertive civil disobedience against what he considered to be an improper mode of worship. He is engaging in a prophetic act of the kind used by the ancient Hebrew prophets to make a point

29. Mark 11:15–16.
30. John 2:15.

not with words but with actions.[31] Jesus here commits symbolic actions against sacrificial worship. He commits no physical act of violence against any person. The money changers and the sellers of animals may have been frightened. Jesus probably appeared to them to be quite mad. Most of us would flee an apparent lunatic barging into our places of business and disrupting our work. His actions are the moral equivalent of the actions of so many Christian peace activists who block the entrance to the School of the Americas, or lie across the railroad tracks to stop the movement of a train carrying nuclear weapons. Faithful Christians are arrested every day for conducting sit-ins in government offices to protest war, unjust laws, and destruction of the environment. The Rev. Dr. Martin Luther King Jr. led a throng of people across a bridge in Selma, Alabama, right up to the police lines that had formed to stop the civil rights marchers. Those police officers were probably afraid. There were a lot more marchers than there were police, and the police probably were not all that confident that the marchers would remain peaceful. The fact that acts of civil disobedience in the name of justice may create fear in the hearts of the defenders of injustice does not make those acts of civil disobedience violent. Nonviolent civil disobedience has a long and honorable tradition in Christianity.[32] The story of Jesus overturning the tables of the money changers and driving out the sellers of animals from the temple is the Biblical model for that civil disobedience. It is in no way a justification for the use of violence.

There is another rationalization for Christian violence that is sometimes advanced. I know a very conservative Christian layman, a member of a large, Evangelical church. He attends my church's men's group, not because he shares our progressive theology (which he certainly does not) but because he is a friend and co-worker of one of our members. It seems he likes the fellowship, or maybe he thinks he can convert us. I don't know, and it doesn't matter. One night we got into a discussion of Christian nonviolence. This Christian man dismissed the whole matter by saying that Jesus' prohibition of the use of violence applies to individuals not to governments, and it is governments not individuals who engage in war. He seemed totally innocent of any awareness that "government" is an abstrac-

---

31. A classic example is the Prophet Jeremiah walking around with a yoke around his neck to symbolize the coming subjugation of Judah. See Jer 27:2.

32. My denomination, the United Church of Christ, recognizes this fact in the disclosures it requires those seeking a pastoral call to make. We must disclose any criminal record we may have *except* convictions for acts of civil disobedience.

tion and that the acts of violence that make up warfare are committed by individual men and women not by an abstraction. He cited no Scriptural authority for this surprising position, but his statement reminded me of Paul's statements in Chapter 13 of his Letter to the Romans. There Paul notoriously states, "Let every person be subject to the governing authorities; for there is no authority except from God, and those authorities that exist have been instituted by God."[33] Perhaps our Evangelical friend who has no problem with Christians engaging in war because, as he views it, it is governments not individuals who do it, had this passage in mind. It is a troubling passage, and it deserves closer attention.

The first thing we must concede is that the passage says what it says.[34] There is no exegesis of the passage itself that will change its apparent meaning. In it Paul does indeed tell us to be subject to the existing governments of the world because they are of God. The passage certainly seems to rule out civil disobedience, and it is not too much of a stretch to read it as meaning that we should obey and follow our government even when it leads us into war.

The passage says what it says, but that does not mean that we have to take it at face value or to give up our commitment to Christian nonviolence because of it. It has been suggested that the passage refers to only one specific historical circumstance, that Paul is merely urging the Christians in Rome not to engage in acts of mob violence against Rome's Jews that the Roman government was trying to suppress.[35] That may be,

33. Rom 13:1. I once asked John Dominic Crossan at a public lecture he gave in Seattle how we should respond when this passage is used to refute his contention, with which I fully agree, that both Jesus and Paul were radically anti-imperial. He began his answer by saying that we have to recognize that Paul made some "stupid generalizations." His statement at Romans 13:1 that "there is no authority except from God, and those authorities that exist have been instituted by God" is clearly such a stupid generalization.

34. We do not, however, have to admit that this passage actually comes from Paul. There is good reason to believe that it does not. Perhaps the primary reason for believing that it is pseudonymous is that it so contradicts what we know about Paul's life and other writings, as I explain in the main text at this point. Beyond that, Romans 13:1-7 appears to be an insert into an earlier text. If we take out those verses, the text from Romans 12:9 flows smoothly and logically to Romans 13:8. Romans 13:1-7 on duties toward the state breaks that flow. Those verses don't fit here, and they don't sound like Paul. They may not, therefore, be Paul. In the discussion in the main text that follows I assume that they are Paul for the sake of argument, but the reader should consider that they may not be.

35. Introduction to The Letter of Paul to the Romans in *The New Oxford Annotated Bible, Third Edition,* Michael D Coogan, ed. (Oxford and New York: Oxford University Press, , 2001) 242. In his answer to my question mentioned in footnote 33 above, Crossan

although the text certainly seems to lend itself to wider application. It is more important to note, I believe, that Paul's statement here is inconsistent with other Biblical statements on Christians' relations to the secular authorities, including other statements by Paul himself. At 1 Corinthians 2:6, Paul says that "the rulers of this age" are "doomed to perish." At 1 Corinthians 15:24, he says that at the end time every ruler and every authority and power will be destroyed. These statements certainly seem to contradict the statement in Romans 13:1 that all earthly authority that exists comes from God. Perhaps more importantly, Paul's actions belie his words in Romans 13:1. He was often punished by the earthly authorities for his preaching of the Gospel of Jesus Christ.[36] The Christian tradition teaches that Paul was eventually martyred by the Roman state because of his apostolic work. Paul was hardly a model of obedience to the Roman empire. He preached the Gospel against that state, and it cost him his life. In all he did, Paul preached the Kingdom of God against the kingdoms of the world, especially Rome.[37] It is also certainly true that the earliest Christians understood that Jesus' teachings prohibited violence whether it was individual violence or government sanctioned war, as we saw in our discussion of the Christian just war theory.

What then are we to do with Paul's statement that we should be obedient to the secular state, perhaps even to the point of supporting and participating in its wars? We are to do with it what we are to do with all Bible passages. We try to understand it first of all in its historical context. We try to understand what its words meant in that context. We ask after the specific historical situation to which the words were addressed. Once we think we understand what the passage means, we search it to discover its meaning for us in our historical context, if any. We take the passage not as the words of God but as a human statement that, we assume, reflects the spiritual experience of the person making it.[38] We then seek to discern

---

said that Paul was here trying to prevent Christian-on-Roman violence, something he greatly feared, occasioned by an oppressive tax measure of the Roman government.

36. See 2 Cor 11:23.

37. On the anti-Imperial nature of Paul's teaching see John Dominic Crossan, and Jonathan L. Reed, *In Search of Paul: How Jesus' Apostle Opposed Rome's Empire with God's Kingdom* (San Francisco: HarperSanFrancisco, 2004).

38. That may not, of course, clearly be the case, as Paul's statement at Romans 13:1 certainly seems to contradict the weight of his own spiritual experience, as we have just remarked.

whether the passage is consistent with and supports what we understand to be the larger message of Scripture on the issue. And we seek to discern whether the spiritual experience that the passage seems to express is consistent with our own spiritual experience of God.

When we do that with Romans 13:1, we quickly conclude that it is neither Paul's final word on the subject nor is it consistent with his own life. We conclude that it is inconsistent with other Bible passages. We conclude that it is inconsistent with the teachings of Jesus in the Gospels. And we conclude, or at least I and many other Christians conclude, that Paul's words at Romans 13:1 are inconsistent with our own spiritual experience of a God in Christ who is a God of justice and nonviolence, values that hardly reflect the established authorities of the world. We therefore conclude that Romans 13:1 is not God's binding word for us. It is not true myth for us. We have taken it seriously as we must, but in the end we set it aside as not being a valid expression of the Gospel of Jesus Christ.

Every rationalization at which Christians grasp in an effort to avoid Jesus' teaching of nonviolence ultimately fails. Their efforts to avoid that teaching are understandable. Violence is the way of the world, and we live very much in the world. Maintaining a commitment to nonviolence isn't easy. The world calls us idealistic and unrealistic. It says nonviolence won't work. That statement isn't true, and it is morally irrelevant. Yet those of us who are committed to nonviolence are constantly challenged, as I was one night at the men's group I mentioned: "How many September 11s will it take before you'd fight?" My interrogator intended the question as rhetorical. He was fully prepared to fight after only one. I thought of Peter's question to Jesus: "Lord, if a member of the church sins against me, how often should I forgive? As many as seven times?" And I thought of Jesus' answer: "Not seven times, but, I tell you, seventy-seven times."[39] Nonviolence is not something we maintain when it is easy. It is a way of life. It is the way of the Christian.

2. JESUS' DEMAND FOR ECONOMIC JUSTICE

In the Gospels, Jesus says absolutely nothing about homosexuality, but he says a great deal about justice. Jesus' ministry was largely about justice for the poor. This theme appears strongly in The Gospel of Luke. Luke states this theme of his Gospel at the very beginning, in the birth narrative with

---

39. Matt 18:21–22.

which the Gospel begins. The famous Magnificat, Mary's hymn of praise upon receiving the news that she would give birth to "the Son of the Most High",[40] contains this prophetic line: "He [the Lord] has brought down the powerful from their thrones, and lifted up the lowly; he has filled the hungry with good things, and sent the rich away empty."[41] Thus, Mary announces that lifting up the poor will be a major theme of the life of her son and of the Gospel that follows. In Luke, the good news of Jesus' birth comes first to the poor. That is the significance of the angels bringing good tidings to the shepherds.[42] Shepherds were among the poorest of the poor in Jesus' time. In Luke's account, the good news of Jesus' birth is not good news for the wealthy. It isn't even good news for Gentile sages as it is in Matthew.[43] It is most of all good news for the poor.

Luke makes this point powerfully in his version of the Beatitudes. The first of them reads, "Blessed are you who are poor, for yours is the kingdom of God."[44] Luke will have none of Matthew's spiritualizing of this blessing.[45] In Luke, when Jesus says poor he means poor—economically poor, lacking money and resources, living at a subsistence level, in economic need. Poor people are hungry people, so Luke also has Jesus say, "Blessed are you who are hungry now, for you will be filled."[46] To drive the point home even more powerfully, Luke adds "woes" as a counterpart to the blessings of the poor and the hungry. His Jesus says, "But woe to you who are rich, for you have received your consolation. Woe to you who are full now, for you will be hungry."[47] Luke drives the point home. God cares about the poor. Especially in Luke's presentation, God not only cares for the poor but rejects the rich. Clearly Luke is telling us that as Christians, we too are called to care for the poor. In our context that call certainly means that we are called not only to provide for the material needs of the

---

40. Luke 1:32.
41. Luke 1:52–53.
42. Luke 2:8–14.
43. The reference is to the story of the "wise men" in the Gospel of Matthew (Matt 2:1–12).
44. Luke 6:20.
45. Matthew's version of the same saying reads, "Blessed are the poor in spirit, for theirs is the kingdom of heaven" (Matt 5:3).
46. Luke 6:21a.
47. Luke 6:24–25a.

Christian Social Ethics: The Teachings of Jesus for Our Time

poor but to work to change the social, economic, and political structures that create poverty in the first place.

Luke is not the only Evangelist to express Jesus' concern for the poor. The Gospel of Mark contains the famous story of the rich man who asked Jesus what he must do to "inherit eternal life."[48] When the man assures Jesus that he has kept the commandments of the Law his entire life, Jesus says to him, "You lack one thing: go, sell what you own, and give the money to the poor, and you will have treasure in heaven; then come, follow me."[49] Pastors usually assure their shocked parishioners that Jesus didn't really mean sell all you own and give the money to the poor. They say he just said it to shock this one man out of his smug self-righteousness. Perhaps, but that's not what the text says. The text is at the very least a strong admonition that caring for the poor is a necessary element of, even a prerequisite to, the life of faith.

In Mark's telling of it, Jesus wants to make sure the point is made; so he doesn't stop with telling the man to sell all he owns. He adds a commentary on wealth that shocks and puzzles us to this day. After his exchange with the rich man, Jesus says, "How hard it will be for those who have wealth to enter the kingdom of God!"[50] And, "It is easier for a camel to go through the eye of a needle than for someone who is rich to enter the kingdom of God."[51] Over the centuries Christians have exhibited great creativity in their efforts to explain this statement away. Those of us who are wealthy (wealthy at least when compared to those who are truly poor around the world) don't like it much. Yet we cannot deny that in the Gospels Jesus expresses a preference for the poor.

The social teaching of the Roman Catholic Church, which understands this fact better than most of us Protestants do, expresses this truth by saying that God has a "preferential option for the poor." Jesus' teaching is quite clear. God loves all people, but God especially loves the poor. God wants justice for all people, but God especially wants justice for the poor. As Christians our undeniable call is to care for the poor and to work to alleviate their poverty and the systems that perpetuate it.

---

48. Mark 10:17–22.
49. Mark 10:21.
50. Mark 10:23.
51. Mark 10:25.

The last judgment scene of Matthew 25 is nothing less than a constitution for all Christian social justice work.[52] That vision of Jesus judging the people at the end time is Matthew's great contribution to our understanding of our call as Christians to care for the poor. It is a frightful picture. It envisions Christ returned in glory, sitting upon a throne. "The nations" appear before him.[53] Christ separates the people as a shepherd separates the sheep from the goats. He puts the sheep at his right hand and the goats at his left.[54] The sheep inherit the kingdom. The goats inherit eternal fire. The difference between them is that the sheep saw and cared for Christ in the persons of the poor. Jesus says to the sheep, "For I was hungry and you gave me food, I was thirsty and you gave me something to drink, I was a stranger and you welcomed me, I was naked and you gave me clothing, I was sick and you took care of me, I was in prison and you visited me."[55] The righteous sheep are perplexed because they can't remember ever having done any of those things for Christ. Christ replies, "Truly I tell you, just as you did it to one of the least of these who are members of my family, you did it to me."[56] He tells the goats who are being sent off to hell, who are equally perplexed by their fate: "Truly I tell you, just as you did not do it to one of the least of these, you did not do it to me."[57]

Matthew's parable (for that is what it actually is) makes the teaching perfectly clear. Christians are called to care for the poor. We are called to care for all who are in need. We are called to do nothing less than see the face of Christ in the homeless mother struggling to provide for her children, the refugee fleeing genocide in some war-torn country on the other side of the

---

52. Matt 25:31–46.

53. Matt 25:32. The import of it being "the nations," that is, the Gentiles, that appear before Christ is that God's demand for justice for the poor is universal. It applies even to Gentile nations who are not Christians.

54. Matt 25:32–33. I have never understood what Matthew has against goats, but I suppose it doesn't really matter.

55. Matt 25:35–36.

56. Matt 25:40. Scholars sometimes claim that the reference to "the least of these who are members of my family" refers only to Christ's disciples. See for example the study note to Matthew 25:40 in *The HarperCollins Study Bible* (New York: HarperCollins, 1993). Even if that is what Matthew intended, surely the meaning of the phrase is not so limited for us. Those who in the eyes of the world are "the least," the poor, the marginalized, and the imprisoned, are hardly limited to Christians.

57. Matt 25:45.

globe, the inmate in our prisons whom we are so comfortable condemning and whom we would rather forget exists. We can pretend that we are not called to do so, and we usually do. The Jesus of the Gospels, however, will not let us ignore his call for long. The Christian life is a life of caring for the poor and working for social and economic justice for all people.

One tragedy of contemporary American Christianity is that it has forgotten this truth. The "religious right" arouses the passions of the faithful against abortion and against the equal rights and dignity of God's gay and lesbian children. Christian values get reduced to caring more about the survival of a fetus regardless of the circumstances of its conception than about the welfare of poor children living without adequate housing, clothing, food, medical care, and education. Rather than demand that society be transformed into a place of justice for the poor, Christians mobilize to prevent justice being done for sexual minorities. If Jesus were in his grave, he'd be spinning in it.[58] Liberating Christianity clearly requires

---

58. In March, 2007, The Discovery Channel, a cable TV channel, aired a film, and HarperSanFrancisco published a book, in which Simcha Jacobovici, an Israeli documentary filmmaker and amateur archaeologist, claims to have discovered "The Lost Tomb of Jesus." The claim rests upon the discovery in 1980 of a first century CE family tomb in Jerusalem that housed ossuaries inscribed with the names, among others, of "Jesus son of Joseph" and "Maria." Most serious scholars have dismissed the claim that this tomb belonged to Jesus' family as pure speculation based upon bad science and bad archaeology. I too believe that the claim that this tomb belonged to Jesus and his family and that one of the ossuaries contained his bones to be very unlikely as an historical matter. I leave the critique of the science and the ancient linguistics of the claim up to the experts in those fields. I will only point out that Jacobovici's argument that an ossuary with the name "Mariamne" in Greek is the ossuary of Mary Magdalene seems particularly weak, based as it is upon the use of that name in the Gospel of Philip, a late second century or third century gospel that can hardly be considered a credible source for the history of the first century. Beyond that, it seems nearly conclusive to me that this tomb was in Jerusalem and the Holy Family wasn't from Jerusalem. They were from Nazareth. If they had a family tomb at all it would be in that Galilean city, not in Jerusalem. Moreover, as the family of a "*tekton*," usually translated "carpenter" but more properly "stonemason," they would have been too poor to have had a family tomb at all. Yet the more important point is that even if this claim is true it has no significance for liberated Christianity. I agree completely with John Dominic Crossan, who appears in the film. He is asked if the claim, if true, would destroy Christian faith. He answers, somewhat bemusedly, "it would not destroy *my* Christian faith." The truth of Christianity properly understood is symbolic and mythic not literal and factual. It does not depend upon the historical factualness of a physical resurrection that left Jesus' tomb empty. We can therefore comfortably leave the question of the "lost tomb of Jesus" to the amateur archaeologists and filmmakers. It certainly doesn't matter to us.

us to call the faith back to what it really stands for, justice for all people, and especially for the poor.

3. JESUS' RADICAL INCLUSIVITY: PURITY VS. COMPASSION

If Jesus' ministry on earth was about anything more than it was about justice for the poor, it was about inclusion for those whom society excludes. It was about putting compassion over personal piety or purity. It is difficult for modern people to understand just how radical Jesus' message of inclusivity and compassion for all was because we have forgotten how people in Jesus' time lived. We have forgotten what the religious and societal norms of his day were. In short, we have forgotten the power that the Levitical purity or holiness code had over the religious and social life of the people in Jesus' time. At that time, Judaism was largely about purity. The function of the Law, meaning, of course, the Law of Moses especially as it is presented in the Book of Leviticus, was to distinguish between people who were ritually pure and those who were not, and a great many things could render a person ritually impure or unclean. In those days almost everyone was poor, and almost everyone who was poor was impure for one reason or another. Failure to pay the Temple tax made one ritually impure, even if paying it meant you had nothing left to live on.[59] Women were not impure per se, but a woman was impure during her menstrual period. Non-Jews were impure. Shepherds were impure simply because they were shepherds.[60] Anyone who collaborated with the Romans was impure. Anyone who committed an immoral sexual act was impure. Persons with a great variety of illnesses, from skin diseases to mental illness, were impure. The list went on and on.

Being considered impure had consequences. Being impure made one a sinner. Purity was what was required for a person to be right with God. A person who was impure could not enter the Temple to offer the required sacrifices to God. A person who was impure was socially shunned. The "righteous," that is, those who met the requirements of the purity code, were not to associate with them in any way. Contact with an impure person rendered the person having the contact impure and

---

59. We have already considered this dynamic in our discussion above of the story of the "widow's mite."

60. Luke's making the first announcement of the birth of Jesus come to the shepherds takes on added meaning in light of this fact.

required that person to undergo some kind of cleansing ritual, perhaps involving a ritual bath or a specified animal sacrifice. The purity system is the background, for most of us the lost background, of most of Jesus' ministry as it is reported in the synoptic Gospels. A few examples will perhaps make the point clearer.

We've probably all heard of the charge against Jesus that he "ate with tax collectors and sinners." Thus in the Gospel of Matthew, we read, "When the Pharisees saw this, they said to his disciples, 'Why does your teacher eat with tax collectors and sinners?'"[61] What so appalled the Pharisees, those guardians of the purity laws, was that Jesus was associating with people who were considered impure. That is what "sinners" here means, people who somehow were out of compliance with the purity code. The Pharisees could not understand why Jesus, a teacher and presumably someone who himself was ritually pure, would violate the purity code by associating with those who were not. An understanding of the operation of the purity code in Jesus time affects our understanding of many of the incidents and parables in the Gospels. We will look at two of them to illustrate the point, the story of the woman with the twelve-year flow of blood from Mark and the Parable of the Good Samaritan from Luke.

The story of the woman with the twelve-year flow of blood is short. It reads:

> Then suddenly a woman who had been suffering from hemorrhages for twelve years came up behind him and touched the fringe of his cloak, for she said to herself, "If I only touch his cloak, I will be made well." Jesus turned, and seeing her he said, "Take heart, daughter; your faith has made you well." And instantly the woman was made well.[62]

It is probably not clear to us that this story is about Jesus' rejection of the purity code of his time, but it is. The woman was bleeding. Any blood was considered impure, and contact with blood made one impure. Any woman who was menstruating was impure, and the assumption here is that this woman's bleeding was uncontrolled menstrual bleeding. According to the religious and social norms of the day, Jesus should have been outraged that this impure woman, this sinner, dared to touch him. It was bad enough that a woman had touched a man to whom she was not

61. Matt 9:11.
62. Mark 9:20–22.

married in public. That was forbidden too, but this woman was a sinner; she was impure. Her touch should have required Jesus himself to undergo some ritual of purification. Jesus should have condemned and rejected her, but he didn't. He comforted her, he affirmed her, and he healed her. He accepted the outcast. He included the excluded. He rejected purity and replaced it with compassion.

Although most of us take a different lesson from it, the Parable of the Good Samaritan makes the same point.[63] It is a familiar story. Jesus tells of a man who traveled down the road from Jerusalem to Jericho. He was attacked by robbers, "who stripped him, beat him, and went away, leaving him half dead."[64] Two officials of the Temple in Jerusalem, a priest and a Levite,[65] passed by, one after the other. Both of them saw the man but just passed him by. They did nothing to help the unfortunate traveler lying beaten and bloody by the side of the road. Then a Samaritan, that is, a non-Jew from the region of Samaria north of Judea, came along. This man was "moved with pity."[66] He went to the man, bandaged his wounds and cleansed them with oil and wine. He put the man on his own animal and took him to an inn to care for him. The next day, when the Samaritan presumably had to continue his own journey, he gave money to the innkeeper with instructions to care for the man until the Samaritan returned, at which time, he promised, he would pay the innkeeper for any additional expenses he incurred. Jesus affirms the actions of the Samaritan, saying to the person to whom he was telling the story "Go and do likewise."[67]

To us the story is about acting with compassion toward the misfortunate, and indeed it does contain that important moral. Yet in its original setting the story would have had another meaning that we miss because we miss its significance for the purity code of the time, indeed for all religion that defines morality in terms of purity. It is the presence of the priest and the Levite that introduces purity into this story. We usually think of them as heartless, uncaring people, but that is not necessarily the case. As officials of the Temple, they were bound by the purity code in a particularly powerful way. If they became impure, they could not perform their

---

63. Luke 10:25–37.
64. Luke 10:30.
65. A Levite is a kind of assistant to the priests.
66. Luke 10:33.
67. Luke 10:37b.

duties in the Temple without undergoing a purification ritual. Moreover, they were professional guardians of the purity code. The reason they did not help the beaten man is not because they were heartless. They may or may not have been. Either way, they did not help the beaten man because, regardless of what they may have felt, under the purity code they could not. They could not risk becoming defiled and impure. The victim of the robbers had been beaten and left "half dead." We can assume that he was bloody. Contact with blood would have rendered the Temple officials impure. They may have thought he was dead. Contact with a dead body also rendered a person impure. They *had* to pass by on the other side. The purity code required it of them. In passing by rather than stopping to help the beaten man, they were simply being true to their religion.

And Jesus would have none of it. He didn't care that the priest and the Levite were being faithful to God's will as they understood it. For him compassion trumped purity every time. The point is made even stronger because the person in the story of whose actions Jesus approved was himself unclean. He was a Samaritan. The Samaritans traced their ancestry back to the patriarch Jacob, but the Jews did not consider them to be co-religionists. The Jews of Jesus' day despised the Samaritans and avoided all contact with them. That a Jewish teacher would approve the actions of a despised Samaritan over the actions of righteous guardians of the law, a priest and a Levite, was simply outrageous. Jesus didn't care. For him, compassion trumped hatred every time. The Parable of the Good Samaritan is a radical rejection of purity as the standard of righteousness and correct faith as the standard of morality.

In his rejection of purity as the standard of morality, Jesus included where his society and the religious authorities of his time excluded. He reached out where they pushed away. He acted with compassion where they acted with judgment. He calls us to do the same. No religion that claims to act in the name of Jesus Christ can ground its ethics, personal or social, in anything other than inclusivity and compassion. Jesus reached out to the poor, the powerless, and the marginalized in his society and told them that God loved them and accepted them. He even told them that they were God's favorites. He stood the social and religious conventions of his time on their head. His culture saw poverty, illness, and disability as signs of God's disfavor. He saw God's compassion touching all who needed it. He calls us to do no less. No social ethic of judgment and exclusion can claim him as its Lord.

4. HOMOSEXUALITY: THE DEFINING ISSUE OF OUR TIME

Jesus' rejection of the purity code of his time has direct significance for the most heated and the most visible issue dividing Christian churches in America today, the issue of the proper Christian understanding of and relationship to homosexuality. The common perception is that Christians consider homosexual behavior to be immoral per se. The leaders of the Christian right have had great success spurring their followers to effective political activity on behalf of conservative causes by raising the specter of "gay marriage," which they claim (with no rational justification) is a threat to "traditional marriage" and "family values." They have organized successful efforts in many states to pass amendments to state constitutions limiting marriage to traditional heterosexual couples, denying all the while that they advocate discrimination against God's gay and lesbian children.[68]

Many Christians today understand the matter differently. Their views have received considerable publicity because of the struggles that are going on within some of the traditional Christian denominations in the United States over the issue. The Presbyterian Church U.S.A. and the United Methodist Church in particular have been wracked with controversy. It may well be that the only reason these denominations have not fractured over the issue is their connectional polity, in which the local churches do not own their own buildings and other property. It is therefore extremely difficult for a congregation that disagrees with the decisions of the national body, whether in favor of full acceptance of gay and lesbian people or against it, to break away from the denomination. The Episcopal Church has gotten a great deal of publicity over its decision in 2003 to consecrate an openly gay priest as bishop of the New Hampshire diocese and the virulent reaction against that decision by some Episcopal churches and dioceses in the United States and a great many other churches of the Anglican Communion around the world, especially in Africa and Asia. My own United Church of Christ has been a pioneer in the full acceptance of gay and lesbian people, but even here the matter has not been without controversy. The UCC has lost membership and churches over the actions of its General Synod in support of the "Open

---

68. For the sake of brevity I will refer to gay and lesbian people. I do not mean to exclude bisexual and transgendered people, as I know that those ways of being are also naturally occurring varieties of human sexuality. The analysis of homosexuality here applies to these people as well.

and Affirming" movement, the gay acceptance movement in the denomination. Most recently, we have lost people and churches because of the decision of the 2005 General Synod to endorse same-gender marriage.[69] The issue of homosexuality has become the hot button issue in American Christianity today.

My experience working on this issue in the Pacific Northwest Conference of the UCC has convinced me that, as important as the issue of homosexuality is in its own right, it has become as volatile as it has because it goes directly to the heart of a more fundamental issue for Christians today. Any discussion of homosexuality in the church leads immediately and directly to the issue of the nature of Biblical authority. It leads directly to that issue because, although the matter is more complex than it may appear on the surface as we shall see, it cannot be denied that the very few Biblical references to homosexual acts view such acts negatively and even harshly condemn them. The opponents of the equal rights and dignity of gay and lesbian people cite those few references and consider that these proof texts (as they see them) end the discussion. I have already discussed the issue of Biblical authority at some length in this work. I will not repeat that discussion now. For liberated and liberating Christianity as I have developed it here, the mere fact that some passage in the Bible supports, or can be made to seem to support, a particular position is in no way dispositive. Yet discussion of the issue between the opposing sides is made difficult not merely by the fact that people disagree about homosexuality but because they disagree about the nature of Biblical authority. The issue of homosexuality in the church will never be resolved as long as a significant number of people believe that Biblical condemnations of homosexual acts end the discussion.

That being said, there are still reasons for looking closely at those few texts. We will examine the two most important of them, Leviticus 18:22 and Romans 1:26–27. Before we do, however, we need to deal with one other Biblical issue. The story of Sodom and Gomorrah in the Book of Genesis[70] is sometimes cited as a Biblical condemnation of homosexuality. We can state unequivocally that it is not. In that story two angels, who

---

69. We have also gained churches as a result, most notably the Cathedral of Hope in Dallas, Texas, a predominantly gay and lesbian congregation that became the fourth largest church in the UCC when it was accepted into membership by the UCC's North Texas Association in 2006.

70. Gen. 19:1–26.

appear simply to be men, come to Sodom. A man named Lot sees them and invites them to spend the night at his house. After some urging the men agree. Later that evening, "the men of the city, the men of Sodom, both young and old, all the people to the last man, surrounded the house; and they called to Lot, 'Where are the men who came to you tonight? Bring them out to us, so that we may know them.'"[71] The phrase "so that we may know them" means that the crowd wanted to gang rape the visitors. Lot refuses to turn his guests over to the mob. The men then warn Lot to get his family out of the city because God was about to destroy it for its wickedness. They get their host and his family out of town, then God destroys both Sodom and Gomorrah with "sulfur and fire from the Lord out of heaven."[72]

The story of Sodom and Gomorrah has nothing to do with homosexuality. There are two bases for this conclusion. The first is that because the mob that threatened Lot's visitors included all the men of the city, most of those men were straight, not gay. Statistically, most men are straight. There is no reason to believe that this mob would have been any different. Certainly the author of the story believed them to be what we would call straight since, as we will discuss further below, the ancient world had no conception of homosexuality as a naturally occurring variety of human sexuality.

Beyond that, the dynamic of the story is not about sex, it is about hospitality. In the ancient Middle East there was, and indeed in the desert cultures of the Middle East to this day there is, a powerful ethic that requires the people of a settled area to provide food and shelter to alien travelers in their midst. The reason for this ethic is clear enough. Without it no one would be able to survive traveling across that arid and rugged country. Being left without food, water, and shelter was, and is, a sure death sentence. In extending his hospitality to the two men, Lot was complying with this ethical demand of his culture. The story teller in Genesis reinforces Lot's commitment to this ethic by having the two men first decline his offer of hospitality and then accept it only after Lot presses it upon them.[73]

---

71. Gen 19:4–5.
72. Gen 19:24.
73. Gen 19:2–3.

The sin of the men of Sodom then is not homosexuality or even a desire to engage in a homosexual act with the visitors. Their primary sin is that they violated the ethic of hospitality. Lot had extended to the men the protection of his home. The mob wanted to take that protection away from them. The fact that they wanted to gang rape them simply makes their violation of the ethic of hospitality all the more egregious.[74] So let us leave the story of Sodom and Gomorrah off to the side where it belongs. It has nothing to do with the issue of the morality of homosexuality.

The primary text that opponents of gay rights use to support their position that all homosexual behavior is necessarily immoral in all contexts is Leviticus 18:22, which reads, "You shall not lie with a male as with a woman; it is an abomination." Less often cited except by extreme bigots like Fred Phelps is the corollary passage, Leviticus 20:13, which reads, "If a man lies with a male as with a woman, both of them have committed an abomination; they shall be put to death; their blood is upon them." We cannot, and do not, deny that these passages condemn as worthy of death sexual relations between two men. On their face they do. The issue for us is not what the words of Leviticus are but whether those words are the eternal and binding will and law of God, as those who would continue the church's legacy of hatred toward gay and lesbian people contend.[75]

The answer surely is that they are not. Perhaps the major reason that this condemnation of all homosexual acts between men[76] is not binding on us is that the ancient world had no conception of homosexuality as a nat-

74. It should be clear that the most that can be said about any condemnation of sexual behavior in the story is that it condemns gang rape. Of course gang rape is immoral, and no moral person would dream of arguing otherwise.

75. I am, of course, well aware that Christians who condemn homosexuality as inherently sinful generally deny that they hate homosexual people, or perhaps better, people who have engaged in homosexual behavior (since these Christians generally deny that homosexuality is a natural and inherent personal characteristic for some people). Having given the matter much thought, I have concluded that these denials of hatred are unconvincing. The Christians who make them may not feel the emotion hatred toward homosexual people. The fact remains, however, that they condemn and reject an intimate and intrinsic part of these persons' humanity. In doing that they necessarily condemn and reject the people themselves, since our sexuality cannot be separated from the rest of our being. If condemning and rejecting a person is not hatred, I do not know what is.

76. The author of Leviticus apparently did not care enough about women even to condemn their homosexual acts as he did the homosexual acts of men. Or perhaps he really did not consider lesbian acts to be the abomination that he thought sexual acts between men were. Either way, Leviticus 18:22 and 20:13 can be used to condemn lesbian acts only by analogy. They don't mention them.

urally occurring variety of human sexuality. That understanding is of very recent origin. Only in 1973, for example, did the American Psychological Association remove homosexuality from its Diagnostic and Statistical Manual of Psychological Disorders. People in ancient times simply assumed that everyone was what we would call heterosexual. They did not even have words for homosexual and heterosexual. Cultures do not produce words for concepts they do not have. Leviticus 18:22 does not say "homosexuality" is an abomination. It calls lying "with a male as with a woman" an abomination. The assumption is that sexual relations between men and women are the norm for everyone. One reason Leviticus condemns male homosexual acts is that they were considered unnatural, for everyone. We know better. We know that while same gender sexual relations are not natural for the majority of people, for those whom we call heterosexual, they are natural for some people. The Levitical condemnation of male homosexual acts is grounded in and reflects an ancient anthropological understanding. That understanding has changed. The modern understanding of human sexuality has rendered Leviticus 18:22 irrelevant.

The text of Leviticus itself reveals another reason Leviticus condemns same-gender male sexual acts. Leviticus 18:22 is part of the Levitical holiness code, the same holiness or purity code that Jesus so forcefully rejected.[77] One of the primary purposes of the holiness or purity code is to keep the Hebrew people separate and different from the Canaanites, the people of the land the Hebrews were to inhabit. Thus the code states, "You shall not do as they do in the land of Egypt, where you lived, and you shall not do as they do in the land of Canaan, to which I am bringing you. You shall not follow their statutes."[78] Leviticus is a book written by and to a considerable extent for Jewish priests after the return from Babylon in the late sixth century BCE. Their concerns are not our concerns. Maintaining the identity of sixth century Jews is not a concern of ours. Indeed, it is not a concern of at least the more progressive of our Jewish brothers and sisters, many of whom have views on homosexuality similar to the one

---

77. The term holiness code means the same thing as purity code. It comes from the frequent admonitions in Leviticus that the people are to be holy. Leviticus 19:2, for example, reads, "Speak to all the congregation of the people of Israel and say to them: You shall be holy, for I the Lord your God am holy."

78. Lev 18:3.

expressed here.[79] Leviticus deals with ancient concerns on the basis of ancient understandings. It is not God's law for us.

The frequent use of Leviticus 18:22 by opponents of the equal rights and dignity of gay and lesbian people raises another significant issue, the issue of the selective use of Scripture. As we have said, Leviticus 18:22 is part of a much larger holiness code. That code contains numerous prohibitions and requirements that no one today (except perhaps the ultra-Orthodox Jews in Israel who want to bring back animal sacrifice because it is commanded in the Bible) pays any attention to. The Leviticus holiness code prohibits all contact with a woman during her menstrual period.[80] It condones the purchase and ownership of slaves, provided only that they come from neighboring nations.[81] It prohibits eating seafood that does not have scales and fins, i.e., shellfish.[82] It provides that no person with any physical defect may serve as priest.[83] It prohibits planting two different crops in the same field or wearing garments of mixed fibers.[84] These are but some of the prohibitions in the holiness code of Leviticus that even the most vehement opponents of the rights of gay and lesbian people ignore. Indeed, in my experience, most of them are not even aware of these other provisions of Leviticus. I do not deny accepting some of the Bible as authentic and authoritative and rejecting other parts as false. I have tried to explain my basis for doing that in this book. The problem with those on the other side of the gay rights issue is not that they read Scripture selectively. The problem is that they deny doing so, or, in the case of many less sophisticated Christians, are not even aware that they do so.[85] They there-

---

79. The only Jewish wedding I have ever attended was a "wedding" of two women in a Reformed Jewish synagogue.

80. Lev 15:19–24.

81. Lev 25:44.

82. Lev 11:10.

83. Lev 21:16–21.

84. Lev 19:19.

85. After my church had received considerable local publicity for being Open and Affirming, a woman who I do not know called me up and asked me how I could claim to be a Christian pastor if I teach things contrary to Scripture. During that conversation I asked her if she ever wore clothes made of mixed fibers, a cotton-wool blend for example. She said yes, she supposed that she did. I told her that Leviticus prohibits that too. She said incredulously, "It does?" I assured her that it does. She was surprised, but I will give her her due. She at least tried to be consistent. She said, "Well then I suppose we shouldn't do it."

fore do not articulate the basis for their selection, something that makes discussion with them all the more difficult. A great many Christians use Leviticus 18:22 selectively to harm gay and lesbian people by denying their full and equal God-given human dignity. Liberating Christianity in our context requires that we expose the fallacy and even the hypocrisy in their use of the Bible.

Some unsophisticated Christians, unaware that the Christian tradition condemned Marcionism as a heresy more than a millennium and a half ago,[86] counter any rejection of Leviticus by saying something like, "Well, it's in the Old Testament. So you can ignore it. But the New Testament says the same thing." In making this claim they are referring primarily to Romans 1:26–27. Opponents of the equality of gay and lesbian people also use this verse to say that because the New Testament affirms Leviticus 18:22 but not much of the rest of the Levitical holiness code that one verse from the code remains valid while the others do not. Upon examination, however, it turns out that Romans 1:26–27 does not support their position either.

Unlike Leviticus 18:22, Romans 1:26–27 is a very complex passage. In the first chapter of Romans, Paul contends that even pagans who have not had the Jewish law to guide them are accountable for sin because "what can be known about God is plain to them, because God has shown it to them."[87] God's "eternal power and divine nature" have always been revealed "through the things he has made."[88] Paul's argument is essentially one from natural law, in which the truth about God is evident to all who will seek it. Yet the pagans did not seek and discover the truth about God in God's works of creation. Instead, they descended into idolatry: "Claiming to be wise, they became fools; and they exchanged the glory of the immortal God for images resembling a mortal human being or birds or four-footed animals or reptiles."[89]

Because of their idolatry, which they could have avoided though they were without the Law, God inflicted punishment upon the pagans. Because

---

86. Marcion held that Christ had superceded the Law and that Hebrew Scripture was therefore no longer Scripture for Christians. The Church held otherwise. The Hebrew Bible is also part of the Christian Bible. We cannot dispose of things in it simply by saying that it is the "Old Testament" and therefore not applicable to us.

87. Rom 1:19.

88. Rom 1:20.

89. Rom 1:22–23.

they "worshiped and served the creature rather than the Creator ... God gave them up to degrading passions."[90] Those degrading passions included homosexual acts. In a passage that includes the only reference to lesbian sexual acts in the entire Bible Paul wrote:

> Their women exchanged natural intercourse for unnatural, and in the same way also the men, giving up natural intercourse with women, were consumed with passion for one another. Men committed shameless acts with men and received in their own persons the due penalty for their error.[91]

The first thing to note about this passage is that homosexuality is not itself the sin that Paul is condemning. He is condemning idolatry. Homosexual behavior is the penalty, not itself the sin. Beyond that, the reason that Paul considers homosexual behavior to be a punishment is that it is unnatural. Paul assumed that both female and male homosexual relations were unnatural for the people who engaged in them. We know, however, that that is not true for men and women with a naturally occurring homosexual orientation. For them, heterosexual relations are unnatural and homosexual ones are natural.

Like everyone else in the ancient world, Paul had no such understanding. The only male homosexual behavior with which he was familiar was probably the Greek practice of pederasty, in which an older man took a young man or even a boy essentially as a sex slave. If that practice is your only image of homosexual behavior, of course you condemn it. Paul simply had no awareness of natural homosexuality. He had never experienced the kind of loving, mutual, committed, and faithful same gender unions with which we are, or if we'll just look can be, familiar today. Like Leviticus 18:22, Romans 1:26–27 is not an expression of the immutable will of God. It is an expression of an ancient cultural understanding leading to what we call prejudice.

We have insisted in this work that the Bible becomes true myth for us; that is, it truly connects us with God and God with us, when we hold it up to the mirror of our own experience of God to see whether or not a particular Bible passage agrees with and confirms or contradicts that experience. Because all truth is grounded in perception and experience, including even Biblical truth, we can and indeed must trust our own ex-

---

90. Rom 1:25–26.
91. Rom 1:26b–27.

perience of God, even when the Bible seems to contradict it. The passages we have examined here, and the very few others that mention homosexual acts, contradict my experience of homosexuality. They contradict the experiences of a great many people today, both straight and gay. For me, as a heterosexual man, homosexuality is unnatural. For my many gay and lesbian friends, it is natural. It is an intrinsic, God-given part of who they are in exactly the same way that my heterosexuality is for me. The use of the Bible to condemn these children of God simply for being who they are is an abuse of our tradition's holy book. It will not stand. Because it is such a major obstacle to faith in our context today, liberated and liberating Christianity must and will overcome it.

Questions for Reflection and Discussion

A. JESUS' "THIRD WAY" OF CREATIVE NONVIOLENCE.

1. What does Jesus teach us about nonviolence as an imperative of the Christian life:

    By his words?

    By his life?

2. Are Jesus' teachings on nonviolence binding on Christians today?

    Why or why not?

3. Are Jesus' life and death a model of nonviolence for Christians today?

    Why or why not?

4. Is it ever legitimate for Christians to use violence?

    If so, under what circumstances?

    How, if at all, do you reconcile any resort to violence with the teachings of Jesus?

    Is there a Biblical basis for a Christian use of violence?

    If so, what is it?

    If so, why did Jesus reject the attempts of some of his followers to save him from arrest through violence?

5. Is Jesus' teaching on nonviolence a call to passivism, to passive acceptance of evil?

    Why, or why not?

6. Is there a danger of perpetuating suffering and injustice in Jesus' teaching on nonviolence?

    If so, what is it?

    How can we avoid it?

7. Does it matter who is urging nonviolence on people?

    If it is an advocate for victims of injustice?

    If it is a defender of oppressive social, economic, and political systems?

If so, is it legitimate for victims of oppression to resort to violence against their oppressors?

Why or why not?

8. Can you think of any war in human history that fits all of the criteria of classical just war doctrine?

Which war?

9. Many people who like the idea of a commitment to nonviolence nonetheless resist making the commitment out of a belief that violence is more "effective" than nonviolence.

Can you think of cases where violence has effectively brought about peace and justice?

How, if at all, could the same result have been achieved through nonviolent means?

Can you think of cases where nonviolence has effectively brought about peace and justice?

Do you agree that nonviolence is ineffective?

Why or why not?

Does effectiveness matter in making a moral decision?

B. JESUS' DEMAND FOR ECONOMIC JUSTICE.

1. Is the Gospel political?

    What does political mean?

2. What does "justice" mean in the Bible?

    Due process?

    Fairness in business deals?

    Giving charity to those in need?

    Restructuring societies to remove the causes of poverty?

    All or some of the above?

    Something else entirely?

3. Read Amos 4:1–3, 5:10–13 and 21–24; and 6:4–7; Micah 4:1–4; and Isaiah 1:16–24.

    What is the image of God in these passages from some of the great eighth century BCE writing prophets?

How did Jesus relate to Bible passages like these?

Was their God his God?

Do these Biblical passages shed any light on Jesus' teachings about economic justice?

About the nature of that teaching?

Or about its sources?

4. Do you see the face of Christ in the homeless person begging on the street corner?

Do you think you should?

5. In the Sermon on the Mount, Jesus says, "Give to everyone who begs from you" (Matthew 5:42a)

Do you?

Why?

Why not?

C. JESUS' RADICAL INCLUSIVITY

1. Does God require purity from us?

If so, what is that purity and why does God require it?

2. Are there modern day Pharisees, that is, those more concerned with compliance religious laws than with compassion?

If so, who are they?

Why do you think they place so much emphasis on compliance with laws?

3. In the Parable of the Good Samaritan:

Who today are the priest and the Levite who pass by the beaten man?

Who today is the beaten man left beside the road half dead?

Who today is the Good Samaritan?

D: HOMOSEXUALITY: THE DEFINING ISSUE OF OUR TIME

1. What did you learn about human sexuality as you grew up?

What specifically did you learn about homosexuality?

2. Regardless of what your personal sexual orientation is, did you:

   Choose it at some point?

   Discover it as part of your humanity as you matured?

3. Christian social conservatives often say that contemporary American society favors homosexuals and encourages homosexuality.

   Do you agree or disagree?

   Why?

4. Christian social conservatives say that same-gender marriage threatens traditional heterosexual marriage as an institution.

   Do you agree?

   Why, or why not?

   If you are in a traditional heterosexual marriage, do *you* feel threatened by same-gender marriage?

   Why or why not?

   If you disagree with the claim that same-gender marriage threatens traditional heterosexual marriage, why do you think that the Christian right insists that it does?

5. Some socially conservative Christians operate what they call ministries that aim to "cure" a person with a homosexual orientation and to change that orientation to heterosexual.

   Do you believe that such a change is possible?

   Why, or why not?

   Do you believe that such a change is desirable?

   Why, or why not?

Epilogue

What Do We Do Now?

THE CHRISTIAN FAITH IS in crisis in North America today. In this work, I have tried to analyze what I see as the basic causes of that crisis and to suggest ways in which the crisis might be resolved. Resolving the crisis in American Christianity must begin with recapturing the reality of the spiritual along with the symbolic nature of all religion. With that renewed understanding of the fundamental character of faith we can overcome the Biblicism, the unacceptable theology, and the reactionary social ethics that act as barriers to the Christian faith for a majority of people in our context as the dominant culture in North America. Liberating Christianity must begin with such a re-envisioning of Christian theology. Theology is foundational. It is indispensable. No religious movement can long endure without a solid theological foundation that appeals to the people of the movement's context and that makes the religion accessible to those people. I hope that this work will be at least a modest contribution to that necessary effort.

Liberating Christianity begins with theology, but it cannot end with theology. Theology far too often remains a matter solely of academic interest. Academic theologians far too often speak only to other academic theologians. Indeed, our faith finds itself in such a crisis today in large part because the insights of academic theologians over the last century or more have not been widely disseminated in the church. As I noted in the Introduction, academically trained ministers of the church have largely declined to share the theological learning they acquired in seminary with the lay people of the church out of fear that the people will not accept new and challenging ways of understanding the faith. We professional ministers have far too often played the role of Dostoevsky's Grand Inquisitor, protecting the people from the truth rather than sharing it with them. The result has been that Biblicist Christianity has swept the field, leaving us Christians with a better vision on the sidelines wondering what hit us. Biblicist Christianity, with its bloodthirsty God demanding the shedding of innocent blood and with its narrow morality grounded not in grace and love but in ancient cultural prejudices, has monopolized the popular understanding of the faith because those of us with a better vision have remained too silent for too long. In our silence, we have been complicit in the hijacking of our great faith by reactionary elements that fear the accomplishments of the human spirit and seek to tie Christianity up in a straightjacket of literalism and narrow, judgmental morality. We have yielded the floor to the voices of those who define Christian values as opposition to the equal dignity of gay and lesbian people and to the right of women to make their own reproductive decisions. We have stood far too quietly by as Christ's values of nonviolence and radical justice have been ignored at best and perverted at worst.

The time for our silence is over. If we truly wish to save Christianity, we must now speak up boldly, loudly, constantly, and in great numbers. We must tell the world every chance we get that Christianity does not require us to deny our God-given intellectual capacities, as the anti-intellectualism of popular American Christianity insists that we do. We must tell the world every chance we get that Christianity properly understood calls for the recognition of the equal rights and dignity of *all* people and not only of those who live in a way that the vociferous leaders of the religious right insist is the only moral way, an insistence that truly is nothing but ancient prejudice wrapped up in a covering of Bible verses chosen not because they truly express the will of God but because they reinforce the prejudices of our culture. We must tell the world every chance we get that true Christianity does not support American imperialism abroad and policies that favor the rich at the expense of the poor at home. We must advance the Christian values of nonviolence and radical justice as powerfully as others have advanced the un-Christian values of war and economic exploitation of the powerless and marginalized at home and around the world. We must tell the world every chance we get that true Christianity celebrates the world's religious diversity and rejoices when people find their connection with God, be that through Christianity or through another of world's great faiths. We must tell the world every chance we get that true Christianity supports the separation of church

Epilogue

and state because it treasures freedom for all of God's people. The time for our silence is over. We must speak up.

But how? It isn't easy. Those of us who are members of a Christian church can begin by speaking up in church, by calling our church and our denomination if we have one to fidelity to true Christian values. If your pastor preaches against homosexual people, call her on it. If your denomination adopts resolutions at any level that discriminate against any group, support war, or support unjust economic policies and policies that despoil the environment, get involved. Demand that your denomination change course. If all else fails, withhold your financial support until your church adopts positions more in tune with true Christian values. Far too often, a decision to continue supporting a group with which we disagree so we can "work from the inside" to bring about change only helps perpetuate the stagnation of an institution badly in need of transformation. Our churches will not become more faithful to the Gospel of Jesus Christ until we show that we will not continue to support them until they do.

Yet speaking up inside the church is not enough. Christianity is in crisis only in part because of what the churches are doing. It is in crisis mostly because so many people stand outside the churches refusing to have anything to do with them. The task of Christian apologetics is to reach those people, and to reach them we must venture outside of our churches and into the larger public arena. Doing that can be far more difficult than speaking up in the familiar and relatively safe environment of a church. We can do it individually by talking to the people we know, writing letters to the editor of our local papers identifying ourselves as Christians and advocating progressive social and political policies, and letting our elected leaders know that not all people of faith are social conservatives. We can become active *as Christians* in local politics, speaking out for civil rights protection for all people, for example, and opposing attempts by Biblical literalists to hijack the public education system.

Education is the key. If you found this book helpful, lead an adult education series on it at your church. Or lead a series on one of the other very helpful books that are available to introduce people to non-Biblicist Christianity. Marcus Borg's book *The Heart of Christianity*, that I have mentioned and cited several times in this work, is particularly useful. If you have friends who call themselves spiritual but who resist or reject Christianity, invite them to your series. If you don't feel up to leading a series yourself, ask your pastor to do it or find someone else who can and

Epilogue

will. We will never liberate Christianity by quietly acquiescing in the perpetuation of the Biblicist version of the faith. We must teach people both inside the churches and outside them that there is a better alternative.

All of these individual things are important, yet individual action alone is not enough. That is why organizations like Jim Wallis' Sojourners, The Center for Progressive Christianity, and Rabbi Lerner's Network of Spiritual Progressives are so important.[1] Collective activity is always more effective than individual activity. Joining and supporting local and national progressive spiritual organizations is an important way of spreading the word that spirituality can be, and indeed in its best forms is, progressive. In addition, all of the so-called mainline denominations have within them groups of people who are working to advance progressive Christian values, especially around the issue of homosexuality. Find out who that group is in your denomination. Join it. Work with it. Start a local chapter. Our denominations will respond when enough people speak up.

The task is a daunting one, but it is not hopeless. Our faith today needs nothing short of a new Reformation, but Christianity has been reformed again and again throughout its long history. Indeed, the faith's survival over two millennia is due largely to its ability to speak to people in vastly different times, cultures, and circumstances. It can speak to people in our context too. Our faith can speak a saving word to all spiritual seekers. Our call is to present Christianity in a way that speaks to them. If we will do that, our great faith will continue to connect people with God in powerful, life-saving and life-transforming ways. If we will do that, our great faith may even be able to save the world. With trust in God and in the power of the Holy Spirit we can do it. Let's get on with it.

---

1. I mentioned Jim Wallis and The Center for Progressive Christianity in the text of this book. Rabbi Michael Lerner is rabbi of Beyt Tikkun synagogue in California and editor of the journal *Tikkun*. He is founder of the Network of Spiritual Progressives, an interfaith organization the works for progressive spiritual values. He is one of the most powerful voices for progressive spiritual values in our country today. For more information, go to www.tikkun.org and www.spiritualprogressives.org. That Rabbi Lerner is Jewish not Christian, of course, matters not at all from the perspective of liberated Christianity.

A Philosophical Appendix

The Meaning of Is:
The Essential Nature of Knowledge and Truth

THIS STUDY IS BASED upon a particular philosophical understanding. I explain that understanding in this Philosophical Appendix. As the title of the Appendix suggests, that understanding has to do with the nature of human knowledge and the nature of truth examined from a philosophical perspective. I hope that you will find this Appendix interesting and helpful. I am quite sure you will find it challenging. I trust that you will find it to be worth the effort.

1. THE ISSUE

During the scandal over his affair with White House intern Monica Lewinsky, President Clinton was widely ridiculed for his claim about the truth of a certain statement by one of his lawyers that "it depends upon what the meaning of the word 'is' is." In the context in which the President made that remark, it was truly absurd, and he deserved all the ridicule he got. Yet in the context of a discussion of the crucial foundational question of the nature of truth, of what constitutes truth and of how and to what extent we can know truth, the question of the meaning of the word "is" is the most profound question that we can ask. This work is a consideration of the nature of Christianity, of what it is and is not, of what it can be and what it cannot be. That consideration must be based upon an understanding of the very nature of human knowledge and truth, of the meaning, in effect, of the word "is."

People making claims about the truth of Christianity and of the Bible use the word "is," or some other form of the verb "to be," all the time. They say, "Christianity *is* the one true faith" and "the Bible *is* the revealed word of God." They say, "the Bible *is* literally true and inerrant" and "Jesus Christ *is* the incarnate Son of God." These and many other claims about the faith use the word "is" all the time, yet in our American culture people never stop to ask, What does it mean to say that something "is"? Or to ask, How can we know that something "is"? We don't ask those questions, yet a claim that something "is" necessarily implies certain assumptions about what it means for something to be. A critique of any claim that something "is" will be superficial if it does not begin with an examination of the claim's assumptions about what "is" means. Put more philosophically, a critique of any claim that something "is" will be superficial if it does not begin with an examination of the claim's ontology, that is, of its understanding of the nature of being. A closely related and equally important question is the question of what the philosophers call epistemology, the question of how and to what extent we can know that something is. Epistemology is the question of how and to what extent we can know what is real.

These questions may sound silly and insignificant to you, but they are not. They probably sound silly and insignificant to you because in our dominant culture in North America today we do not teach people to think philosophically, or even critically. We all have operating assumptions about what is real and about how we know what is real, but we are never taught to examine those assumptions even to see what they are, much less to see if they hold up to close critical scrutiny. Yet if we are truly to understand the nature of faith and of the truth of faith, we must undertake such a critical examination of our assumptions about what is real and how and to what extent we can know what is real. I know that the discussion that follows may seem obscure to you. It may seem theoretical and lacking in practical significance. It used to seem that way to me too, but please bear with me and follow along closely. This stuff really is important to our task of liberating Christianity.

2. THE OBJECTIVIST ASSUMPTION

We all live every day in a world that is presented to us by our sense perceptions. We see people and things. We hear sounds. We smell odors and taste flavors. We touch objects. All the while we assume that what we perceive through our senses corresponds to something objective, to something outside ourselves that exists independently of our perception of it. We've probably all heard this question: If a tree falls in the woods and there is no one there to hear it, does it make a sound? I'm willing to bet that the immediate answer that sprang into your head when you first heard the question was: "Of course if does!" I know that that was my immediate answer to the question the first time I heard it. What you may not have thought about was the fact that there is a reason why you immediately wanted to answer that question "yes it does." Once it's pointed out to us, we get it that there can't be a sound without an ear to hear it. Nonetheless, we answer the question yes because we go through life assuming that what we perceive corresponds directly to something objective, something "real" that exists outside of and apart from us. We assume the objective reality of the things we perceive precisely because we perceive them. We think: How could I perceive something that isn't "really" there?

I will call that assumption the "objectivist assumption." It is the assumption we all make that, when we perceive something with our senses, there is, in fact, an object that corresponds to our perception of it. It is the assumption that what we are perceiving has its own independent, objective existence. It is the assumption that there is an object that we are perceiving that would be there whether we perceived it or not and that, barring some physiological abnormality that distorts our perception, that thing exists as an objective fact the way we perceive it.

3. THE FALLACY OF THE OBJECTIVIST ASSUMPTION

You may find it difficult at this point to see the objectivist assumption as an assumption, but in the eighteenth century the British philosopher David Hume demonstrated that the objectivist assumption is precisely that, an assumption, and that it cannot possibly be more than that. Indeed, he demonstrated that the objectivist assumption is a fallacy when it claims to "know" that what we perceive has objective reality apart from our perception of it. To help you understand Hume's hypothesis, let me lead you through a brief exercise.

Pick an object nearby (actually, what appears to be an object—the objectivist assumption is so deeply ingrained in us that it is difficult even to talk about it without falling back into it), a book, a lamp, a table, or a chair for example. Look at it. Or if you prefer or need to because of a physical limitation, touch it. It doesn't matter which sense you use for this exercise. See it. Feel it. It seems real to you, doesn't it? You see its shape, its size, its color. You feel its hardness or softness, its texture, its warmth or coolness. And so you *know* that the thing is really something out there, a separate object with its own being, its own reality. It was there before you looked at it or touched it. It will be there after you look away or remove your hand. You know that all of that is true.

Or do you? Think about the matter a bit more. What do you really know? You know that you looked and saw, that you touched and felt. You know that you perceived something. You know that you experienced a sight or a touch. You experienced an object as real. Hume's great insight was to see that that is all you know: that you experienced a sight or a touch. Because all you really know is that you *experienced* a sight or a touch, you cannot "know" that there is indeed an object out there that corresponds to your experience of a sight or a touch. When you think you *know* the objective existence of the object, what you're really doing is *assuming* that there is such an object. You cannot *know* that such an object exists apart from your perception of it. Perception is all you have.

At this point in a critique of the objectivist assumption, most people throw up their hands and cry, "That's ridiculous! Of course the thing I was looking at, the thing that I was touching, is real! I saw it! I felt it!" Yes, but that's just the point. You believe that the thing is objectively real, that it really exists outside of your perception of it, because you perceived it. The Germans have words for this understanding. They say you did not see or feel *das Ding an sich*, the thing in itself. You saw or felt its *Phenomenologie*, its phenomenology, that is, the phenomena of the thing, that which you experienced of it. Yet what you experienced was not the thing itself but your perception of it. What you really know is that you perceived it, and the fact of the matter is that that is all you can know! Because we humans perceive the world from a center that we call our self, because as humans we have no other way of being in the world, all we can know is what we perceive, what we experience. What is real is our perception, our experience. Whether anything beyond that is real, we simply cannot know.

Try thinking of it this way for a moment. Have you ever heard a sound that no one else heard? When the people you were with said they heard nothing, did you ever think "maybe I'm just hearing things," meaning maybe you heard something that wasn't really there? Maybe the sound corresponded to something real. Maybe it didn't. Either way, it sure sounded real to you. Was it? Wasn't it? All you know is that you heard it.

A Philosophical Appendix

It's the same with *every* perception we have. All we know, and all we can know, is that we had a perception, that we experienced something.

My father Lloyd Sorenson, a brilliant man retired many years now from his position as a history professor at the University of Oregon, once tried to explain the fallacy of the objectivist assumption to a former graduate student of his. The former graduate student, himself an intelligent and educated man, replied indignantly: "Are you trying to tell me that my wife and children aren't real!?" His response indicated that he didn't understand the fallacy of the objectivist assumption at all. His response in fact reflects the objectivist assumption. He used the word "real" to mean having independent, objective existence. Hume's analysis leads to a different definition of the word "real." In this analysis, the graduate student's family is real to the extent that he perceives them to be real. They are real to the extent that he experiences them as real. He cannot know that they have objective reality because all he really knows is that he perceives them, that he experiences them.

4. REALITY AS SUBJECTIVE AND EXPERIENTIAL

The point is not actually that my father's former graduate student's family isn't real. The point is that we need to refine and deepen our understanding of what "real" means. And here's the really big point to all this: Because as humans all we have is our perception, our experience of things, all reality is subjective and experiential. The only reality that we humans can know is subjective, experiential reality. Reality is subjective for me because *I* experience it. Reality is experiential for me because I *experience* it. I know what I experience through my senses. I cannot know that my senses do not deceive me. Indeed, I know that sometimes they do.

Perhaps you've seen the movie *The Matrix*, starring Keanu Reeves. In that movie computers have taken over the world. They have enslaved all humans so they can use the electrical current every human body produces to run themselves. The humans, however, or at least most of them, don't know that they live in little pods hooked up to machines feeding the computers because from birth the computers have manipulated their consciousness, their perception, so that they perceive what we would call a normal human existence. They have homes and families. They have jobs. They live the way we live, except they really don't. They only *perceive* that life, they *experience* it, and so, to them, it is real. The movie shows us that their perceived life is in fact objectively unreal. The point that we have to come to terms with is that *we cannot know that the same thing isn't happening to us!* All we have is our perception, our experience of reality, and our perception and experience are what make "reality" "real" for us.[1]

Subjectivity and experience are all we have. It simply is part of our nature as human beings that we live inextricably in subjectivity. It simply is part of our nature as human beings that reality for us is experiential not objective. Objective knowledge is not given to us. It may be possible for God, but we aren't God. Objectivity is not possible for us.

5. THE EXISTENTIAL NECESSITY OF THE OBJECTIVIST ASSUMPTION

Please understand that I am not suggesting that we all start assuming that what we perceive, what we experience is not real. What we experience as real seems so objectively real to us because assuming that it *is* real works. It gets us through the day. It makes our life possible. Acting in response to our perceptions and experiences as real generally speaking facilitates our existence. Experience tells me that if I treat the car that I perceive bearing down on me as I cross the street as real and hurry out of the way my existence will be facilitated. If instead I put on my philosopher's hat and say that I'm just perceiving that car and that I can't know that it is real and therefore continue to amble leisurely across the street I'm likely to experience my existence coming to an abrupt end. But does that prove that the car has objective existence? No. It proves that that is true which we experience as facilitating our existence. It proves that that is true which experience shows us is true.

Even David Hume didn't live his life as though what he perceived and experienced wasn't real. He said that every morning he got up, took his morning walk, came home, and ate his very real breakfast. The point is not that what we perceive and experience isn't real. The point is to understand that "real" does not mean that we know that what we perceive and

---

1. The movie *The Matrix* has a limitation as an illustration of our point. It actually makes the objectivist assumption itself because it shows us what is supposed to be an objective reality very different from the perceived reality of the captive humans. If you watch the movie again, ask yourself: How does Neo know which reality is real? How does he know that the reality the rebels are showing him isn't as manipulated and false as the reality he knew when he was hooked up to the computers' machines? The simple answer is, he doesn't, and he can't.

A Philosophical Appendix

experience has objective reality. "Real" means that subjectively we perceive and experience something as being real. The objectivist assumption is an existential necessity for us humans. That truth, however, does not change the fact that philosophically speaking the objectivist assumption is just that, an assumption that we make. Objectivity is not something that we can know.

6. SCIENTIFIC AND RELIGIOUS TRUTH

At this point you may be thinking, "Well, OK. I can get it that *religious* truth is subjective and based on perception and experience, but surely *scientific* knowledge is different. Science gives us objective, verifiable facts. It gives us reliable information about the world, about the universe, right?" Well, in a sense yes and in a deeper sense no. Scientific knowledge is human knowledge, and, like all human knowledge, it is grounded in perception and experience. It has to be. It is knowledge gained by humans, and by our very nature we humans exist in subjectivity. The sense perception of scientists may be assisted and amplified by an impressive array of scientific instruments and mathematical calculations. Scientists may be able to replicate the experiments and observations of other scientists, but in the end scientific observation comes down to subjective observation by a human being. Just as all you could know about the thing you were perceiving in our earlier exercise in this Appendix was that you observed it, so all the scientist can know is that she observes her instruments and her mathematical calculations and what she perceives them to be reporting.

Still, it is commonplace among us to make a sharp distinction between the facts revealed by science and the beliefs of faith. We say that scientific truths are objective and verifiable. We can *know* them, or so we believe. We say that the truth of religion is different. We say that religion is about belief not fact. We say that we can't know the truths of faith, we can only believe them. Our analysis here of the nature of all knowledge and all truth establishes that at the most fundamental level this distinction is false. Scientific truth is not objective because *no* human truth is objective. The truth of religion is subjective, but *all* truth is ultimately subjective. There is a difference between scientific observation and the experience of the spiritual in that ability we just mentioned of scientists to reproduce the experiments and the findings of others, but at a more fundamental level scientific truth and religious truth are both subjective because both rest on human perception and experience. Therefore, there is no ultimate ontological difference between scientific truth and religious truth. Both are grounded in perception and experience.

The crucial point is this: Because subjectivity is all we have, and because all truth is therefore subjective, all truth is ultimately grounded in experience. That is true which we experience as true, whether we are talking about the truth of the desk I'm writing on that I observe or the truth of a God Who I experience in my life. Does the desk have objective reality? I don't know. I can't know. It doesn't matter. I experience the desk as real. Treating it as real works for me. That's what makes the desk real for me. Does the God I experience in my life have objective reality? I don't know. I can't know. It doesn't matter. I experience God as real. Treating God as real works for me. That is what makes God real for me.

Yet, perhaps in order to avoid misunderstanding, more needs to be said about the distinction between scientific truth and spiritual truth that I just mentioned briefly above. It is true that scientific truth ultimately rests upon human observation and perception and is therefore subjective. It is also true, however, that science creates knowledge of the world of sensed phenomena through the processes of the mind working upon data acquired through perception or sensation. Within the realm of science itself knowledge can be considered objective if that knowledge is found through repeated experimentation to be consistent with the data thus acquired. In that sense, and only in that sense, scientific knowledge may be considered to be objective knowledge. It is not objective as I have defined objective here as meaning having independent existence apart from human perception and experience. Because scientific knowledge, like all human knowledge, rests upon human perception and experience, we cannot know whether scientific knowledge has that kind of objective existence just as we cannot know that any human knowledge has that kind of objective existence.

Religious knowledge does differ from scientific knowledge in that it is not subject to this kind of repeated testing of data acquired through our senses. Rather,

> Religious truths, which seem to glory in mystery—that is, in instances often contradictory of what we know about the sensory, the phenomenological world—cannot meet this test, nor do religious people, even liberals among them, who take inspiration from the Bible's miracle stories.... Unlike the scientific mind, the religious

A Philosophical Appendix

mind is not limited by the logical principle of consistency nor by any other rational principle. Instead, it wanders freely through the various images and conceptions imagination comes up with, taking a bit here and another there even as poets do, and weaves them into a fabric containing metaphorical, mythical truths of a spiritual order it deems existentially superior to the truth science confirms objectively about its phenomenological world.[2]

On a certain level, therefore, religious knowledge is different from scientific knowledge. It is freer and more creative because it is not bound by scientific method or by a need for logical consistency. Yet as we acknowledge and work with this distinction between religious and scientific truth we must never forget that both types of truth are ultimately grounded in human perception and experience. Both are therefore ultimately subjective as I have used that term here to mean existing in or arising from human perception and experience and the processes of the human mind.

I can't stress enough that this understanding of the nature of reality does not diminish the truth of God for me. Rather, it puts the truth of God for me on the same level as the truths of science. It acknowledges the essence of both truths, that they are both grounded in experience. What does it mean for me to say that my desk is real? It means I experience my desk as real. What does it mean for me to say my God is real? It means I experience my God as real. I cannot know the objective reality of my desk or my God. I experience both as real. Experiencing both as real works for me. It facilitates my existence. Therefore, both are real—for me.

7. THE SUBJECTIVIST UNDERSTANDING MATTERS

This understanding of the nature of human knowledge and truth, which we can call the subjectivist or the radically empiricist understanding, has profound implications for our understanding of Christianity and our critique of Biblicism. Biblicism treats the stories of the Bible as objective fact. It treats its understandings of the Christian faith as objective truth. It considers those truths to be universal, valid, and binding for all people whether those people experience them as true or not. Philosophically, that is, at the deepest levels of the nature of being and of human existence,

---

2. From an unpublished letter to me from my father Lloyd R. Sorenson of January 25, 2007, in response to an earlier draft of this Philosophical Appendix.

those contentions of Biblicistic Christianity are ontological impossibilities. Bible stories cannot be about objective facts because in the sense of the term we are using here (which is the same sense the Biblicists use) there are no objective facts. Christianity cannot be objective truth because there is no such thing as objective truth. This analysis of ontology and epistemology, of what is real and of what we can know of the real, makes Biblicism impossible.

Most popular critiques of Biblical literalism do not plumb the subject to this depth. They talk about the historical nature of the books of the Bible. They present some of the conclusions of modern Biblical criticism about source theory and the editing history of the various books. They point out the scientific impossibility of the first Genesis creation story and of God causing the sun to stand still in the sky. They talk about translation issues and the time gap between Jesus' death and the earliest Christian documents that we have. These are all matters of great significance, and I have dealt with some of them in this book. They are not, however, the most fundamental reason why Biblicism is wrong. Biblicism is wrong in the first instance because given the nature of being and of human existence *it cannot be right*. Its assumptions about the nature of reality and of human knowledge, almost always tacit and unexamined, are simply false.

A proper understanding of the nature of truth and human knowledge rules out Biblicism, but it puts faith properly understood on a solid ontological and epistemological basis. It shows that the nature of religious truth is not radically different from other types of human truth. It shows that all truth is subjective and experiential.

Glossary

Biblicism: As used here, the understanding that the Bible is to be understood factually and literally and that the Bible's authority derives from its supposed divine origin.

Classical Theory of Atonement: A soteriology that holds that we are saved from our sin by Christ's suffering and death in which Christ atones for our sin in our place because only He as the Son of God is good enough to make sufficient atonement for human sin. It includes the belief that God requires a sacrifice before God can forgive sin. It is the most common soteriology in our context today.

Deism: A rationalistic religion from the Enlightenment that saw God as "the great clockmaker" who created the universe, set it to run according to universal natural laws, then withdrew from creation to let it run on its own.

demonstration soteriology: The understanding that we are saved by the demonstration of God's love, particularly by Christ's demonstration of that love on the cross.

divine: Another word for the spiritual.

Enlightenment: A period of European intellectual history in the seventeenth and eighteenth centuries that emphasized reason as the standard for truth in any area of human endeavor.

epistemology: The study and understanding of how we know things. The epistemology advanced here is that we know things through perception, experience, and the workings of the human mind on what we perceive and experience. Knowledge understood this way is subjective not objective.

materialism: An ontology that holds that only the material or physical is real.

myth: A story of the gods, or of God, and of humans' relationship to the gods or God. Myths are stories that act like symbols in that they connect us with the divine and the divine with us.

Glossary

Numinous: Another word for the spiritual or the divine.

objective: Having independent existent apart from human perception and experience.

Objectivism, or objectivist assumption: The belief or assumption that reality has objective existence.

ontology: The study and understanding of the nature of being or of reality, of what is real. The ontology advanced here is that that is real which we perceive, experience, and process through our minds. Reality understood this way is subjective not objective.

Scientism: A materialist ontology that holds that the real that can only be established through the methodology of science.

soteriology: A doctrine or understanding of salvation, of how it is that Jesus Christ saves us.

spiritual: As used here, the spiritual is that dimension of reality that both transcends and is immanent (inherent) in the reality of ordinary sense perception that we perceive and experience differently from our perception and experience of ordinary reality but that we nonetheless experience as real. Synonyms for the spiritual are the divine and the numinous.

subjective: Existing in or arising from human perception and experience and the processes of the human mind.

symbol: An object from the world of ordinary sense perception that connects us to the divine and the divine to us. The cross is the central Christian symbol.

synoptic Gospels: The Gospels of Matthew, Mark, and Luke, so called because their many similarities allow them to be "seen together," which is what synoptic means.

Theology of the Cross: A demonstration soteriology that holds that on the cross Christ demonstrated to us God's presence and solidarity with us in all aspects of human life, including suffering and death.

www.ingramcontent.com/pod-product-compliance
Lightning Source LLC
Chambersburg PA
CBHW070249230426
43664CB00014B/2459